THE
MAFIA
PHILOSOPHER

TWO TONYS

SHAUN ATTWOOD

For Niki

ACKNOWLEDGEMENTS

A big thank you to my proofreaders: Penny Kimber, Claire Bishop, Mark Coates, Grant Davidson, Hannah Burton and Jane Dixon-Smith for typesetting and cover design

SPELLING DIFFERENCES: UK V USA

This book was written in British English, hence USA readers may notice some spelling differences with American English: e.g. color = colour and = jewelry = jewellery

SHAUN'S BOOKS

English Shaun Trilogy
Party Time
Hard Time
Prison Time

War on Drugs Series
Pablo Escobar: Beyond Narcos
American Made: Who Killed Barry Seal?
Pablo Escobar or George HW Bush
The Cali Cartel: Beyond Narcos
We Are Being Lied To: The War on Drugs (Expected 2019)
The War Against Weed (Expected 2019)

Un-Making a Murderer:
The Framing of Steven Avery and Brendan Dassey

Life Lessons

Pablo Escobar's Story (Expected 2018)
T-Bone (Expected 2022)

SOCIAL-MEDIA LINKS

Email: attwood.shaun@hotmail.co.uk
Blog: Jon's Jail Journal
Website: shaunattwood.com
Twitter: @shaunattwood
YouTube: Shaun Attwood
LinkedIn: Shaun Attwood
Goodreads: Shaun Attwood
Facebook: Shaun Attwood, Jon's Jail Journal, T-Bone
Appreciation Society

Shaun welcomes feedback on any of his books.

Thank you for the Amazon and Goodreads reviews!

CONTENTS

INTRODUCTION BY SHAUN ATTWOOD

As a business-studies graduate moving to Arizona from the UK, I hadn't planned on ending up in prison, where a Mafia associate classified as a multiple-homicide murderer serving 141 years would save my life. Two years before the incident, and a few days before meeting Two Tonys in late 2004, I was on the way to a Christmas visit with my parents, when I was attacked by a burly gang member. In a crowded corridor, he approached from behind and punched my kidneys. All of the inmates stopped walking to watch my reaction.

If you don't hit back, you are classified as a punk, which means you're going to spend the rest of your time inside cleaning people's toilets, performing sexual services and getting rented out as a prostitute. If you do hit back, the guards can arrest you, put you in a prison inside the prison called lockdown, where you lose all of your privileges including your visits, and they can add more time onto your sentence.

Not wanting to become a punk, I threw some punches, which felt as if I were hitting a big bag of cement. After reeling from more blows, I ended up on the floor, injured.

When my cellmate found out about the attack, he suggested I meet Two Tonys, who was at the top of the prison hierarchy for murdering rival gangsters and capable of offering protection – the respect each murderer had depended upon the nature of his crimes. Under the convict code, murderers of women and children were classified as KOS – Kill On Sight – and the prisoners would try to kill them upon arrival. Two Tonys operated under the old-school Mafia code of not harming women or children.

Waiting to meet Two Tonys over a game of chess, I was

conscious of my heartbeat revving and sweat trickling down my sides. I thought, *Maybe this isn't such a good idea. If I beat him, I might be next on his hit list.* My cellmate arrived with Two Tonys, bespectacled and in his early sixties with hazel eyes and slicked hair greying at the sides. Slightly under six feet and with a medium build, he wasn't physically intimidating, but as he approached, and I heard his voice and saw his eyes, I felt uneasy. His gaze was fearless and aggressive. I sensed that if he were pushed, his response would be limitless. The hardcore in prison communicated in gangster lingo. Being a fish, a new prisoner, I worried I might say the wrong thing. My voice betrayed my nervousness as we chatted, until Two Tonys asked in a mock UK accent whether I'd ever had tea and crumpets with the Beatles.

After the game, I shook his hand. "I won because you kept speaking your mind. It gave me an advantage."

"Me and my big mouth," Two Tonys said, slapping the side of his head.

I didn't know that the game had been a test of my character. To stay alive, Two Tonys had to judge people fast. After chess, Two Tonys said he felt that I was an honest person and asked if I'd write his life story – my cellmate had previously told Two Tonys that I was writing a prison blog, Jon's Jail Journal. I felt honoured.

When Two Tonys was ready to start work on his autobiography, I took a pad and pen purchased from the inmate store to his cell in Tucson prison, located in a dust bowl of the Sonoran Desert, sixty miles north of the US border with Mexico. For several months, almost daily, I visited his cell on the bottom floor of a run-down two-storey building. Inside were two bunks, a stainless-steel combination sink/lidless toilet and a tiny table and stool, where I sat for hours, hunched over my writing paper, sweating next to a hot cement-block wall. An oblong window at the back offered a view of security cameras on giant poles, coils of razor wire glistening in the mirage-inducing sunlight and a patch of desert cleared of vegetation, so that anyone attempting to escape could be shot. Outside of the cell door, prisoners wearing sunglasses and nuclear-orange outfits were roaming around in racial groups, some exercising on pull-up and dip bars, a few sweeping or mopping.

Two Tonys disclosed that his story included unsolved murders. With no statute of limitations on murder, he was worried that the guards, who did regular cell searches, might discover something that I'd written about his murders that could be used as evidence against him. He wasn't worried about extending his multiple life sentences, but about being uprooted from Arizona to Alaska for a murder trial that could last for years. I offered to write in a chicken scratch that only I could decipher, and to mail my manuscript to the UK via the British Embassy, so it would be classified as legal mail, which the guards couldn't open. I showed him my scrawl. He seemed satisfied. As a precaution for some murders, he requested that I write down that other people had done them, but verbally he'd tell me the truth, which I could add after my freedom.

Perched on a circular steel seat bolted to the wall, I wrote rapidly, listening with fascination as Two Tonys described his upbringing in Detroit and how his early dealings with the Mafia involved shining their shoes. I was struck by his introspection, his attention to detail and the eloquence of his descriptions. Every time a guard did a security walk, I had to exit the cell as visiting was prohibited. Even though Two Tonys stationed prisoners outside to watch for guards, I was sometimes caught inside, but we managed to talk our way out of receiving disciplinary tickets. Writing had to be halted when his visitors arrived throughout the day, mostly big tattooed men, some gang members, others murderers, all paying respect to Two Tonys. Telling them that I was his official biographer, Two Tonys helped to raise my stature on the yard. Some of the respect his visitors harboured for him rubbed off on me.

One day, I found him chatting to a Mexican American with a weatherworn face, bespectacled and soft-spoken, seemingly a polite and gentle older man.

"Pico, this is my friend, England. He's a good dude," Two Tonys said, getting off his bunk.

"Pleased to meet you, Pico." Smiling, I shook his hand.

"Pico here saw I was reading your book," Two Tonys said, "*The Great War for Civilisation*. He's wondering if you want to sell it to him."

"It's a good read," I said. "A blog reader sent it to me for free, so I can't sell it. You can have it."

Pico's brows shot up. "That's real nice of you, England. Are you sure I can't give you anything for it?"

"No need. I've got to keep my book karma intact."

"I like you, England," Pico said. "Listen, if anyone ever fucks with you, you tell me." Pico fished a bandage from his pocket and wrapped it around his left hand. Holding a fist out, he said, "Look, I'm always ready to go. I don't give a fuck who it is. I don't give a fuck what time of the day it is. I'm always ready. I've got your back."

"I appreciate that, Pico," I said, taken aback. Pico left.

"You just made a good friend with that one," Two Tonys said, sitting on his bunk.

I sat on the stool. "Why? Who is he?"

"He's Old Mexican Mafia. All the Mexican Americans listen to him. He's one of the most dangerous motherfuckers you'll ever meet. He's doing life for murders, and while he was in the joint, he shanked two guards to death in Cell Block 4. The cops tortured him for years. They denied him medical and he lost a kidney."

"Why'd he kill two guards?" I asked, wide-eyed.

"Him and some others were high. The guards busted them, so him and his homies cut them to pieces. He's a killer, but he's a sincere guy, an old convict. No one disrespects him. He's a good fella to have in your corner."

Writing in prison was dangerous. Some prisoners praised my activism, whereas others barged into my cell and said they would happily kill me if I ever posted their activity online. Even though I never blogged about anyone without permission, some prisoners told others that I had done so just to try to get them to attack me. With Two Tonys support, I was viewed less suspiciously and more prisoners revealed their stories.

My parents posted some of Two Tonys' anecdotes to my blog. We were amazed at how quickly he gained a following at Jon's Jail Journal, which was inundated with questions and comments for him. One reader asked about the death of his father, Joe Hootner. In his response, Two Tonys solved the murder, which had been sanctioned by the Bonanno Crime Family.

My blog readers warmed to Two Tonys' voice, which this book is written in. In the media, gangsters are typically portrayed as uneducated thugs, which Two Tonys had transcended by spending decades reading in the Arizona Department of Corrections, rendering his voice a blend of Mafia associate and philosopher. That's why this is no ordinary true-crime book. Towards the end, during his more reflective years, he questions the meaning of life and deconstructs many belief systems with his unique wit and gallows humour.

We spent so much time together that by the fifth year of my incarceration, Two Tonys said that I was like the son that he had never had. Writing this book, reminiscing about our time together, there were moments when I had to clear away tears. The same happened when I said goodbye to Two Tonys at the chain-link fence just before my deportation. I still rely on his life lessons such as appreciating the small things instead of seeking excitement in the wrong places.

Meeting Two Tonys was a blessing because there was much more to him than his rap sheet. By using his influence with the gangs, Two Tonys saved several lives in prison, including mine. He got a hit called off that had been sanctioned by an Aryan Brotherhood gang leader who I had unwittingly made an enemy out of by blogging about how prisoners were purchasing items from the inmate store to make syringes to inject drugs. For two days, my adrenaline pumped non-stop as I braced to get stabbed at any moment. At nights, I could barely sleep. Half of the two-hundred prisoners on the yard wanted to smash me, whereas the other half were offering protection. Every time our cell doors opened, friends, including Two Tonys, arrived to guard me. My parents had just flown over from the UK. Straining to hide my fear at Visitation, I struggled to shield them from the events unfolding. A redneck high on crystal meth and heroin, and drunk on hooch, approached my cell with a shank but was disarmed by an almost six-and-a-half-foot ex-Marine friend of mine and Two Tonys. Eventually, Two Tonys called in a favour, which "squashed the beef" – ended the threat.

One of his most impressive qualities was his devotion to his daughter, Niki, and his grandchildren who came to visit. He also had a relentless appreciation of life. When prisoners complained about breakfast being cold or recreation not commencing on time, Two Tonys would jest that it was worse in the Siberian gulag, where they fought over fish eyeballs in the soup, and his favourite character from literature, Ivan Denisovich, resided. The Russian prisoners were worked to death in temperatures so cold that they lost fingers, noses and ears to frostbite. Those who refused to work were dragged to death by horses or thrown off cliffs.

In this book, Two Tonys never complains about getting caught nor makes excuses for his crimes. He backs up his stoicism with quotes from the legends of military history, the myths of Ancient Greece and philosophers such as Aurelius, Machiavelli, Nietzsche and Schopenhauer, whom he affectionately referred to in gangster nomenclature as "The Schop". His favourite authors included Tom Wolfe, John Updike, Haruki Murakami, Gore Vidal, Hemingway, Tolstoy and Steinbeck. He even aspired to be a book critic.

As amazing as it was to experience Two Tonys' humanity, I never lost sight of the horror of his crimes, which were to various degrees business decisions and drug-fuelled outbursts. As a teenager, he recognised his affinity for violence, and so did the Mafia, which he eagerly joined. To kill or be killed is the ethos of gangsters, and he saw little difference between that and his contract with the US government during his days in the Navy.

Knowing that he could be murdered by a rival at any time, he was quick to kill those scheming against him. He credited that foresight for keeping him alive. The murders started after Two Tonys' cocaine use, and he constantly urged me to never resume drugs. Working for the Bonanno Crime Family in the 1960s, Two Tonys was indoctrinated into a world of old-school Mafia values. In contrast, the powerful Mafias of today, such as the Mexican Cartels, have decapitated entire families and posted online videos of their atrocities. I'm not making excuses for homicide. I'm just trying to put Two Tonys' actions in context.

During a recent interview, I was asked, "As a guy that was well into love and the rave scene, you spent a long time documenting the life of a killer who you cared for. How do you square that?"

"Prisoners are human beings," I said. "In prison, I realised there is good and bad in everybody. I try to focus on the good in the belief that it helps it to come out."

All of the crimes in this book happened, but for legal reasons, the names and descriptions of some of the people and locations had to be changed. Composite characters have been used to hide identities and to provide continuity.

PROLOGUE

Sometimes at night, I lay on my bunk, staring at the flies and mosquitoes splattered on the grimy ceiling, reminiscing about the pieces of shit I whacked, which gives me weird thoughts. Probably not weird in the way you're imagining. If you're thinking that any of my victims might have been the next Bill Gates or might have discovered a cure for cancer or might have been the first person to walk on Mars, no, let's be real. They were the kind who might have blown your face off during an armed robbery or sold heroin to your kids. For almost two decades, I got away with putting schmucks to sleep. It all ended after my arrest in the early nineties, so before I set the table for my story, let's take a peek there.

In 1994, I was reading *The Bonfire of the Vanities* in my cell – books keep me alive, they keep me from fucking dementia – when the peep slot on my door slammed open, and a pair of eyes gazed in. "You've got a legal visit. Back up to the door and don't try anything stupid." A key rattled, a latch clicked and a hatch unfastened.

Glad to get out of my shithole, I put down my book, got up from the metal bunk, put my hands behind my back and fed them through the hatch. Handcuffs clicked on tight. Two pairs – a practice reserved for dangerous motherfuckers, like the big dudes in here who work out all day, and are into cage fighting or are ex-Marines, and have the strength and knowledge to get out of cuffs. I ain't in that group. But there is another group of guys who ain't physically intimidating, but their files say that based on their criminal and prison history, they'll kill you in a heartbeat with a weapon. That's more like me. But if I got free, I ain't gonna whack a guard. I'd stab a child molester at a kids' playground, lusting over a six-year-old girl on a swing, or a politician trying to poke a pageboy: slimeballs like that.

"Step away from the door." The metal door screeched open. "Come out with your back to us. Any sudden moves and we will face-plant you into the concrete." I ended up between two overgrown hillbillies, trained to remain aloof, probably told, "If you slip and fall, don't think a prisoner won't grab your gun and kill you." They were not gonna talk about who won the ball game or where the nearest pizzeria is. Chains jangled around my belly and ankles. The door clanged shut and was locked. "Down the corridor. Go!"

Curses and dank smells wafted from the cells as the guards marched forward. When they guided me past Visitation, I knew something was up. "Where're we going?"

"We can't tell you for security reasons." They brought me to a small room and opened the door. "Can we bring him in, lieutenant?"

"Yup."

"Go!"

I shuffled inside: beige walls, a fluorescent strip light, no windows, a creaky fan.

"Three homicide detectives and a county attorney from Anchorage wanna talk to you," said another fat redneck, who stood sweating through a tan uniform. "Have a seat." He slid a plastic chair my way, which scraped the concrete.

Restricted by chains, I sat slowly, relishing the better air. "Do I have to talk to them, lieutenant?" I asked, playing dumb.

"No."

"Then I don't wanna talk to them."

"I'll call the gate to see where they're at." He got on his radio. "They're on their way up. When they get here, tell them you don't wanna talk to them." That was his ploy to get me in a room with them.

Dwarfed by the guards, the detectives and lawyer came in, eyeing me like a prize. With the three Alaskans was Dirk Taylor, a Tucson homicide detective I'd been jousting with for almost two decades. In a beige shirt, brown pants and snakeskin boots, he tilted his cowboy hat, revealing his face, leathery and tanned, with a bulbous burnt nose. "How're you doing?" Dirk's south-western drawl was less rustic than the rednecks'. It was polite and coaxing, designed to get fools to incriminate themselves. But behind his charm, he hid the tenacity of a hunting dog.

"Just fine, but I don't wanna talk to you."

"We're just looking to close some old cases," said the Alaskan attorney, a spindly twerp. "We're not gonna charge you with any crimes. We know you're never getting out. Indicting you would be a waste of taxpayers' money."

Dirk steered his brown eyes, small and severe, towards the lieutenant. "Can you make him talk to us?"

I kept my expression deadpan, but every fibre in my body itched for me to say, "What is it you wanna talk about?" But if you ask that question – I was taught a long time ago by the Mafia – you run the risk of dialogue with them, so you say nothing. It's always best to plead the Fifth, even if they only ask for your address. To come all the way from Alaska to Arizona, it had to be serious. Someone must have ratted me out for whacking members of The Brothers, a biker gang that tried to muscle in on my cocaine business. So what if I left a few bodies along the highway? Those punks all had it coming.

The lieutenant shrugged. "OK, you can go."

Glad to get away from them, I stood.

"Wait! Don't you wanna save yourself from the death penalty?" Dirk busted open a manila folder and slapped down a photo of a big bald dude on a hotel-room bed. He was a fucking mess, blood coming from his mouth, some of it congealed, his eyes closed, one foot on the floor, one on the bed, most of his brains on the ceiling. "We found your prints at the scene. Is there anything you'd like to tell us?"

Gazing impassively, I thought, *Who's Dirk trying to fool?*

Dirk slapped down another photo: a biker stabbed to death in a prison cell. "How about this one?"

I shook my head.

Slap! Slap! Slap! Bodies unearthed from the Tucson desert. "How about these?" Dirk snatched a folder from the county attorney. He slapped down another photo: a biker frozen in Alaska with a chunk of his head missing. "How about this one?"

I shrugged.

Slap! Another frozen biker. "And this one?" *Slap!* A biker with his throat slit. "This one?" Dirk gathered the pictures together like a hand of cards and shoved them at my face. "You left a trail of corpses from Arizona to Alaska. Tell us something, anything."

"OK. I have something to say." Their gazes intensified. The detectives' eyes were as cold as the corpses I'd left behind in Alaska. I wondered if hunting motherfuckers like me had injected ice into their hearts. "Don't ever show up here uninvited without stopping at McDonald's and bringing me a Big Mac and a Coca-Cola." I smiled at Dirk, who sneered. With them all glowering, I said, "Hey, it's not like I asked for a T-bone steak with mashed potatoes, sour cream and chives." I paused to enjoy their expressions. "Can I return to my house?" I asked the lieutenant. He nodded at the guards to take me to maximum security.

Just as I was about to leave, Dirk said, "When they sentence you to death, would you prefer the gas chamber or lethal injection?"

I didn't even turn my head to look at the motherfucker.

PART 1

BEFORE DRUGS

1941–1972

CHAPTER 1

Decades before facing the death penalty, I was raised in the smoky shadow of the Chrysler plant on the east side of Detroit – the industrial capital of the world – strictly bona fide blue-collar territory. As a kid, I told the time by listening to the whistles blowing in the factories. My earliest memory is of soldiers returning from World War II. Germany and Japan were in ruins. Even England was bombed out.

Our neighbourhood was Irish and Italian. Detroit was booming, really jumping, a lot of people were making money. Malls didn't exist. If you wanted to eat out, you went up Jefferson Avenue – six lanes wide with red streetcars that looked like trains running down the middle – and stopped in one of the greasy spoons, little bullshit restaurants here and there. No Denny's. No International House of Pancakes. No fucking chain corporations.

My Italian mother stayed at home and my Irish father was an industrial serf, an assembly line worker for Chrysler for twenty-five years, a life sentence. God bless him. Out of my two sisters, the one sixteen years older than me got married early. The one thirteen years older – who I shared a back bedroom with – married when I was ten. We lived downstairs in a two-storey house. Other people lived upstairs. The houses in my neighbourhood were so close, I could take my hands and press them against the opposite walls. A milkman would bring bottles right to our door, set them down, and nobody would filch them. A sheeny man would come around and blow his horn to see if we had any rags or stuff to sell. We'd hang out on the back of his wagon. He'd yell at us and run us off. It was a time when families ate together, and kids played outdoors and appreciated nature. These days, people's brains aren't rolling right. They're too plugged into shit like *Entertainment Tonight* to see whether Britney Spears or Paris Hilton are wearing panties.

As a paperboy, selling the *Detroit Free Press* at night, I saw a lot of bar fights, especially among drunken servicemen. It was normal to see violence. I also worked as a shoeshine boy, and a stock boy for Socrates. Just about every fucking corner in our neighbourhood had a Greek market on it. As a stock boy, I put soda bottles on shelves and stuff like that. Socrates gave me a few dollars, but I was always a hustler.

Across the street from me on Kitty Corner was Honky John, an old man who sat on his front porch all day, retired. A lot of guys hung out there who were sort of thuggish: Jimmy Damasco, Billy Fox, the DeMarco Brothers, Cato Pasco. They weren't mobsters, just tough guys in their early twenties. Only twelve, I could go over there and get in. I couldn't join the conversation, but I'd get to listen. Billy Fox lived up the street from me. I'd see him washing his cars, and I'd help him. I started developing awe for guys like that when I should have been looking at my dad as a role model or people working at the Chrysler plant who paid their bills and didn't go to bars and get drunk all of the time. Instead, I admired those pieces of shit who wanted to go out and beat people up. I started knowing those guys, and they started knowing me.

My fondness for that type of person in my preteen years was the beginning of my development into what I became: homicidal. Just like they wrote in my presentence report: I have a propensity for violence. Even now I walk around prison – where I'm serving 141 years – and look at motherfuckers who I'd like to take a lead pipe to and bust them across the nose with and knock their teeth out. But what stops me is I'm too old and liable to get my ass whupped, and I don't want to go back to the conditions in the hole – a dungeon they throw you in for breaking the rules – where I've already served enough time. The act of violence does something inside of me. It makes me feel good.

Looking back on things – I'm no psychologist or nothing – but there's a time in a kid's life when you shouldn't whip him even though you might think that you're helping him. I ask myself the question sometimes: what the fuck makes me like this? The bottom line is as a kid I got whipped a lot by my folks. I don't know why they whipped me. It would start with me sassing my mom, nothing heavy, just kid shit. My mom and pops would take me into the basement. She'd whip me with an ironing cord. There was a rack with towels on it that I grabbed. I can still visualise her whipping me. The whip would go *crack-crack-crack* as she hit me until I shut the fuck up. I was thinking, *I'm gonna kill you someday. I'm gonna get a shotgun and blow your fucking head off.* My dad whipped me with his belt even though I never sassed him. My mother stuck a big ol' two-pronged turkey fork in my neck one time, and said, "I'll kill you." You don't think that had an effect on me? I was just a little guy.

I take full responsibility for whacking motherfuckers who had it coming, but the point I'm making is that a combination of the neighbourhood, the bar brawls, it being such a violent time in society, and the whippings turned me into a violent motherfucker. Even now in my old age, I feel it. When I first arrived at one prison, I cut a motherfucker's finger off. That's who I am, but I'm trying to change. That's what Mafia bosses look for: guys like me who've been kicked around a bit.

As water seeks its own level, the kids I hung out with in Detroit were just like me, baby thugs running around with greased-back hair. A guy approached us for a favour. There was a shop with a scab barber cutting hair for less than a dollar a head, so the guy contracted us to go there with fucking rocks, throw them through the windows, and try and hit the mirrors, which we did. And what did we get for that? We all went bowling.

In the fifties, when I was sixteen, I frequented Richard's Drive-In. In those days, you'd go around in your car, three or four of you, and drive in the drive-through all night long. It didn't stop. That was the craze. One time, we saw some friends fighting some guys, so we jumped out of our car and got into it, fighting in the middle of the drive-in. I had a little knife. A guy bigger than me came at me, so I took my knife out and stabbed him in the belly a couple of times. Luckily for him, the blade wasn't long enough to go in deep. We got away, but one of our friends got caught. He told me, "The cops wanna talk to you about that stabbing," so I went down there with my brother-in-law, Harper Woods, a cop out of Detroit. He talked to the cops and a judge he knew. He told the judge I was gonna join the military. The judge said he would give me a break if I joined the service, so I signed up for the Navy.

At seventeen, I left home for the Navy. I got in a lot of fights, especially bar fights, and – this part I'm not proud of but I'm going to tell you anyway – I developed a penchant for stealing. I stole a Navy car in Okinawa and headed for a whorehouse, drunk. I rolled the motherfucker end over end three times, and put my buddy from Eureka, California in hospital. I was OK. I walked away from the motherfucker, not a mark on me. At a special court martial, I was sentenced to 180 days hard labour in the brig and given a fine of $160. I was a two striper, and they busted me down to one stripe, but everything had to be approved by the captain of the ship. He cut everything in half, so I got ninety days, a fine of $80, and I kept my two stripes. I was told not to go ashore until we got to the continental limits of the United States.

In the Philippines, our ship, the USS *Vesuvius* – a 7,700-ton grey ammunition ship that had been awarded two battle stars in World War II – had a change of command. The new captain declared an amnesty on the four or five of us who couldn't go ashore. What do you think I did? I went ashore that night. My first time out in two months, I got drunk, shacked up with a hooker, and stayed gone for four fucking days even though I was supposed to have been back at midnight on the first night. I ran out of money, but my buddies came off the ship and found me. We went drinking and to a whorehouse. I eventually got tired. I'd run out of gas. I had no money, and the hooker was looking at me funny, so I decided to go back aboard. The boat I took to get back pulled up to the USS *Vesuvius*. I went up the gangway.

At the end of the gangway was the XO, executive officer,

second in command, a strapping guy with a mean face. "What did you do, get hungry?"

Smiling, I said, "What's for supper?"

I had to go to a captain's mast, a disciplinary hearing with the captain as the judge. He gave me more hard labour, and I couldn't go ashore until the continental limits of the United States. I had to report to a master-at-arms, a ship cop who arranged hours of extra work, which could be at any time of the day or night. People were going to watch a movie, and he'd be sending me to work. Next I got a summary court martial for sleeping on watch. I'd hit the duty station and fall asleep. My stealing got worse. I wasn't by myself: two or three of us were doing it. My fighting got worse. I'd go ashore and get into it with guys from other ships and have fights on board.

I lived on the USS *Vesuvius* for three years, seven months and ten days. *Vesuvius* is the volcano that destroyed Pompeii, Herculaneum and Stabiae in the year 79 AD. They found bodies of motherfuckers sat at tables and in bed who'd died quickly 'cause a pyroclastic cloud had swarmed their lungs. There's a lot to be said about living dangerously. And I'm not knocking employees of Walmart, Sears or KFC. It's not easy going into a heavily armed hotel room at two in the morning and blowing a guy's face off, but it gives you a feeling of living on the edge. Look at the footballer, Pat Tillman, the Arizona Cardinal, an NFL player, a college grad. He gave up a multi-million-dollar contract to join the military, went to Afghanistan to fight the Mujahideen in the Hindu Kush Mountains, and got his ass blown off by friendly fire. Some say it was patriotism, but I say it was for fucking excitement.

I got an honourable discharge from the Navy on 5th March 1958. Towards the end of my hitch, I was thinking, *What are you gonna do back in Detroit?*

At the foot of our street was the Harbor Bar built on old pilings. I was twenty-one, just out of the Navy, when I went there with three friends. After talking drunken shit, we got into it with five guys bigger than us. A friend and I flat put it on the motherfuckers, and fought until the end. We had that Irish in us – know what I mean? – and I had my Italian slyness. I slipped out before the cops arrived. I was in the back of a convertible when we hit a roadblock. The cops walked up to the car and did a knuckle check. Mine were bloody, so they took me to the jailhouse. What did I do? I dropped my cop brother-in-law's name. They talked to him on the phone – he knew them all – and they let me go. The cops told me that the customers watching the fight were in awe of us. After that fight, I knew in my heart and soul that I'd end up making a career out of violence.

CHAPTER 2

Each neighbourhood in Detroit had a guy you went to if you had problems with someone. The guy worked for the Mafia, which was set up for the benefit of the top guy, the apex, and there were multiple levels right down to us teenagers. To qualify for the upper echelon – bosses and made guys – you had to be of pure Italian descent, which I wasn't 'cause of my Irish father. A made man had to go through a secret-society ceremony, which included pricking your trigger finger, bleeding on a picture of a saint and taking a vow of silence called omertà. If you broke omertà, the Mafia would whack you. Anyone who messed with a made man would be whacked. Then there were associates, guys like me who were almost confirmed as made men. Henry Hill in *Goodfellas* was an associate of the Lucchese Crime Family. There were also wannabes and hangers-on – the type of motherfuckers who didn't have the heart or balls to be used for anything heavy or half-ass light. The ones with the nuts had to take a few risks every now and then as they were always trying to get a pat on the head or an attaboy from the higher-ups.

As a young man, I entered the inner world of the Mafia through my relationship with the Licavolis. In 1962, I first saw Teddy Licavoli in a pizzeria where we both knew the owner in Grosse Pointe, Michigan, one of the most exclusive neighbourhoods in the US, home of the big shots of the auto industry like the Fords and the Dodges, and gangsters like the Zerillis and Licavolis, who lived on Mafia Row. Teddy's dad, Peter Licavoli, was a mob boss they arrested for murder seven times, only for him to be released every time. His wealth came from gambling, liquor-smuggling and boot-legging operations. Teddy was my age, twenty-one. He had dark hair sprouting from a low brow, parted at one side and greased back. His eyes, big and brown, had a hustler's gaze. He'd been to Grosse Point High and military school in Florida while his dad was in the joint for tax evasion. There was a big difference in his lifestyle and mine, but we attracted. He was looking to get a little thug in him, and I was looking to hang out with the big boys. In order to hang out, I had to have a little something-something to offer, a little charisma, a craziness, a ballsiness, so they'd think, *I can use this guy for something.* Working in the suit department at a men's clothes store, I was dressed sharp. I had a 1956 Chevy convertible outside of the pizzeria next to Teddy's new Corvette.

So I got talking to Teddy, and we clicked. We went to a restaurant. Everyone knew who he was. We didn't have to pay for a thing. They were like, "I've got this. How's your father? Give him my regards." Which was good for my ego and prestige. After that, we hung out at a pool hall with about fifty others from all over, some big-shot gangsters' kids and blue-collar motherfuckers like me. Teddy said he was going to Arizona. He asked if I'd pick up his twelve-year-old brother and take him to a saxophone lesson at their house. Before long, I was driving down to Grosse Point twice a week.

I wasn't doing anything other than driving the Licavoli kid to sax lessons when Sal Spinola, a friend I'd made through the Licavolis, suggested, "Let's go to LA and live." Sal was a smart, good-looking kid, real dark and wiry, with thick hair. His brothers were hooked up with the Licavolis in the numbers racket, the Italian lottery, an illegal form of betting that allowed people to pick three numbers that won if they matched numbers drawn the next day. Due to the small size of the bets, it was popular in blue-collar neighbourhoods.

"Fuck it! Let's go!" I said.

We packed his red 1958 Plymouth Fury convertible, said our goodbyes – "See you later. We're going to LA!" – and took off. We cruised along Route 66 with the top down, two young guys pumped up on adventure. Before Las Cruces in the New Mexico desert, we hit a strip of road past Roswell, and saw a sign: NEXT TOWN 100 MILES.

"Let's make it in a fucking hour!" Sal yelled.

"Let's go!"

We set our watch timers and Sal punched the gas. The Fury blazed down the little two-lane road, no freeway, no lights, hemmed in by sand dunes. We were doing it, going 110 mph. The Fury was wide open. We made it but fried the engine up. Coughing from the stink of burnt oil and rubber, we pulled in at White Sands, where the dunes looked like snow.

In Las Cruces, a mechanic said it would take a week to get the parts to fix the Fury. We checked into the Lorna Hotel. In a glass case, the old register had the signatures of Billy the Kid and the lawman who'd shot and killed him, Pat Garrett. The hotel even had the cell where Garrett had locked up Billy the Kid. There were no room keys. The bathroom and bathtub were down the hall.

"Fuck waiting around here for a week. The Licavolis have got a ranch in Tucson," Sal said.

We took a Greyhound bus to Tucson, admiring a panoramic view of a desert with the odd shrub and cactus. On the way, we called Mike Licavoli – Teddy's older brother, a bit bigger than Teddy, but with the same dark hair and complexion – who picked us up. Going to the Triple H Ranch, Mike drove through the University of Arizona, all tall campus buildings, palm trees and well-watered grass. The sun was shining and college girls were smiling at us. The warm breeze had the scent of desert flowers blooming. Can you imagine the impression that had on me coming from dark and smoky Detroit to cleanliness and fresh air? I fell in love with Arizona right away.

The ranch building was spread across the desert with cactuses here and horses there. Papago Native American maids with lustrous black hair were cleaning rooms and cooking. Snowbirds – old wealthy guests from out of state – were staying there, paying monthly. An old-time Jewish gangster managed the ranch. When he took his top off, he revealed a pastiche of bullet holes and scars on his back from shootouts during his days in the Mayfield Road

Mob, based out of Cleveland's Little Italy. Most of the people running the ranch were from Ohio, including ten goombahs from Youngstown. With them, we went to the Grace Ranch every day while living at the Triple H. With a beautiful Olympic pool and a bathhouse, the Grace Ranch was thick with mobsters on the lam, walking around with no necks, their noses all on the sides of their faces, their wives with them and their Cadillacs. Only twenty-one, I was more than impressed. It was like taking a kid off a baseball sandlot and putting him in the Yankee locker room with his favourite players. While waiting for the Fury to be fixed, I was swimming and eating well every day. The dining room at the Triple H had twenty tables and wood walls with knotty-pine panelling and south-western motifs. The Papago Native American maids served us. Mike Licavoli, Sal and I always ate there. There was no bill, but we had to eat what they fixed for the day, bunkhouse style.

One night when we were all drunk, Mike took us out on the town. Stopped at a red light on Speedway Boulevard in an old station wagon, Mike got into a yelling match with some guys. We pulled in at the Flamingo Hotel, got out and started fighting the guys. I grabbed a FOR SALE sign from the back of the station wagon and started swinging it and hitting them. All at once the guys took off, but cops arrived in plain clothes. They showed us their badges: liquor-control agents. They knew who Mike was and were laughing. After asking us what we were doing and all that shit, they let us go. During the fight Mike had noticed that I was a thumper. He liked that.

When it was time for me to leave Tucson, I told Mike, "I'd like to come back out here to live and work with you."

"Let me clear it with the old man first," he said, referring to his mob-boss father.

We went back to Las Cruces to get the Fury. The bill was $600. "Don't drive it over 50 mph for the first 100 miles," the mechanic said. Like a couple of numb-nuts, we were driving over 100 mph, heading back to Detroit now, fuck LA. Outside of

Amarillo, Texas, the car started making funny noises and stinking. We sold the motherfucker and got on a train.

In Detroit, I went to see Teddy Licavoli. "I'm going back to Arizona to hook up with your brother. He told me to come back."

Teddy gave me his blessing, so a few months later, I said my goodbyes again, got on a plane with Sal and arrived in Arizona in Easter 1963, aged twenty-two. At Tucson airport, we just walked off the plane down a ladder. There was no covered concourse. Mike was waiting for us at the gate.

Right away, we went to work with Mike at a golf driving range. With a couple of Native Americans, we were up at the butt-crack of dawn – the coolest hours for construction – building the driving range, digging ditches, painting the inside of the pro shop and planting palm trees. The Licavolis owned a motel by the Rillito Park Race Track, a shabby two-storey joint with truckers and hookers roaming around. We collected rent from deadbeat motherfuckers behind on their payments. Mike and I told them, "You've gotta pay the rent or get the fuck out. This is no picnic. No free ride."

The ranch we were staying at had a bathroom with four fucking walls of mirrors. We'd bust Sal in there greasing his thick hair and admiring himself from all angles every night. The boss, Peter Licavoli, arrived with his wife, his daughter and son-in-law. They stayed in the plush penthouse at the top. Mike Licavoli, Teddy Licavoli, Sal and I picked up some women, and brought them back to our rooms. A Papago maid saw a woman coming out of Sal's room and ratted him out to Peter Licavoli.

Sal and I were at the golf range, renting out clubs, selling buckets of balls, and all that shit when Peter Licavoli drove up, a stubby double-chinned guy in his early sixties. If I was typecasting for a gangster movie, I wouldn't choose Peter Licavoli. He looked thuggish, but he didn't look like a boss compared to the other bosses. When he wanted to emphasize a point, he tilted his head to the side. Even in his Detroit Police Department mugshot, his head is cocked. His favourite saying was, "Find out and let me know." Despite the way he looked, he wasn't a person to fuck with. He had the heart of a mountain lion and an army behind him. Walking up to us, Peter scowled at Sal. "You had some fucking broads in my ranch last night."

"Yes, sir," Sal said, caught off guard. Guys like us could never call him Peter. We called him Mr Pete or Mr L.

Peter cocked his head to the side. "You had some whores in my house where my wife and children sleep." He was raised in the old Italian customs. You don't shit where you eat in that society. "Pack your stuff. I want you out of here in the morning. You disrespected my family." That's a run out – when the boss tells you to get the fuck out of town and move on. He looked at me. "What about you? Were you with him?"

Having heard him scold Sal, I was ready to brown-nose the old man. "No, sir, Mr Pete. I wasn't with him." He believed me. He turned around and walked away. The next morning, I had to take Sal to the fucking airport.

In the summer of 1964, I returned to Detroit with Teddy Licavoli. After a few weeks of hanging out, Teddy got engaged to the daughter of a wine distributer. They planned an elaborate engagement party. The old man, Peter Licavoli, rented a big ball-room. Teddy started acting crazy, and told me, "Fuck it! I don't wanna get married." Instead of settling down with his fiancée, Teddy rented us an apartment in an old mansion, charged a bunch of stereo equipment to his old man and partied.

In late 1964, things weren't looking good for the marriage. I was hanging out at Peter Licavoli's art gallery, Vesuvio, helping unload paintings. Vesuvio is Italian for Vesuvius. Remember the Navy ship I was on for three years, USS *Vesuvius*, living danger-ously? Omens were following me around, but I was too young to notice. I was unwrapping a painting when Peter Licavoli came out of the back office and walked up to me. "Put that down!" He cocked his head. "Get the fuck out of here and don't come around here no more! Stay away from the house! Stay away from Teddy. If you go around Teddy, I'll break your fucking legs."

Flabbergasted, I had no idea what was up, but I knew not to give him no shit. "OK, Mr Pete, but do you mind if I ask what I did to deserve this?"

"You're the cause of Teddy not getting married!" He was mad 'cause of the money he'd spent on the wedding, and his loss of face after sending out the invitations. He thought I'd cast a spell on Teddy, but Teddy was leading me. In his eyes, his kids were never to blame.

That same night, still upset with Peter Licavoli, I went down to the Checker Barbecue, famous for its food in a black part of town where the in-crowd went after the bars closed. Inside were gangsters from all over Detroit, the singer Marvin Gaye and the founder of Motown Records. It wasn't a place for lames or truck drivers. Sitting at a table, having drinks put me in a good mood. Teddy arrived with his head in his ass as usual, and sat at the next table.

At 2 AM, Peter Licavoli's bodyguard, Black Tony, came in, about sixty, with black hair sprayed down, and a dark blue over-coat right down to his ankles, average height, but as wide as a wall. He had no fucking neck, and his nose was smashed in like he belonged in *Wise Guys*. "Get up!" he yelled at the kid next to me, so he could sit down.

Drunk, I didn't give a fuck about being run off by Peter Licavoli. *Fuck these guys.* Black Tony sat down. "Hey, how're you doing, Tony?" I asked.

"OK." Pointing at Teddy, Black Tony said, "I thought the old man told you to stay away from this kid."

I was gonna say, "He ain't with me," but I never got the fucking chance. Black Tony backhanded my face. My head hit a pole behind, stunning me.

"Get outside now!" he yelled. In Black Tony's eyes, I could see my own death. The whole fucking joint started staring, gangsters and black rock 'n' roll musicians.

I got up and went outside with him right fucking behind me. Scared, I was thinking, *This is it. I'm gonna die on Brush Street.* I turned around.

"I'll blow your fucking brains out if I catch you around Teddy again!"

I knew I couldn't fight this guy. Even if I whupped him, it would have been a one-way ticket to the bone yard. Fifteen guys were watching by now, none of them rooting for me, all for Black Tony.

All at once, Black Tony's nephew yelled, "What are you fucking with this guy for?" The Zerilli Crime Family was grooming Ronnie Morelli to be somebody. He had all of the charisma in the world. He looked like he was born and raised for *The Godfather*. He even had a screen test in Hollywood. "If you wanna slap someone, slap Teddy 'cause he wants this guy with him everywhere he goes."

Suddenly, Black Tony got real fucking humble. "I didn't know that. The old man didn't want him around." Thanks to Ronnie, the beef was squashed.

I got a job at a new club in Greektown, which was real authentic in those days, mysterious. People were afraid to go down there. The Pink Panther opened in an old building, a 1960s lounge with valet parking, plush carpeting, no tables or chairs but little couches with coffee tables in front, beautiful paintings, a hat-check girl, a hostess, six waitresses in uniforms, a band – Tony Thomas and the Tartans – and two bartenders, of which I was one, wearing white shirts and black vests emblazoned with big pink panthers. The place reeked of atmosphere. Every gangster in Detroit came to that motherfucker. They had to come just to be seen. All except for the Licavoli outfit. My job involved setting up the bar, cutting fruit and getting the cherries and olives ready, and serving drinks. I was getting tips like crazy, making good money, staying out of trouble.

CHAPTER 3

In 1965, fed up working at the Pink Panther, I returned to Tucson, where Mike Licavoli put me up at the Grace Ranch. I still hadn't made peace with his old man, Peter Licavoli, but he was in Detroit, wrapping up business. Mike took me to see my buddy, Sal Spinola, who was back out there. Having not made peace with Peter Licavoli either, Sal had clicked up with the Bonanno Crime Family. With his dark eyes, brownish skin and square jaw, Sal looked the part in a light-grey three-piece suit. Only twenty-three, he'd become the president of Tucson Vending Company, a jukebox and cigarette-machine operation owned by the Bonannos, one of the five families dominating the Cosa Nostra.

The Bonannos were far more powerful than the Licavolis. Their boss was Sicilian-born Joe Bonanno Sr, whose exploits inspired *The Godfather*. Following a purge of the Mafia by Mussolini, Joe had fled Italy by stowing away on a Cuban fishing boat heading to Florida. At twenty-six, Joe had risen through the ranks in the 1920s to become one of the youngest-ever Dons. He was a founder of the Mafia Commission and one of the longest-running bosses. While many of his contemporaries were whacked, Joe ruled for decades, making millions from bootlegging, loan-sharking, book-making, numbers running and other crimes. He prided himself on being a man of honour, tradition, respect and dignity. When the Feds broke up a Mafia meeting in New York in 1957, Joe gained a national reputation as "Joe Bananas," a name he fucking hated. Despite the heat, he was never convicted of a serious crime. The stuff Mario Puzo used for Don Vito Corleone included Bonanno wanting his son to succeed him, and his old-school attitude of not profiting from drugs. Joe owned a funeral parlour back east with double-decker coffins, enough room for two stiffs, so he could dispose of the people they'd whacked.

The Bonannos had Sal fronting only in name. He did what he was told by the Bonanno lieutenant, Charlie "Batts" Battaglia. One day, Sal said, "Batts wants you to do him a favour."

"What is it?" I asked.

"Pick up some dynamite. There's a guy who sells dynamite out of his house. He has a licence to buy cases of the shit."

I picked up a case of dynamite sticks, fuses and detonation caps, which was dangerous to transport 'cause radio frequencies could have set the caps off. A few nights' later, Johnny Paulus' restaurant on East Speedway was bombed. The windows were blown out of the fucking place.

That earned me an attaboy from Batts, who I was in awe of. With his hair slicked back over his big head, his fat mouth always chomping on an Antonio and Cleopatra cigar, wearing dress slacks, alligator shoes and pinky rings, Batts was the epitome of a gangster. Unlike Sal, he had the cold gaze of an executioner, showing about as much emotion as a fish strung up on a hook. In prison, we call it dead eyes, like you see on these neo-Nazi Aryan Brotherhood psychos – who I'll introduce you to later on.

The grunt work from Batts was a test. When it comes to clicking up with a family, there is no job interview. They give you tests – busting in a head here, collecting a debt there. After proving myself as a strong-arm guy by doing a few pistol-whippings and twisting a guy's arm behind his back until it cracked – I wanted to beat him with his own arm, but it wouldn't snap off – I graduated to helping Batts dispose of people the Bonannos had whacked. An expert at getting rid of bodies, Batts had whacked motherfuckers from coast to coast, and was never busted. I learned a lot from him, which came in useful later. He had a preferred plot in Tucson he liked to use by Rocking K Ranch.

When the Mafia whack a guy, they rarely do it in the streets like in the old Al Capone days with Thompson submachine guns. They wanna take a guy out somewhere he just disappears, ground up in a sausage machine or a wood chipper or fish bait in Jamaica Bay or in a junkyard in the trunk of a beat-up car crushed to the size of a cigar box. With no corpse, it's hard for the cops to prove there was a crime. The exception is when the Mafia are trying to send a message. Some bodies are meant to be found. The body of a snitch, also known as a rat, a canary, a stool pigeon, might be dumped on the side of a street with a canary or a pigeon stuffed in his mouth as a warning to others. Before the rat's whacked, his tongue might be cut out. A more elaborate way is by placing a guy's feet inside of cinder blocks, filling them with cement and throwing him in the water. That's where the expression "sleeps with the fishes" came from.

One of the problems of transporting a body is the stink. It releases gasses and fluids and crap. It's best wrapped in plastic sheets that catch paint drops, so you don't get a trace of blood on your car or clothes – which could be used as evidence against you – and transported in a sleeping bag as camouflage in case you get pulled over. If you're in a truck, you can use a fifty-five-gallon industrial drum. If the corpse is too big for the drum, you might have to saw an arm or a leg off. Ideally, you cocoon the corpse in plastic sheets like a mummy with its hands at its sides before rigor mortis kicks in. A corpse rots underground, destroying the evidence. It rots faster in the heat, so summer is the best time to whack someone. Heat will rot a corpse down to a skeleton in a few weeks, so it's easier to get away with whacking someone in Arizona than Alaska. I ran into problems in Alaska 'cause the motherfuckers froze and what I'd hoped for didn't happen: bears eating the corpses. In heat, worms and maggots chow-down on the evidence.

For premeditated killings, it's best to dig a hole in advance 'cause of the time it takes to get deep enough: about five or six feet. We ain't talking about no little sandpit here. Digging a hole is hard fucking work. You don't wanna get caught with a shovel loitering off some dirt road in the boonies with a stiff in the trunk. If you don't dig deep enough in Arizona, monsoonal rain might wash the soil away and expose the corpse, or coyotes might dig the motherfucker up and start chomping on an arm or a leg. In Tucson, bears and lions come down from the mountains when they're hungry. There's more rain in Tucson than Phoenix and it's slightly cooler, so you've got better desert soil to dig. In Phoenix in the summer, the desert is baked so hard that it's impossible to dig.

A good trick is to bury the stiff several feet under the grave of a large dead dog or any other big carcass. If the cops come out with cadaver dogs, which pick up a corpse's scent, they'll stop digging when they discover the carcass. Once you've got your corpse buried, take a look at the spot and see how obvious it looks. Camouflage it by raking sand or soil.

If you whack someone on the spur of the moment and you need to get rid of the stiff fast, take it to the nearest cemetery. Find fresh-looking graves, and check no cameras are scoping you out. Dig a grave up and drop the corpse in. Who the fuck's gonna notice that? Or better yet, invest in a funeral home like the Bonannos.

After proving myself, I was introduced to the godfather's son, Joe Bonanno Jr, a pretty boy and snazzy dresser. We hit it off right away. At that time the godfather, Joe Sr, had disappeared off the face of the planet to avoid going to a grand jury. I was approved to move into Joe Jr's house on Elm Street, and asked by Batts to watch out for him. I bought a Corvette. I was partying with college girls and thriving.

One night, Joe Jr came home and said, "Man, I just met this guy, Walter. He wants to buy me a Corvette."

"Is he bullshitting you?"

"No. He's got all kinds of money."

"Let me meet this fucking guy."

"I'll bring him up here for dinner on Friday night."

Sure enough on Friday they came in. Joe Jr introduced me to Walter, a soft-spoken guy in a business suit and tie, who was going bald. Behind horn-rimmed glasses, he had sharp blue eyes.

I assumed he was blowing smoke up Joe Jr's ass about having money. But two days later, Joe Jr showed up with a brand new blue 1966 Corvette with a hard top and a hatchback.

A few days later, I met Batts at a coffee shop. He was with a killer called Tony the Snake, a big fat Turk with a bushy moustache. "What's going on here?" Batts was a real loud-talking motherfucker. "This Walter guy buys the kid a car and pays cash." Batts could smell Walter's money, but he was faking it like he was looking out for the kid.

"Hey, Charlie," I said. "What do I know? Walter wants to take the kid to San Francisco now."

"What the fuck are they gonna do in Frisco?" Batts said, his mind working. "Can you go to Frisco with him? If you can find out what the fuck's going on, I wanna know." He was giving me an assignment.

I found out that Walter was the comptroller of Complete Auto Supply. I didn't know if he was pilfering or not. On the way to California, I said, "Do you think this Walter guy is trying to put moves on you?"

"Fuck no! I don't know what his game plan is."

On the way to San Francisco, we stopped in Monterey, where Joe Jr's mom and sister were vacationing in a big house with a swimming pool that had a cover on it activated by a button. Their neighbour was Shirley Temple Black.

On a Friday night, we picked Walter up at an airport. I was watching to see if he made any moves. He was leery of me. The three of us got in the Corvette. Out of respect, I crawled in the back. We went to a hotel downtown, and Walter made a reservation for a room with two beds, but he had them put another bed in there. Walter called his boyfriend. The four of us went to dinner at the Fleur de Lys. Walter was putting on a show, ordering wine.

An old buddy from Cleveland – who knew everyone in town – met us at The Fairmont Hotel. In a big black Caddy, he took us to a nightclub in the basement of a building in Chinatown called China Smith's. Outside, people were stood with hats and trench coats on, cigars hanging from their mouths. Richie Fong – a mysterious dude in a copper shirt, pink tie and dark glasses – owned the joint. He greeted us and wanted to hang out. I had a piece on me, a little .38, a five-shotter, but it would do the job. I made sure Walter saw it. He didn't know who the fuck I was, but he knew Joe Jr was a Bonanno. When he saw the gun, a look came over his face, and I realised Walter had a real bad case of gangsteritis. From being an accountant, he was now out in San Francisco with a pistol-packing motherfucker from the Bonanno clique who was bodyguarding the boss's son.

Back in the hotel, I took the middle bed. Never once did I see a move made on Joe Jr. They were never alone. We toured San Francisco for the weekend. On Sunday, we got more dough from Walter and went home.

In Tucson, Sal and I met Batts and Tony the Snake at Bob's Big Boy on Broadway. Four of us sat in a booth. Batts liked to eat as well as talk loud. He was drilling me, asking me questions about the trip.

"Hey, Charlie, I didn't see anything. Nothing went on with those guys." He wasn't buying it. "What the fuck! Are you trying to get me to lie and say something I didn't see?" I said in a shitty tone.

Batts gazed hard. "You know, maybe you should leave the table before you say something that'll get you in trouble." I went out to the car. A few minutes later, Sal came out and said everything was cool.

We went to the Bay Area for a month and came back broke. I told Sal that we had to find a way to get money out of Walter. We told Walter we needed $30,000 to invest in a shady deal, and we'd pay him back $10,000 interest. If you can appeal to a motherfucker's greed and let that override his suspicions about you, you can get him. It was one of my favourite scams. Walter loaned us the money.

I was wary of Batts trying to get in on this action, but at the time he was on trial for extortion. We went to the courthouse.

Batts was in federal court in a hospital bed, with an oxygen mask on his face, faking a heart attack.

"You're still going to trial," the judge said, and made a big deal about us being in the courtroom. "No one better threaten the witnesses. If anyone does, call me immediately."

The victim who was gonna be on the witness stand owned a bowling alley. Orders came down from the Bonannos for us to intimidate the motherfucker. Before the trial, Sal and I went to the bowling alley and cracked the pool tables' slate by dropping bowling balls on them. It went to trial and Batts got sent down for ten years. He posted an appeal bond, which enabled him to remain free for now.

I was hiding my moves from Batts. Before Walter's money, I was living in a $65-a-month shack. I moved to a high-class eleventh-floor apartment on Miracle Mile. It was the in-spot. Paul Newman stayed there when filming *Hombre*. I threw extravagant parties. I hired the maître d' from the Hilton to serve hors d'oeuvres and make drinks. Everybody came, including state senators such as Sol Ahee.

I started hanging out with Katy, who just showed up at one of my parties and didn't leave. We hit it off instantly. She had big chestnut eyes and long wavy brown hair. Her shape and looks made motherfuckers stop what they were doing to check her out. Born in Arizona, she was a florist with a gentle way about her that appealed to my protective side. I'd stop by her joint and watch her arrange flowers. Her fingers worked like magic over a vase. The bouquets she brought home gave my crib a female touch and a sweet scent. She was generous and spontaneous. We went to Las Vegas and Mexico, where Mariachis, a band of strolling musicians in traditional costumes, followed me around as if I was Errol fucking Flynn. I was doing it. I went to riches overnight.

Half of the money from Walter went to Sal, who was getting married and wanted to get his old lady a nose job. She had a big beak and he knew a Los Angeles Jewish plastic surgeon who wanted $5,000 to give her a movie-star nose. Sal and his girl went off to the surgeon in LA, and the rest of us – Mike Licavoli and our girls, including Katy – went to have lunch at the Tucson Hilton.

Tony the Snake was stood in the lobby of the Hilton. "Hey, Charlie's in the coffee shop," the Snake said, referring to Batts. "He wants to talk to you for a minute."

In the coffee shop, Batts said, "Listen, when you get your people sat down in your booth, come back in here. I wanna talk to you." I got everybody situated and joined Batts and the Snake. "Where's your buddy, Sal?" Batts asked.

I couldn't tell him that Sal was on the coast getting his old lady a schnoz job. "He's fishing," I said with a wise-guy attitude like, *How dare you ask me!*

"Let me ask you a question," Batts said, using the typical words that mob guys start their interrogations with. "Where did Sal get the money to go fishing with? Plus, you're living over there in a high-rise when a few weeks ago you were behind the Midway Drive-In."

"Hey, Charlie, we shoot a little pool. We play a little poker. We make a little money here and there."

"That's good to know. Let me ask you one more question."

"Sure, Charlie."

"If you grab a guy in this town and take some money from him, do I have a piece coming?" He must have known that I'd shook down Walter. But I knew not to cop to it. Batts just wanted to stay at home and watch TV with his new baby and young wife and have other guys do things for him. He thought that he was gonna ride the Bonannos' coattails and have us pay homage to him. That wasn't gonna happen.

"Sure, Charlie, this is your town," I said in a sarcastic way. I didn't expect him and the Snake to fuck with me too hard 'cause I had Mike Licavoli with me.

"Well, when your buddy gets back from fishing, you guys call me and we're gonna have a talk all together." He was calling us on the carpet – where you have to stand on a rug in front of the boss and get your ass chewed out.

Sal came back from the coast with his wife with a bobbed nose, black eyes and her head all bandaged up. I told him about Batts. He said he'd call him. Sal arranged for us to meet at Batts' house at 2 PM.

On the way, I said to Sal, "Whatever happens, we don't cop to this. We didn't take nothing from nobody." Sal led me to believe that we'd get whacked if they ever found out. I wasn't thinking about Batts now, but the guys in New York, the Bonannos. Outside Batts' house, I saw Joe Bonanno Jr's car, a Corvette. Batts let us in. We went to the back patio, by the pool and sat down with Joe Jr.

"Let's get right down to this," Batts said. "Did you guys take some money from Walter?"

"Are you fucking crazy?" I said.

"This guy, Walter, is saying you went into his office and took money from him for some kind of bogus deal and you've been using the old man's name," Batts said, which was a lie 'cause I was cautious not to use the old man's name or to say drugs were involved.

"Hey, Charlie, this Walter must be fucking nuts."

"Why would he lie? Why would he make this all up out of the clear blue sky?"

"Look, Charlie, a few months ago, I borrowed two grand from him, and I haven't been able to pay him back. Evidently, he's pissed at me, coming up with this kind of shit."

Joe Jr was starting to look apprehensive. He never had big balls.

"The guy's swearing that you got him," Batts said. "Where are you getting all this fucking money? The apartments! The penthouse and shit! Fishing trips to Mexico! Where's it all fucking coming from?"

"I go out every night and try to hustle the pool tables. I've been doing real good."

"Do you want me to believe that?"

"Charlie, you believe whatever you wanna believe," I said, starting to feel uppity. "Walter's full of shit."

"Well, we're gonna get to the bottom of this."

"You're already at the bottom of this, Charlie." After that, we left.

It was March 1967 and two weeks went by. I was at the apartment with Katy when the phone rang. It was Sal. "Come over here. I gotta talk to you right now."

"I don't have a ride."

"Mike Licavoli's coming over. He'll bring you here. It's important."

We drove to Sal's little track home. A blue classic Buick was parked outside. Sal opened the door. Mike and I went in. Bill Bonanno – a heavyset guy with a big oval head, dark hair and a swaggering look in his eyes – was sat at a table. The wedding in *The Godfather* had been based on Bill's wedding. With Joe Bonanno Sr still missing, Bill had assumed a higher role, which, combined with tension over Joe Sr's decision to stay away from drugs, had led to a war within the Bonanno clique the media called the Banana Split. With Bill were Batts and some rough-looking goombah we'd never seen before, dark and thick and looking the part. Bill introduced him to us as Hank. Formalities commenced. "How are you doing?" *Wah-wah-wah.*

Bill said to Mike Licavoli, "How's your father? How's your family?" *Wah-wah-wah.* "Hey, Mike, with all respect to you, I've got business to do with these guys, and it's better you not be here. Out of respect to you and your father, can you give us an hour alone with them?"

Mike looked at me real funny as if he didn't know what to do. "It's all right, Mike. Come back in an hour," I said. Mike left.

From directly across the table, Bill gazed at me with big Hank to his right. Batts was at the head of the table, his arm in a sling, broken cleaning his swimming pool. "The reason I called you guys here is 'cause you took some money from a guy that belongs to us," Bill said. "We want the money or we want your lives. I don't wanna hear no stories or bullshit."

The Bonannos expected certain things from Sal and me as

associates. They included beatings, threats and extortion, which I excelled at, but also laying down money at their feet for the privilege of being able to operate, which I wasn't so good at. When you're called to the carpet by the boss, you're supposed to show nothing but respect and kiss some serious ass, but that's never been in my fucking nature.

Sal had been there with them for an hour before I'd arrived. In situations like this, his heart pumped Kool-Aid, so there was no fucking telling what he'd told them. I looked at Bill. "That's it, Bill, end of story? You don't wanna hear what the fuck I've got to say?"

Batts frowned. "You just heard what the fuck he said. He don't wanna hear no stories. Now, where's the fucking money?" Over the years, Batts and I had developed a dislike.

"What money?" I said sarcastically, scowling at Batts.

Batts turned to Hank. "If that motherfucker says that again, knock him off that chair." I didn't get a chance. Hank knocked me down – *bam!* – a hard hit, too. I was tough in those days, twenty-six, I could take an ass-whupping and blows and all that shit, but here I was on the carpet.

Sal jumped up. "Not in the house! Not in the house!" he screamed, the fucking punk that he was. Right there – *bam!* – Hank knocked Sal's two front teeth out. Bill and Batts jumped up. They were all standing over me. Sal was laid out. Batts started kicking me in the ribs.

"OK! OK! I'll get you the money!" I started yelling.

"Where is it?" Batts asked.

"I'm almost broke now. What's left is in the fucking bank. I can't get it until Monday morning."

"Get on your knees," Bill said.

Thinking they were gonna whack me, I got on my knees.

Bill cocked a .45 and rested it on the bridge of my nose. "You listen to me and listen to me good. Monday morning, you get a hold of the money and you get a hold of this man."

"I've got it in the bank," I said, aware of how close to death I was.

"Just for the record, I don't give a fuck who you know or who you think you know," Bill said, referring to the Licavolis. "Everybody in this town is our guest. This is our town. If one word of this leaves this room, I'll whack you myself." They left.

Sal jumped up, bleeding, his front teeth gone. "Man, I've gotta go to the dentist. Between my teeth and my old lady's face still recovering from the surgery, how the fuck are we gonna get married?"

With no money to pay the Bonannos, we were still close to getting whacked. I asked Sal to take me to see Peter Licavoli. Sal drove us to Peter's office. Peter and Mike Licavoli were inside. I told Mike I had to speak to the old man. He said OK. I told Pete the whole fucking story. In a roundabout way, I was asking for help from the old man.

He frowned at me. "I can't get involved in this for reasons I don't have to explain to you. But keep this in mind for the future: where was I when you took this money? You didn't come around and see me. You didn't even take me to lunch. The only thing I can do is give you some advice: don't let the Bonannos get the drop on you" – by which he meant not to let them draw their guns. I left determined to get ready for the worst.

The next day, Sal got a hold of me with temporary teeth in his mouth. We recruited a little crew, including Blake, a 6-foot-4 musclebound motherfucker who loved to fight. He had blue eyes, light-brown hair, a strong jaw and broad shoulders. He was deadly with his fists and looked the part. He was a loyal motherfucker, who'd back me up under any circumstances. The kind of guy I'd want to share a foxhole with.

I told my crew, "Hey, look, I'm gonna get strapped down." I had no money to give these motherfuckers, but I'd taken care of them in other situations. In my home, the phone rang. "Hello," I said.

"I thought you were gonna get a hold of me at ten," Batts said. I hung up. He called back. I told Katy not to answer the phone. I called the phone company and had them change my number.

Sal's dad, an old dago barber, used to cut Joe Bonanno Sr's hair. He informed us that the Bonannos had gone back to New York on Sunday night, including Bill and Hank. They had their hands full with the Banana War. Except for Tony the Snake, Batts was on his own. I was ready to shoot Batts if he showed up at my apartment, but he never came.

Two weeks later, Hank was all over the newspapers, shot down in front of Rose's Delicatessen in New York City. Buying a packet of Chesterfields, he'd got four in the head. They'd tried to get him into a car. Hank had tried to fight them off and he was whacked on the spot.

Katy and I moved from the high-rise to a one-bedroom cottage with a sunken living room out in the desert next to a little meandering wash with a Palo Verde tree in the front yard. She knew I was broke, but didn't bail, so I knew she had my back. With all of the enthusiasm of a newbie to relationships, I was in love. She liked the excitement I provided, but hadn't figured out that I'd joined a society of killers.

I leased a brand-new 1967 Chevy from a guy with gangsteritis, who agreed to the first and last payment and then fuck all. Every night, I was out with Katy or Sal or Blake, bar hopping, buying drinks on tab, broke, but wearing a tailor-made Italian silk suit, a pair of alligator shoes, a ruby pinky ring and a Patek Philippe watch. When you're hustling, you can't let motherfuckers know you're broke or else you're finished. You've gotta make them think you're rolling, and then they're gonna want your company at their nightclubs and wedding receptions. If they have gangsteritis, they'll tell their friends and mistresses they're close to the mob. Every now and then, you catch one who wants to put a few dollars in with you, just so he can be part of *us* and tell his old lady that he's in on the action. One guy even told me, "You know what I like about you. I can't tell when you've got money in your pocket or you're broke 'cause you're always the same."

My Saturday morning ritual was to spend an hour in Walgreens, going up and down the aisles buying toothpaste,

SHAUN ATTWOOD

aspirin and various shit. Down an aisle, I reached for Listerine and put it in my cart. I looked up and saw the godfather, Joe Bonanno Sr with Bill Bonanno. Joe Sr's re-emergence had been like the Second Coming of Christ. The boss saw me. *Is Bill still gonna whack me himself?* I knew they wouldn't shoot me in Walgreens. I also knew why they were there. When they called New York, they used payphones. Bill carried quarter rolls in his car for this purpose. They were waiting for a call on the Walgreens' payphone.

"Good morning, Mr Bonanno," I said.

"Good morning," Joe Sr said cordially. "You're a good boy."

"Dad, excuse me a minute," Bill said. "I wanna talk to him and I'd rather you not be here."

"Sure, I'll go over there." The boss went to the next aisle.

"Listen," Bill said. "Have you been reading the newspapers? You know we've got problems back east that might drift out here. You guys are on the street all day and night. You know the people. You know this town. I've got some guys with me now, but they don't know who's who. I'm gonna give you guys a clean slate. The past is the past. All I want from you guys is if you see somebody who looks out of place like they're from back that way, use your heads. Maybe they're asking questions they shouldn't be asking. If so, get a hold of me. We're back in Tucson now and we're here to stay. But I'm gonna tell you something. If you grab a guy in this town and take some money from him, go on record with me before you do it 'cause the guy might already belong to us. And if the guy don't belong to us, I'll tell you to go ahead and do it, but throw me a bone. We're in all the newspapers, riding the heat and you guys are running around here using our name, making your scores. I want you to make money. I just don't want you taking anything out of our pockets."

"Yeah, Bill, no problem," I said, thinking, *It's a wonder I'm alive.* "I'm sorry things got out of hand."

42

CHAPTER 4

I believe the purpose of life is procreation. That's why if Angelina Jolie is laying in a thong by a swimming pool with a pitcher of Margarita, and she's calling me over by crooking her finger and giving me the look, I can't deny it, I will get a certain tingle. Most men feel the same when a woman in a tight skirt walks by. The rest of the baggage – love, support, protection, monogamy – is what we brought on the set. We are here to keep the species going. I like the rest, the love and partnership of a good wife, but that's not what nature intended.

When Katy told me she was pregnant, I thought, *Wow! A kid of my own!* It was a big fucking deal. I was determined I'd be there for my kid no matter what. *If it's a boy, I'll make sure he doesn't fuck up. He'll have a different life from me. If it's a girl, I'll make sure she has everything and I'll protect her from all of life's bullshit.* Happy as fuck, I wanted to ask Katy to marry me and to be a real father, but I didn't have any cash for a ring. It didn't take long to come up with an idea.

I took my 1966 Chevy onto a lonely desert road, followed by Blake in his car, with dust billowing up behind us. I got out and rolled the windows up. Blake took out a .45, shot the windows out and put four slugs in the door. He jumped in his car. I went the other way. I pulled in at a gas station with the car all shot up. Breathing really hard, I said to the attendant, "Where's your payphone at? They're trying to kill me!"

"Right over there," he said, pointing.

"Don't call the police!" I walked over and acted like I was calling someone. The attendant went inside and called the cops. The cops who showed up knew me. "I don't know what the fuck is going on," I said. "I was at Sabino Canyon when all of a sudden a blue Caddy pulled up and started shooting at me. Can you please keep this out of the news?"

"We'll keep it out of the news. Don't worry."

Sure enough, the next day, the five o'clock news reported that a local hood had been shot at. I wanted that. Now that I was in the newspaper and on TV, who did I call? Walter. "I'm in a little bit of trouble. I wanna talk to you."

"I saw it on the news."

"When can we get together?"

"Well, I'm gonna be taking Mom and Dad to the Iron Mask Restaurant. We could meet there at seven." He lived with his parents in an old house in the same cul-de-sac as Evo DeConcini, a Superior Court Judge who I later bombed.

At the restaurant, the two of us sat at a table in the bar. "Walter, they're trying to kill me. Let me explain. I picked up a package I was supposed to take to San Francisco to Richie Fong. I was supposed to get paid and then pay the guy in Nogales, but when I got to San Francisco, Richie Fong didn't have the money. It was going to take him three weeks. I tried to explain this to the guys in Nogales. They didn't want to hear it. They want their money."

"How much?"

"Look, I can pay you back in three weeks when Richie Fong pays me, plus I'll give you interest of $5,000."

"How much?"

"Twenty grand."

"Come by the office in the morning, I'll have the money for you."

The next morning, Blake and I drove down to Complete Auto. In the back office, Walter handed me a large manila envelope. "Thanks a lot. I'll see you in three weeks." We left. In the car, I pulled out the envelope. The $100 bills were all crisp. They weren't new, but they'd been pressed and ironed. We split the money.

At a classy jewellery joint, the sales guy was all over me. He suggested a two-carat-diamond gold ring. With the mother-fucker burning a hole in my pocket, I stopped by a swanky joint called the Arizona Inn. Back in 1965, Princess Margaret had stayed there. I told the family who owned it that I was gonna do a marriage proposal. They had a special plate to hide the ring and they reserved a secluded table.

When I arrived with Katy, a cellist was playing. On the table was a bouquet of pink and red roses with sliced oranges in the vases, giving off a citrus fragrance. A waiter lit candles. Throughout the meal, Katy kept looking as if she knew something was up, but I didn't give her a fucking clue. "Are you pleased about this baby?" Katy asked, scanning my face.

"I sure as hell am," I said, casually. When we were done eating, the waiter brought the bill in a small leather envelope on the special plate. I reached into my pocket as if to find my wad, and acted like it wasn't there. "Oh shit! I've got no cash. Can you take care of it and I'll pay you back later?"

Katy looked peeved. I felt her mood drop. "I've got no cash either."

"Well, can you at least look how much the bill is?" Straining not to fucking smile, I was hurting inside. Reluctantly, she reached for it. When she opened the envelope, her face lit up. I dropped down on one knee with motherfuckers all over the joint watching me. "Will you marry me, Katy?"

Her face turned red. "Yes, I will."

A week later, we took off with Sal and his fiancée to all get married in Vegas. I was Sal's best man and he was mine. Our honeymoon was in Cancún.

A month later, I had lunch with Walter. I told him that the deal with Richie Fong had gone bad. "I'm sorry about what happened. If there's any way I can ever get you that money back, I will," I said, schmoozing him real good, ripping his fucking face off. He seemed receptive. Aware Bill Bonanno was in San Francisco, I said, "Look, Walter, I've got a chance to buy a club for $20,000. All I need is ten grand to get me in the place and I can do what I have to do and start to pay you back and make a decent living, but the Bonannos can never know about this."

"Don't worry now about paying me back. I'm sure you'll make a lot of money down the road. I'll get the money for you."

With the ten grand he handed over – all in ironed and pressed C-notes – I went and bought the Cabaret Lounge in Katy's name. I gave the owner six grand and carried a $16,000 mortgage. I used four grand to remodel the joint. I took the kitchen out and sold some of that stuff. With Blake, the most reliable of my strong-arm guys, I made a pool room. I brought in Falcon Vending and a little band. I told all of my friends that Katy's dad had given her the money to buy the place. I was the manager and the liquor licence was in her name. It was an ingenious move on my part. Even Sal didn't know that I'd got Walter again.

On the opening night, the Bonannos came sniffing around. I told them, "My girl's old man put up the money. He's retired in Nebraska."

The band came on: The Howard Bromberg Trio – blues, funk, jazz, rock. The Licavoli faction was there. The cops were all over the place, seeing who was who and checking out licence plates. I was tending bar and the joint was bustling.

I gave Bill Bonanno a tour. I showed him the pool room, my office, the storeroom and the pizza oven. Bill squinted at the oven. "Does that work?"

It took a month to find out why he'd asked. He said he wanted to give one of his guys a job selling slices of pizza out of my joint. In those days, I ran with my antennae up all of the time. In this situation, I knew the camel was trying to get its nose into my tent. If his guys were cooking pizza, they'd all be constantly in my joint, mooching pizza, wanting to drink all day, running tabs and shit they'd never pay for. I told Bill, "Jeez, that sounds like a swell idea, but I've gotta check with my girl's old man in Nebraska. I'll get back with you on that." I waited for a week and told Bill, "Hey, he don't want anything like that going on in here. It's only for Katy."

I had a Mexican-American waitress working for me, Nogales Alice. She needed money to support her kid. One night she showed up with a lot of make-up on, trying to disguise a fat lip, a black eye and bruises. "You been in a car wreck or what?" I asked.

"Jimmy got crazy with me," she said, referring to her on-and-off car salesman boyfriend.

I hate those pieces of shit who beat their wives or their kids for crying or acting up. The same kind of motherfucker never jumps on a man who will kick his ass or bust his fucking jaw. Everybody checks their wild-beast side and reason takes over when confronted with superior strength, especially wife beaters. Back in the day, we had a rule if we got robbed: never let a motherfucker tie you up. Tell him, "Here's the goods." Fortunately, I never had to try that out. My point is when a person is helpless before you and at your mercy, that wild-beast shit comes out in some assholes such as Jimmy. It's a power trip, a real control thing, like rape isn't always a sex thing 'cause a guy can buy a hooker. Fuck that wild-beast shit coming out of wife beaters and fuck Jimmy.

"Where the fuck's Jimmy at?"

"He's hanging out at the Tropical Inn."

"I'll be right back."

It was time to do my bit for women's lib. For thousands of years, women were treated as fucking prisoners. In Ancient Greece, while the men were sodomising unbearded youngsters, women were items to have alongside goats and cows, low on the scale unless it was one of their heathen gods like Athena. You may be thinking, *So how come Helen caused the Trojan War?* Well, men have been fighting over women, cows and sheep, right up to modern times. Women didn't then, and in a lot of countries still don't have a fair shake at life, from honour killings and funeral pyres to getting burnt alive for witchcraft. Many cultures didn't want girl babies and even snuffed them out. Women are not less than men. They just have different strengths and weaknesses, and I'm not talking about the art of lying in caves, pregnant, boiling up rabbit guts. As much as I wouldn't wanna be in Tora Bora fighting the mujahideen with Hillary Clinton or Nancy Pelosi watching my back, look how Margaret Thatcher crushed the Argentinians. She left their intestines floating in the South Atlantic Ocean after she sent her Limey sailors to the Falklands. She had more guys whacked than the Bonannos, all without leaving Downing Street – like a true pro. It's thanks to women's lib that during the past century, women have been encouraged to think for themselves. The bottom line is: we've all gotta think for our fucking selves. Look at how many dumb motherfucking men there are in this world. My advice to young women is: get yours – it's that simple.

I picked up Blake and went over to the Tropical Inn. Jimmy was at the bar with a friend. Of average build, Jimmy had scruffy thinning hair, big sideburns and dark circles around his eyes. "How're you doing, Jimmy?" I bought them beers. After chatting, I went outside and waited with Blake. Eventually, they came out.

"Hey, Jimmy!" When he looked at me, I hit him in the head with a beer pitcher. Then, I nailed the fuck out of him. Not once or twice, but all over, in the jaw, eyes, nose ... Bleeding badly, his face was all busted up. His friend did nothing. The final blow pushed him back against a wall, which he slid down as if drunk. "Hey, Jimmy, so you like to beat these women up. If you put your hands on Alice again or ever go by her business without her inviting you, I'm gonna plant you under a fucking cactus!" They wound up back together, but he never beat her again.

In the spring of 1968, Bill Bonanno arrived at my club by himself. "Who's back in your office?"

"Nobody. It's locked."

"Go back and unlock your office door and come back here and talk to me. Someone's gonna put a package in your office and I don't want you to see them." I unlocked the door and returned to Bill. "When you go back in your office," Bill said, "there's gonna be two packages. I need you to do me a favour and put them in places for me."

"Where do you want them?"

He gave two addresses in Walter's neighbourhood, so I thought they were something to do with Walter. One address was a house and the other was the Wig Beauty Salon. "On the street address, I don't want nobody hurt. I just want the bomb to make some noise to send a message. Try and do some serious damage at the Wig."

"Yeah, Bill. I can do this." Even though there was no money changing hands, I was still making a lot of money from these guys, not directly, but from them being behind me.

In my office was a paper grocery bag with two fucking bombs. In the old days, bombs were crude. These motherfuckers were seven or eight sticks of TNT wrapped up with masking tape with a crimper, a detonator and a three-minute fuse. I got a hold of Blake.

We arrived at the house first. Down an alley, I went up to the back fence, lit a cigar and touched it to the fuse, which started going off. We took off. We were a few blocks away when *badd-abing!* We drove over to the Wig Salon, a stylish place with a fountain with a bird spurting water from its beak. It was closed, so no one was gonna get hurt or knocked off. I put the bomb in the patio amongst the shrubbery. I lit the cigar again. It did a good job. The blast broke all the glass mirrors. Everyone got away. It went well.

The next morning, the newspapers were cooking with the headline: the house of Evo DeConcini, a Superior Court judge, had been bombed. I'd bombed his carport while he was chomping down on pasta. DeConcini had been a character witness when the feds had tried to deport the godfather, Joe Bonanno Sr, but he'd drifted away from them after they got bad press. The Wig didn't get that much play in the news.

The next night at my club, I was playing host, shaking hands when the owner of the Wig came in. "I gotta talk to you."

I was nonchalant. I had a .38 on my side. "Yeah, I'll be with you in a minute." I followed him into the pool room.

"Why did they do that to me?" he asked.

Now I knew he was boffing Batts' wife, while Batts was in the joint serving ten years. It had started after she went to the Wig to get her hair done. "What the fuck are you asking me for?" I yelled, irritated. "Don't come down here asking me questions. I've got nothing to do with that shit. Next time you come in here, buy a fucking drink and spend some money. This conversation is over."

He turned and walked away. "Go fuck yourself!" he yelled.

Heads were turning in the bar. I couldn't let that slide. I went after him through the door. "Hey, motherfucker, I'll blow your fucking brains out if you ever come here again. Do you understand me?" I pulled out my .38.

"You ain't gonna shoot me," he said.

Stood right in front of my club, I had to give him credit for that. People were parking. I couldn't just shoot him there. When you whack a motherfucker, the place you do it is even more important than where you bury the body. My philosophy has always been: no witnesses, no crime. The Iceman got away with whacking people for so long 'cause he knocked off not just his victims, but all of the witnesses, including his former crime partners and even fellow hit men. My preferred place to whack someone is indoors: a disused house or a business, a hotel room. Putting on a trench coat and a big black Russian fur hat and blasting someone in a steakhouse was never my thing. The Colombians shook things up and had real success for a while using two dudes on a motorbike: a driver and a pistolero. They'd wait until rush-hour, when the target was stuck in traffic, drive up with a MAC-10, spray the motherfucker until he looked like Swiss cheese, and take off again. Wearing helmets disguised their faces. That was popular with the cartels. Personally, I like to do it on my own in private, but sometimes you need a reliable crime partner, someone you're not gonna have to whack for ratting you out.

"Yeah, you're right. I'm not gonna shoot you." I proceeded to beat his skull in with my .38. I opened his head up and beat the living shit out of him. People were watching, but they didn't want to get involved. I slid the .38 to a black guy, a yellow cab driver. "I'll get it later." I washed the blood off my sweater and changed clothes. The hospital sowed and patched his head up.

A week later, someone threw a bomb on the Bonannos' garage roof and down the chimney of the barbecue pit, blowing up the patio. Glass had sprayed all over the sleeping godfather's wife, cutting her up a bit. With a shotgun, Bill Bonanno had blasted one of the fleeing bombers, but the explosion had sent Bill flying. When the cops arrived, the godfather asked them, "Why did they do this to my beautiful barbecue? My barbecue never hurt anyone." Two nights later, the Licavolis' Grace Ranch was bombed, damaging a carport and four cars. The bombings were all over the newspapers. I was wondering what the fuck was going on.

Bill Bonanno and his crew came down to my lounge to meet me and my crew. The Bonannos knew that the Licavolis hadn't done it. The Licavolis knew the Bonannos hadn't done it. They were both hip to the fact that someone was trying to start a gang war, but they didn't know who. Bill was watching my guy, Blake, shooting pool, showing his money roll and buying drinks. Bill and his crew left, but Tony the Snake stayed behind by himself, which was unusual. He approached Blake, saying, "Hey, Blake, loan me $500."

"I ain't got $500, so I can't loan you $500."

"Yeah, you've got it. I just saw it." I realised that the Bonannos suspected Blake for the bombings.

"Empty your pockets on the table," Tony the Snake said.

Blake scowled. "Fuck you!" Hearing that, I felt good for Blake.

"What did you say?" Tony the Snake yelled.

"I said fuck you."

"OK, tough guy. I'll teach you who to tell fuck you to." The Snake walked out of the pool room. He was forty-five, a killer, but not an eye-to-eye killer. The kind of killer whereby you'd go and empty your fucking garbage one night and he'd be in the trash can with a garrotte. The Snake went into the lounge and sat at a booth. He motioned for me to join him from behind the bar. I went over, and he said, "Let me ask you a question. First of all, it don't leave this table. Nobody. Just me and you."

"What's up, Tony?"

"How close are you with this Blake guy? You heard what happened in there."

"Yeah, I heard it. We're real close."

"Well, what if I gave you a destination and asked you to set up a meet at one or two in the morning with this guy? You haven't got to go to the meet. Would you handle it for us?"

"Hey, Tony, I'm gonna be right up front with you. I like this guy a lot. He's a close friend of mine. I did a speech at his wedding. I couldn't do nothing like that, and I don't think you should either."

"OK. I can respect that. Like I said, this stays at this table."

"No problem."

He left and I said nothing to Blake 'cause he would have shot the motherfucker for asking something like that. I called Bill Bonanno. "I gotta talk to you. It's important."

"Meet me at the Lucky Strike Bowling Alley at ten in the morning in the coffee shop."

I met Bill with his goon, No-Neck Navarro. "Bill," I said, "I'm gonna be upfront with you on this. Blake's a close friend of mine. He's done a lot of things for me and he's done some things for you, too. Tony the Snake tried to put a move on Blake and now he wants to kill Blake." I told him the whole story.

"Listen," Bill said, "this Blake guy is walking around flashing a roll of bills. What does he do for a living?"

"He's a carpenter."

"I ain't seen no hammers on the motherfucker."

"That's what he is officially. He's done work for me. He put in work on the bombings."

"Listen, you tell your buddy Blake that first of all, we don't know who's moving on our house. My old man lives in that house. Blake's walking around with a pocket full of dollars, acting like a big shot. Tell him to stay the fuck away from us. Tell him to stay the fuck away from our property or else he's gonna have big problems."

"I'll tell him and he'll stay away." Bill liked my response.

Back at the lounge, I sat Blake in a booth, and said, "Lay low for a little while. Those motherfuckers will be around and we don't want no shoot-outs."

Eventually, I found out that a renegade FBI agent, thinking he was an avenging angel, had hired two nutty kids to do the bombings. Hoping to start a war between the Licavolis and the Bonannos, he wanted them to wipe each other out, but it hadn't worked.

'Cause of my lifestyle, Katy and I weren't getting along. She'd wised up from seeing me as a flashy hip mobster type guy to a hoodlum addicted to living dangerously. I made up my mind to change all of that. I wanted to be a good father and to protect my child. Putting Katy and my unborn baby first, I sold the bar and decided to try to make a career out of selling real estate.

I approached the manager of Rio Rico, a 32,000-acre development in Southern Arizona, forty miles south of Tucson. He sent me to a real-estate school in Phoenix. I went to work on Arizona's border with Mexico. I'd get up in the morning, put on my Louis Roth suit, grab my Samsonite attaché briefcase and get in the carpool heading to Nogales, armed with a Schreiner pen with a Masonic lodge symbol. For once in my fucking life, I was a citizen, licensed by the State of Arizona to sell real estate.

Katy was real proud of the way I'd cleaned myself up. We were both looking forward to the birth of our child. I was doing well until the State of Arizona put two rummy-dumbs on trial for bombing the Bonanno house and Licavoli ranch. One of them admitted to the bombings. When asked about the bombings I'd done, the schmuck sang my name out in court. The supposedly reputable company I was working for – run by hustlers out of New York who'd been selling swampland to blue rinses in Florida – read about my role in the bombings in the newspaper. I got orders to attend the main office in Tucson, where I was fired for being a bad fucking person.

I didn't want to lose Katy by gangstering-up again, so I teamed up with a buddy to sell land in Pahrump, sixty miles west of Las Vegas. I'd sit out there in a double-wide trailer, offering free maps and cold drinks to anyone who'd stop and take a tour of Calvada

Valley. Mr and Mrs mooch on the way back from Vegas would see the free sign and stop. Being mooches they'd want the free drink. I'd show the mooches how we were gonna build a casino and a golf course. Their house would be on the eighteenth green. They were the first lucky people to get in on our empire. For every hundred mooches through the door, we'd close the sale on six per cent. They'd put $1,500 down for a $10,000 piece of property. With the money I made, I bought a house in Scottsdale for me, Katy and my newborn, Niki. She was a real doll. I was proud of myself and my family. Convinced everything was going to be great, I worked in Casa Grande, Arizona, selling real estate.

Not long after Niki's birth, I went to a bar with Sal, Blake and all of our ladies. We were toasting me being a dad, having a great time. Blake's girlfriend went to the bathroom and two guys we'd never seen before said something smart to her and pinched her ass. She came crying to us. We went over and fucked the dudes up bad. I knocked the teeth out of one. We got busted, but they dropped the charges after we offered to pay the $3,000 dental bill.

Seeing that level of violence freaked Katy out so much that she ended our relationship. When she told me, I felt so sick that I went into the bathroom and puked. I've been shot, stabbed, had my ass beat numerous times. My parents have died. My siblings have died. Yet I've never felt such a sense of complete loneliness as when Katy left and took Niki with her.

Even in here, I see how love affects prisoners. A gangster I know stood on a mound for hours on end, for six or seven Saturday Visitation days in a row, looking for his old lady's yellow Caddy to show up at the prison parking lot. And you know what? She never turned up. She gutted him while he was in the joint and he never regrouped. He was always a shell of a man after that.

Now I believe that love is strictly a remedy for loneliness. You don't wanna look at the Grand Canyon by yourself. You don't wanna go to Niagara Falls and ride the Maid of the Mist by yourself. So you fall in love, and you have to pay a price. It's not free. It's expensive – in terms of emotions. I saw my ol' man pay the price when my mom died. It was pitiful.

At the time, Katy ending things and demanding a divorce sent me into a tailspin, but she'd done the right thing, and she raised our daughter, who has kids of her own now and brings them to visit me here in prison. It's always great to see them. I'm so proud of my daughter and her family.

By 1972, most of the Tucson Bonanno clique were in prison, including Bill, Joe Jr, Batts and Sal. The Mafia godfathers, Joe Bonanno Sr and Peter Licavoli, had retired. Teddy Licavoli was in the joint, a heroin addict. After quitting real estate, I pulled various scams. By late summer, I was scratching shit with the chickens again, down and out at thirty-two years of age.

PART 2

DURING DRUGS

1973–1990

CHAPTER 5

An associate, Sherman – a stodgy guy with black hair whose beard was turning white at its sides as if someone had sprayed fake snow on it – was moving to Alaska. I asked to go with him. In April 1973, we loaded up his Cadillac Coupe DeVille and took off for the fucking great unknown. People hear about Alaska and think of igloos, Eskimos, woods and all of that shit. Let me tell you about Alaska. Number one: it was action. In Anchorage, there were three or four poker houses on 4th Avenue alone. Number two: bars were open until 5 AM. Fourth Avenue had a lot of foot traffic going back to the 1930s. Before the pipeline started, the locals didn't give a fuck where you came from or what you were hiding from. It was ideal. Sherman knew a guy from Tucson with a tortilla plant in Alaska. He gave Sherman the keys to his apartment. We drove up on the Alcan Highway, Yukon Territory, a Canadian province, real rugged terrain, lots of woods, until we arrived in Anchorage.

At the Holiday Inn's bar during cocktail hour, a woman called my name. Recognising Nogales Alice from Tucson, I was surprised. She said her kid was sixteen and giving her a hard time. He'd been in and out of juvenile detention. She asked me to talk to him. I went and played the dad role. Over Tall Boy beers, I gave him the ropes: don't get in trouble, steal, do dope ... Yes, it was a little hypocritical of me.

Nogales Alice got me a job at the Holiday Inn tending bar. I was getting good tips, working from 6 PM till 2 AM. At the bar, I met Anna Banana, a big, intelligent woman. She said her girlfriend was coming in from Virginia next week 'cause she'd sold her house and was moving here. At that time, I didn't think any more about it.

Right down the street, Harry Kardinoff – half Russian, half Eskimo – owned poker houses. He liked me and asked me to start moving football tickets. I was meeting people, a few guys here, a few women there. I liked Alaska, but Sherman was homesick after just a few weeks.

Kardinoff opened a bingo game in a country and western bar called Country City. I worked there calling the numbers. Set up on a high table, I was calling shit like, "B-22. C-8." Afterwards, we played poker downstairs in the basement of Kardinoff's house on 4th Avenue. It was unique. Outside, it would be snowing like crazy, but we were glassed in, set in a kind of atrium with tropical plants and heaters. Kardinoff had a plush green felt table, a poker light and there was always food like clam chowder and beef stew. It was designed comfy to keep you there. If you wanted to take a nap, there were three bedrooms.

Sherman and I played poker with Perry Green, a gambler who owned David Green Furs. His father had opened the store in 1922, when he'd arrived in Alaska from a family of furriers going back to the 1800s. Perry bought pelts from hunters and trappers coming in from the bush. In his store window, he had a $1,100 wolf overcoat that played a big part in my life. Natural white wolf made from the backs of wolves, almost knee-length with a Russian-general collar. It had some streaks, grey and black. I knew if I had that coat on and I walked into a joint, people would say, "Who the fuck is that?" Nowadays, I'd never wear it as it's too ostentatious and I have an ecology thing going on, but back then, I didn't know any better. I did a lot of things before I knew any better.

Winter was coming and I had a short leather coat with a quilt lining that was no fucking Alaskan winter coat. I told Perry Green, "What I'd like to do with you is work a deal on that wolf you've got in the window." My hustle was always good. If I wasn't serving 141 years and you and I were parachuted out over Ireland, and you landed with me, we'd be all right. We'd get something going moneywise. I've got that type of personality from living off my wits since I was a teen, not always living top drawer, but I've survived and had damn good times doing it. *Ha ha ha …*

"If you give me the coat, I'm working three nights over there at the Holiday Inn and two day shifts. I'll take the days I work nights and come over here and sell furs for you, and during my day shift, I'll tell people to go across the street to buy your furs." This conversation is bringing back memories now. I'm getting a little sad.

"Let's see how it fits you." Perry Green put the wolf on me. The sleeves were too long. His tailors – some Japanese women and an old Russian-Jewish guy – fixed it.

I started working there, having a good time. Three days a week, I worked at the bar and bingo. I had no overhead, just an apartment payment – that's it. I ate from the Holiday Inn's employee menu. It was good shit and free. I even saved up a couple of grand.

One night, Anna Banana showed up at the Holiday Inn with her friend, Linda, who had on a blue silk dress with a fox stole on her shoulders. The head was still on the motherfucker. Its little B-B eyes were staring at me. Linda's blonde hair was thick and wavy and hung down to her shoulders in a kind of bouffant style that flicked up at the ends. The Holiday Inn was packed. They sat down, but I had to keep working. I noticed Linda occasionally glancing, enticing me with her green eyes. Linda checked into the Holiday Inn. I was working the day shift when she came and sat at the bar during the lunch-time lull. "Hi, how are you?" she asked.

After greeting her, I said, "Listen, I'm running a bingo game out of Country City. Why don't you and Anna Banana come and check it out?"

"We might just do that," Linda said. And they did.

At bingo, Linda won $1,500 and a one-week trip to Lake Tahoe, staying at the Sahara with all expenses paid. I'd worked there for three months, and no one had ever won a blackout card like that. She liked me. We went out drinking and fell in love right away. We decided we wanted to live together, so she went out of state to sell her home. While I continued on with my life, she shipped her car up to Anchorage.

There was an element of Tucson people in Alaska, including a big, tough motherfucking oilman, 6-foot-5, 280 pounds, who loved to fight. One night, the oilman came to the bingo drunk, with his brother-in-law, a little fucking twerp. These motherfuckers bought one dollar card apiece for blackout, whereas the old ladies were religiously spending $20 to $25 a card. Through the dauber, I announced B-22. I called B-19, C-24, D-18 and all at once I heard, "I got it!" from the twerp.

I was thinking, *No, he ain't got it. He's been drinking, and it's a mistake.* I yelled to one of my checkers on the floor, "Check his card, please."

Now everyone was watching. "He's got it!" my checker yelled.

The twerp had won the money and a trip to Reno. The old women thought it was a fix and they quit coming. The owner, Kardinoff, accused me of cheating. "How the fuck could that happen?" he asked.

"I'm telling you, the guy won fair and square. I'll take a fucking lie detector test and the loser pays."

"You ain't gonna take no lie detector. We're through with the game." He tried to shaft me on my pay, so I went to the dart room to get my cut by stealing money. Kardinoff entered the dart room, drunk from too many Crown Royals on the rocks. "What are you doing?" he asked, slobbering. I knew my job was at its end, so I told him to fuck himself, and took $500. The game never reopened.

Around town, I became a local guy. I had my fucking wolf on, looking great. Linda returned and we were an item. She was a wealthy real-estate investor four years older than me. She had a teenage boy and a pre-teen girl, cute kids with shiny light-brown hair. We moved into an $185,000 custom four-level home in Geneva Woods built by a Norwegian craftsman. It had a two-car heated garage, important in Alaska. She owned four apartment buildings. Linda and I went to all the best joints. In dinner houses, we ate crabs, lobsters and juicy thick steaks. I was doing it. I was a polished person. I'd adapted to society.

It's 'cause of this time in my life that if you and I went to an expensive restaurant tonight, I'd know how to order. I'd know which before-dinner and after-dinner drinks to select. I'd ask for the wine list and request a decent vintage. I'd check the cork for dampness, roll my eyes when tasting the wine, and look at the maître fucking d'. Maybe I'd say something like, "Very good. This will be fine." But if I'm not impressed, I'd know how to send the motherfucker back. "I'm not satisfied. Please bring another bottle." And I'm a big tipper 'cause I've been in the business. I demand service.

My long-standing crime partner, Sal Spinola, was released from federal prison for $900 income-tax evasion. Hoping to give him a chance at going legit in Alaska, I flew him up there. Temporarily separated from his wife and kids, he moved into my house and hung onto me like a piece of fucking lint. I had an idea to encourage my stepson, Gary, into the business world. In prison, Sal had learned how to make jewellery from half-assed silver and turquoise. I put Sal in business, buying stones from Tucson. Turquoise was big then. I got Gary and Sal together, and told Gary, "You have a third of the business, Sal a third, and me and Mom a third." They set up shop in the back and put a big sign up that was lit up at night: GARY MAYFIELD JEWELLERY MANUFACTURERS.

Linda hosted a cocktail party at our new house to raise money for Pat Brown, the ex-governor of the State of California. Linda invited me to a fundraiser and birthday celebration for the Lieutenant Governor of the State of Alaska. We went in her car. Wearing the wolf, I had a pocket full of C-notes. It was in a big club with a banquet and a dais upon which the elite sat higher than the regular schmucks. They were gonna roast the Lieutenant Governor, talk crazy about him. Linda was a guest speaker. Linda said, "I've got to sit with the Lieutenant Governor up there on the dais, but I've put you with Ellen and Harold at their table."

"What're you doing?" I asked. "You mean to say we've come here together and you're gonna sit at the big-shot table, and I'm gonna sit with the mooches looking up at you."

"You can't sit at the dais."

Reluctantly, I sat at the mooch table. They were nice mooches. Everybody was drinking, being sociable. I started copping a little buzz. The roasting wasn't that funny. "I was ice fishing with the Lieutenant Governor one time, and he slipped on the ice and fell in the water and shit on himself," and they'd laugh and clap. "The Lieutenant Governor put his wrong argyle socks on back in 1949. *Ha ha ha.* Oh look. *He he he.* Stop it. You're killing me. Oh Lieutenant Governor, we love you. *Ha ha ha.*" I was wondering what the fuck I was doing there. I told Linda I had to go and I got the fuck out of there.

The next day, there were big pictures of Linda and the Lieutenant Governor in the newspaper. Realising we were from two different worlds, I was feeling a little put off. I was trying to do the right thing, not using her for her money and spending my money on her. At work, I received a sealed letter from Linda. It was mushy, saying how much she loved me.

On my birthday, February 9, 1974, I was working. The place was packed. *Badda bing, badda boom.* Five waitresses were demanding drinks from me, "Give me a grasshopper. Two Marty rocks. Two Cutty sodas. Four beers. One frozen daiquiri …" I was pumping the drinks out and being honest. It was one of the few places I didn't steal from.

The phone rang and someone said it was for me. "Hi. How are you?" Linda asked.

"I'm OK. How are you doing?"

"I just wanted to call and wish you a happy birthday. Do you think we can get together for a drink?"

"OK."

Now what I'm gonna tell you may sound bizarre. But what is more bizarre than life? Can you tell me? Linda came down near closing time when the place was thinning out. She got a drink and grabbed a little table. "We were meant to be together," she said. Right then and there, she said we should get married. Marriage was something really serious that I had to think about.

The next day, we agreed to wed. We went to Tucson to get married in style at the Triple H Ranch, in a stone-faced building. We had a famous photographer, Ray Manley. It was a classy wedding attended by a bunch of my associates. Batts was there, out of prison, laying real low. Our honeymoon was in Mazatlán, Mexico, with Peter Licavoli Jr and his wife, and Sherman – who'd gone back to Tucson to manage his parents' hotel – and his wife. We stayed in a four-bedroom condo on the beach and took a parachute ride around the bay. I ate lobster Rockefeller in a white sauce and got sick with Montezuma's revenge. On the plane home, I had diarrhoea and my guts were on fire.

Back in Anchorage, I checked straight into a hospital. They sent me home with strong medication. Up to this stage of the game, I'd never used drugs other than smoked a little bit of weed when I was twenty-eight in Tucson.

"What is it you want to do for a living?" Linda asked.

"You know what, I'd like to get into the club business."

"You would?"

"Yes."

With $10,000 I'd saved up, I started looking for a location. I needed a local partner to help with the work. There was a guy tending bar at the Chef's Inn, a Yugoslav from Idaho. We took a look around. The Green Dragon was for sale for $120,000. For $50,000 down, I could finance the rest. With $40,000 from Linda, I bought it.

By the summer of 1974, the construction of the pipeline was just starting. It was a big deal. Alaska was booming. There was a big market for vice, crime and cocaine. We were kicking ass in the club, having good fucking nights, listening to a rock 'n' roll band that we'd scouted the country for.

The first six months of marriage were pure fucking bliss. It was a side of life as an adult that I'd never experienced so full on even with Katy. The kids expanded to three when I brought my daughter from Arizona to stay with us. She was only three. I was protective of her and I let everyone know it. I wanted to ensure that Niki had a good time, and the other kids treated her right. Linda went out of her way to ensure Niki was happy. Everyone got along great.

I had no financial worries. I bought a red Pontiac Firebird just to be sporty. In Linda's Buick station wagon, we took the kids on a road trip from Alaska to Arizona, which took over a week. We were the perfect suburban couple. I attended PTA meetings and Girl Scout functions. The kids behaved. Gary was fifteen, but thought he was thirty-five. His mail-order gemmologist certificate convinced him that he was an entrepreneur. We bought an additional house in Tucson for $175,000, which made it easier for me to see my daughter. Leaving my Yugoslav business partner to manage the club, we spent winters in Tucson – where I played golf with Peter Licavoli Jr – and summers in Alaska. I was living on easy street, thinking my days of burying stiffs were over.

CHAPTER 6

So far, every time the Irish bartender at my club, Joey, had offered cocaine, I'd always refused. Then one night, he said, "Hey, you wanna try this?" I liked Joey. He was cool. I was comfy around him.

That night, I was at peace with the world. I thought, *Why not try it?* Alarms didn't go off. The sky didn't part or thunder start roaring. "Let me have a shot of that." I snorted coke for the first time. I went numb in my gums. When it kicked in, I'd never felt so high. In my head a nerve ending like a little clit started twitching and making me think, *Man, I'm having a great time. I'm so smart. I'm so handsome. I'm so tough. They're all looking at me in my club saying, "Man, who is that guy?" How can I get more of this stuff? 'Cause I really like this feeling.*

Next Friday, I figured I'd get a gram of coke. I paid $85. 'Cause my competition, the Fanny Moose, had closed down, my club was the number one place for rock 'n' roll in Anchorage. With the pipeline built, there was a business frenzy. More people were showing up doing coke and they all wanted to toot the owner of the club: me. By 4 AM, the place was packed with rock 'n' rollers, Eskimos, Native Americans and bikers.

I had three bouncers working, including Blake, my other long-standing crime partner who'd arrived from Tucson after Sal. Sal's specialty was hustling, whereas overgrown Blake was handy with his fists and as loyal as a dog. Two Eskimo women started fighting. I instructed my bouncers to throw them out 'cause there was a law in Alaska: if somebody got hurt in your club, you're liable. I also covered my ass by calling the cops in case one of them ended up in hospital with a stab wound or something. I had over $100,000 invested in the club that I didn't want to lose over bullshit.

At 4:45 AM, I turned up the lights. Waitresses – including Nogales Alice, who I'd hired – started picking up glasses. By 5 AM, it was bright-ass daylight. After everybody left, six bikers from a gang called The Brothers were still sitting there, grubby guys with beards and all that shit, some of their faces scarred-up from the Vietnam War, their sleeveless leather jackets showing off tattooed arms. On the back of their jackets their patch was a skull chomping on a joint, and above it, the top rocker: an embroidered strip that read BROTHERS. Below the skull, the bottom rocker read ANCHORAGE. Around town they were known for one of their rituals: smoking their dead comrades' cremated ashes rolled up in a joint. Whereas the rest of my customers had wound down to go home, The Brothers seemed hyped-up and ready to start some shit.

"Fuck you!" yelled a Neanderthal-looking motherfucker with long hair and a knife on his side. He had a forearm tattoo: MOTORPSYCHO. "Yeah, you," he said to me.

"What's your problem?" I asked.

"Yeah, go on, call the cops, you snitch motherfucker. That's all you know how to do."

From behind the bar, I got my .38 and returned to the biker. "OK, motherfucker, me and you outside. I'll show you what I know how to do." The Brothers went outside. My bouncers and I headed out. I stopped in the doorway. The biker who'd called me out saw my gun. "Hey, motherfucker, don't come back in this place. You can't drink in here no more."

"Put that gun down and get out here with me. Let's settle this."

"Fuck you. I ain't rolling around in the gravel with you. I'll shoot your ass."

"Well, you're gonna have to shoot me 'cause I'm crazy." With a fearless look in his eyes, he started towards me.

'Cause I'd been snorting coke and drinking all night, I was thinking I was Wild Bill Hickok. *Ha ha.* The sun was in my eyes and there was a big fucking biker coming at me, acting crazy. In my mind, I was calculating putting one between his feet to stop him. I shot. I wasn't sure if I'd hit him. My mind wasn't working so good in this situation. Instead of between his feet, I'd hit him in the foot. It had to hurt. I'll never forget what he did. He stopped and started walking in a circle, talking shit with blood squirting from his foot, painting the gravel red. His motorcycle-gang buddies were standing there. One of them got him off to the side. They put him on the trunk of a car, sat down with a leg propped up.

To protect my liquor licence, I had to notify an ambulance and the cops. I stayed at the door with my bouncers in case there was a get-down. After the ambulance took the motherfucker away, his buddies disappeared into the mist. The cops wanted to talk to me. I figured I had a shot at winning them over 'cause it was a case of businessman versus biker. I ran it down to them from the first time I'd called the cops about the Eskimos fighting.

"Look, we're gonna be real honest with you," a cop said, "you know where you fucked up. You should have shot him in the fucking face. That's Gunner. He just got out of McNeil Island Penitentiary in Washington State."

"Well, Gunner just got shot in the foot," I said.

"No problem. He pulled a knife on you, didn't he? You must have thought that to shoot him in the foot." The cops left it at that.

I got a hold of Big Jim, the president of The Brothers. He came to the club, a tall, big-headed motherfucker with biceps bulging from his leather jacket. He had a beanie cap on, covering a bald patch. A combination of beard and moustache stretched down to his gut. He was a serious guy with an aura of menace. "Hey, Big Jim," I said, "you've been here before. You always conduct yourself as a gentleman. This Gunner guy came in here with his whiskey muscles up. He wanted to be a tough guy in my place of business. Just for the record, you know, I've got money. I've paid some people. If anything happens to me or my family, Gunner is dead. Let him know that."

"Don't worry about Gunner. He's been away for too long." He seemed cool with it, and left.

A week went by. I was in the club, ordering beers and whiskey when the phone rang. "Hey, this is Gunner. Evidently, we know some of the same people. Can I come down and talk to you?"

"Hey, Gunner, if you wanna come in like a gentleman, come in, but don't come in starting no shit." I figured he was trying to turn the tables, trying to get money out of me just like I did with Walter. I was ready for this penny-ante motherfucker. I was strapped with a little .38 – which, from then on, I had with me for most of my life.

On crutches, Gunner arrived with his girlfriend. Up close, I got a better look at the motherfucker. A section of his forehead bulged unnaturally – a wall of rock projecting from his skull that could have done some serious headbutting damage. His blank brown eyes were set too close together and slightly slanted as if he had some Eskimo in him. The rest of his face was buried in hair that needed washing. We sat at a table. I wasn't gonna sweat him. "I'm sorry that shit happened the other night," Gunner said. "I was drunk."

"I was drunk a little bit myself. There ain't no problem."

"Look, I just got out of prison, man. I had a heroin problem and I got cleaned up. I had a job. I was doing good. Now my foot's in a cast. I'm not gonna be able to work for months. I've lost my job 'cause of that. They say you're a good guy. Can you give me some help here with my $2,500 hospital bill?"

"Hey, Gunner. I'm sorry you got shot. Shit happens. But as far as me helping you, I'm not in a position to do that. That's the way it is. It could have been me, not you in hospital. But I'll tell you what." I stood up, reached in my pocket, pulled out a roll of bills and gave him $200. "In no way, shape or form construe this as a sign of weakness. This is from the kindness of my heart. Here's a couple of hundred to buy yourself some groceries." That's what I told the motherfucker. I could see a little hurt in his face, but by now, he was realising that the conversation was over. He got on his crutches and hobbled out.

Months later, Gunner was off his crutches. My club was packed. Gunner was by himself, having a drink. I can see shit in people's eyes when they're contemplating getting ignorant. It may sound silly, but it's there – that look in their eyes. We have an inbuilt early warning system developed since the time of cavemen that alerts us to danger. Paying heed to that instinct has kept me alive on the road of life. Gunner was contemplating getting ignorant. I gave him a look that said, *Don't even think about it*. We didn't even have to speak. He finished his beer and left.

There was a bar in Phoenix called Johnny Ringo's. Its bouncers were super-bad motherfuckers. Interested in one bouncer, I went there. At 300 pounds, Tom – a former football line-backer for Northern Arizona University – was Arizona's strongest man on the weightlifting program. Not one of those peacocks who shaves his legs, smears Vaseline on his chest and struts around for the centrefolds of fucking magazines. He impressed me. Nobody outdid him. He had the heart of a Bengal tiger and the strength to back it up.

A call came to Johnny Ringo's from Nogales Alice at my club. "Do you know what happened last night? The Brothers came in. One of them, Happy Jack, pissed on the waitress station."

"Was Gunner with them?"

"Oh yeah."

After hanging up, I said to Tom, "Hey, dude, do you wanna go to Alaska and work? I'm offering you $300 a week, plus an apartment to live in. All you've gotta do is buy your groceries." He jumped at the opportunity. "I'll get you a ticket."

While in Arizona, I promised to take my six-year-old daughter to Legend City, a south-western-style amusement park in Phoenix. Yes, I was a Disneyland dad. When I picked her up, she was at the window, grinning and excited. She ran out to meet me. Hugging her, I felt guilty for not being there for her all of the time. Katy didn't say much except to warn me to take care of Niki, which I found insulting 'cause if anyone had fucked with

Katy or Niki, I would have strung him up, skinned him alive and blowtorched the motherfucker.

Near the entrance of the penny arcade, Niki spotted a dude in a British bobby outfit on a giant unicycle. She asked me where he was from. I told her about England, the Queen and the Beatles. She liked hearing that stuff. We rode through a gold mine with animated miners. It was high tech in the 1970s. Niki shrieked and cowered from the world's largest carnivorous spider, which was big enough to eat her. Her tiny hand grabbed mine and I shielded her as the ride moved on. The way she looked up to me made me feel good inside. To take her mind off the spider, I took her to the kinetoscope, a box with a peephole that we looked down into and saw black-and-white film clips from the Chaplin era. She laughed at Chaplin's goofy clothes.

Niki's favourite was the River of Legends, where we took a scouting boat through magical caves, and were under threat from cannon fire, prehistoric beasts, earthquakes and falling boulders, all of which we escaped narrowly from, so there was no fucking need to pull out my .38. Passing the Native American Village, Niki braced for them to attack and she was squeezing my hand. When she looked up with her big brown eyes, the love I felt brought a lump the size of a grapefruit to my throat. By the time the boat returned to civilisation, Niki was hyperactive with excitement. After an antique-car ride and a mini-sports-car ride, we finished off on the steam train around the park, raised on brown trestle above the barren desert. She said she had fun. Hell, I had fun.

Dropping Niki off, I said, "Who loves you, baby?" I still end all of my conversations with Niki like that.

"Daddy do!" Niki hugged me, reluctant to let go. Kissing the top of her head, I joked about our trip to ease the pain of leaving, feeling guilty again for being a part-time dad. She waved as I drove away. Even now as I write this, with Niki forty years old, I insist on her replying, "Daddy do!" That's always been our thing, and it always will. Niki deserved better than me, but she has always been a shining star in my dark life.

After dropping Niki off, I flew back to Alaska with Sal, ready to deal with The Brothers. In the club, I told my Yugoslav partner that I was bringing Tom up from Phoenix. "We're gonna handle Happy Jack for pissing in the waitress station. You can't let a motherfucker get a foot in the door and think you're scared of him. This is my place of business." As a half-assed tough guy, I was thinking that no fucking biker gang was gonna control me. I had my own crew and they were crazy, too. I sent Tom his ticket. I called him Toto after the little dog in *The Wizard of Oz* 'cause one night after drinking, I told him, "I feel the same way about you as Dorothy felt about her dog." I said that if I ever pulled my ear in a confrontation, it was a signal for him to knock a motherfucker's head off.

With the pipeline going strong, construction workers from all over the US were in Alaska. The Pipeliners Local Union 798 out of Tulsa, Oklahoma, were rowdy, tough motherfuckers, making thousands of dollars a week in the boonies. You couldn't have a skinny bouncer telling people not to be rowdy. You had to have a head-busting motherfucker who could take care of himself, who looked the part and could be intimidating. Beating the fuck out of people and throwing them out of the door is bad business. You want to use a bit of tact, such as, "Hey, fellas, you're making too much noise." That way you can just keep getting them drunk and taking their money. Valdez, Alaska was the southern terminal for the pipeline. There were teamsters unions, pipe welders, carpenters, cooks, bakers, everything. There were pimps, hookers, drug dealers and gambling joints all over the fucking place. Everybody was out to get their dollars, me included, and I was getting my share.

One night at 11:30 PM, two bikers came in, wearing leather jackets. I now had a rule in the club that they were disobeying: no collars and no motorcycle patches. Big Jim was with Happy Jack, a wild-looking motherfucker with a red beard and hair down to his shoulders. They ordered drinks. Other than Toto, my bouncers were half-assed scared of The Brothers.

"Hey, Happ," I said.

"What's up?" Happy Jack said.

"You know you can't drink in here, don't you?"

"Why's that?"

"'Cause you done pissed in the waitress station. Finish your beer and get the fuck out." I would have happily blown his fucking ass away in my fucking place. I now had $150,000 invested in the motherfucker and no two-bit punk was gonna fuck it up.

"Well, I'm with Big Jim," Happy Jack said, like that meant something.

I looked at Big Jim. "What's it gonna be, Big Jim?"

He never got a chance to answer. Toto pushed me aside. I'll never forget this. God rest his soul. Toto had no neck. All he had was a head resting on shoulders about a mile wide. At 6-foot-1, he wasn't as tall as Big Jim, but he was all muscle. "Hey, do you want both of these motherfuckers out of here, right now?"

I looked at Big Jim. "What's up? Are you gonna leave?"

"Yeah. Let me finish my beer and we're out of here." They finished their beer in thirty seconds and left.

One day at 10 AM, on my way to work, I stopped at a convenience store. Toto came in with a bandage around his head. "Those motherfuckers, The Brothers, came in last night." He'd been hit with nunchucks: two martial-arts sticks joined by a short chain or rope. His head was all smashed up, but he'd fucked a bunch of them up.

The next day at 4 AM, things were winding down in the club, but it was still packed. I was coked-up and carrying a nice pair of brass knuckles that I could have whupped Muhammad Ali with if I got him with my first shot. The Brothers came in, six of them, including Big Jim, Crash, Gunner and his older brother, Koot, flying patches on the back of their leather jackets. "Hey, guys, come on now," I said. "You've got to turn your jackets around. You can't wear your patches in here."

Big Jim gave them the nod to turn their jackets around. They did so, reluctantly. I kept my eye on them with Toto and Blake. I had two male bartenders and some regular hangers-on who just loved to do things for me. Nogales Alice said that The Brothers wanted to talk to me. I approached them.

"I ordered a shot of whiskey and it's too weak," said Koot, the vice president of The Brothers. "I ain't getting my fucking money's worth in here." Koot was a bearded Vietnam vet and demolition expert who'd served time for bombing business owners they'd tried to extort. His face was disfigured from shrapnel, his arms all tatted down with skulls and shit like naked women on Harleys. His cranium was less prehistoric than Gunner's, more Cro-Magnon than Neanderthal, with his features pinched below a big forehead. There were dark circles around his sunken scavenger eyes.

"What did you order?"

"I ordered a screwdriver. Here, taste it." He stuck the fucking glass right up to me like I was gonna drink after the sardine-eating motherfucker.

"I ain't gonna taste it. Hey, Alice, I need another shot of vodka in this." She fixed it and I left. A couple of minutes later, Koot came back. "What's the fucking problem, Koot?" I asked.

"This motherfucking drink ain't got no taste to it. What kind of joint are you running here?"

"I'll tell you the kind of joint I'm running here. Get the fuck out of here! That's the kind of joint I'm running. I don't want your fucking business." I was about to pull my ear as a signal to Toto, but things started moving faster than I'd anticipated.

With a long black beard and a droopy walrus moustache, Crash – their sergeant-at-arms – reached over, grabbed Toto by the cheek and pinched it. "I bet you're a real pussy."

Figuring something heavy was going down, five of us got ready to jump in. Crash and Toto traded blows. It was looking bad for Toto. Crash was a big strong dude who knew how to fight. "C'mon, Toto," I said. "Get in there and fuck him up." Toto grabbed Crash by the shoulder and headbutted him right across the nose. He rammed his forehead into his face. It was the first real headbutt I'd seen. When he pulled his head back, blood spurted from Crash. Did Crash go down? No, but he was fucking hurt.

Koot pushed me. They were all getting up. I was going backwards into a table. I pulled out my brass knuckles. By that time, Blake was getting into it with Gunner – *bam-bam-bam!* A bartender leaped over the bar. Crash had nunchucks. *Crack! Bam!* Toto was shaking his fucking head. I nailed one guy. Toto had Crash's head in a chokehold, a death grip. I cracked Koot in the temple. I could see and feel it. He went down. "C'mon, break it up!" Big Jim yelled.

Koot squinted, too dazed to get up. He was going for his boot for a knife or a gun. I pulled out my pistol. "Motherfucker, you'd better not bring nothing out of your boot."

"Hey, you guys, we're leaving," Big Jim said.

Standing up, unsteady on his feet, Koot said, "You ain't seen the last of us, motherfucker."

"Hey, just stay out of the joint," I said. "I don't want you guys' business."

"I fought a war for this motherfucking country," Koot said. "We'll go wherever the fuck we want."

Blood was flowing out of the top of Toto's head. He still had Crash in a chokehold. Crash's eyes were bulging. I didn't want no killing in my club. "Everybody be cool," I said. "People are leaving the club. This shit's costing me money." Toto let Crash go. He would have killed the motherfucker. The Brothers carried Crash out. The cops arrived. They wanted to make arrests. "C'mon. Let's be serious," I said. "This is just a little beef going on here."

"A little beef. Hell, look at his head." The cops knew me. I donated every year to the policeman's ball. I bought six to eight tickets. I was used to them coming around the club. They let it go.

CHAPTER 7

In 1975, an architect arrived to draw up a plan to remodel the club. It was still 1960s shit, red candles on the tables in bowls, red carpeting and crap like that. He said he needed $3,000 to go back to Phoenix to draw up the renderings. Linda and I were in love with the design. I wanted to call the club The Alaska Mining Company and make it a world-famous joint. As the project progressed, the architect took four draws of $3,000. For financing, we went to the People's Bank in Anchorage, to see the vice president. I needed $150,000. I got $200,000 from the motherfucker. We mortgaged two of Linda's apartments.

We closed the club down to rebuild the motherfucker. The logo was a shovel and pick crossed. Outside, we stationed an ore cart on railroad tracks, with wood and rocks spray-painted to create flecks of gold. Next to the entrance in the foyer, where people would stomp the snow off their feet and be told, "Gentlemen, please remove your hats. The sun is not shining inside," we put an old safe from a ghost town and a potbelly stove. I bought old pictures of mines in North Alaska at garage sales and framed them for the club. I got an old miners scale for $600. I had a gas fireplace with fake logs that was constantly on by a big old Victorian couch. The fireplace cubicles were available for groups of people. The uniform had an Alaskan theme: blue denim vests and shirts for the bartenders, and blue denim vests and shirts and skirts for the waitresses. I put my bouncers in sports coats. The cover was $3. Inside was beautiful and there were different levels. A sunken dance floor. Four speakers in each corner. A $20,000 sound system. Klieg lights with different colours that lit up the dance floor. The sound blasted so hard from the disco booth, it made your hair stand up.

On the opening night, the music was the Bee Gees, Donna Summers, The O' Jays, Van Morrison and John Travolta. I've always appreciated music, but my taste has evolved over the years. Here in prison, I listen to music on my Walkman and new CL10 headphones. All music ain't for me though. Don't give me no country and western with some hillbilly whining about how some granny got drunk and ran him over in a pickup truck. Don't give me no rap with egotistical ghetto stars singing about their bitches' big booties, how much jewellery and money and dope they've got, and how they're driving around in Benzes with a bottle of Cristal in one hand and a crack pipe in the other. I'm not saying I don't like all rap. Tupac was the Elvis of rap. Out of classical music, give me Schubert's "Ave Maria" or Handel's "Messiah" or Strauss's "Thunder and Lightning" – anyone who doesn't like that is a fucking animal, sacrilegious. It really affects me when I'm lying on my bunk with the lights out; it makes me sad and takes me down places that I'm better off not visiting. Nietzsche was right: life needs music.

My band, Predawn Flight, were kicking ass. I'd fly them up on the redeye special from Seattle and pay them well. The big table in the VIP room doubled as a one-way mirror looking at the dance floor. You could snort coke off the table practically at the dance floor. Figuring it was bugged, I stayed out of the VIP room. People rented it for $10 an hour. I put coke dealers in there for free. They liked that. People were doing drugs, mostly cocaine, some weed.

Alaska was still booming. You couldn't fall down without coming up with a C-note. I had to pay waitresses $5 an hour, and they were making $100 to $150 a night in tips. My club was taking in a lot of cash. We skimmed money off the top, so we wouldn't have to pay taxes on it. If I took in $3,000 on a night, I'd skim $400.

The rock 'n' rollers didn't come. They were replaced by young lawyers, doctors, stockbrokers, realtors and pilots. Wally Hickel Jr, the Secretary of Interior for President Ford, was hanging out there. All of the coke dealers dressed up and paid $3. The Brothers stayed away. I didn't know whether they were done fucking with me or were just regrouping.

Jett was a local guy who worked for me as a bouncer. He hunted and was a crack shot. Over a square jaw, he had a short, tidy beard and liked to wear the type of camouflage clothes you see on military groupies. One Saturday night, the club was packed, cooking. A band was playing the hustle: Ain't no stopping us now and all that shit. Jett came in with three Tupperware fucking things in his hand, each the size of a big bowl and full of coke. I couldn't believe it. He walked right up to me and handed them to me. "That's for that OJ you wanted," he said, giving me the look. The place was packed, so we went back to the kitchen to open them. Inside, shales of rock were glistening. "They're for you, bro, 'cause you really did me a solid this morning," he said, referring to a shady deal I'd helped him with. So now I had a problem: four ounces of coke. "You can't snort that," Jett said, "you've got to grind it up."

There's a little more to this guy, Jett, my radar said. We went to his house. We crushed it up and snorted it. "Pull your blinds," I said.

"No, fuck it, man. That's when they suspect something: when you've got your shades pulled."

It was 1976. They'd told us that coke was strictly recreational, that you couldn't get addicted, and it wasn't like that scumbag heroin that made you wanna lie around all day, puking and scratching your ass and balls. They were wrong. Let me tell you something: there's basically three segments to my life:

BD: Before Drugs when I was sharp. I had my game together. I made good decisions. I bought things of value.

DD: During Drugs when my mind was in the fucking ozone layer. The most horrendous and costly decisions I ever made in my life happened DD. People lost their lives. I lost control of my decision-making processes. My values changed completely. I didn't value even life, family, oaths, vows, friendships. I didn't give a fuck about too much, except getting drugs, partying, feeling good. If you didn't do drugs, I didn't wanna hang around with you. I never went to big fucking parties, orgying and all that shit, or injected coke. Certain lines, I didn't cross, although I slid way down. I was mostly in the club, doing drugs, selling drugs, trying to be cool, hanging out.

AD: After Drugs is when you sit around in prison and mope about the things you should have done with your money. I'm stuck on AD for 141 years now, but back then my pleasure value was set on stupid. Vanity had a lot to do with it. Yes, it's nice to be pleasured. That's why Vegas comps big shots. The secret is to have the right pleasures, such as taking the kids to the park. Not drugs and hookers. That leads to destruction. Just look at me. My violent tendencies were exacerbated, but drugs can turn even normal people into monsters. Look at Charles Manson with the women on LSD, driving around LA, putting turkey forks in people's bellies, cutting pregnant women open to look at their foetuses and giggling while they did it. They weren't insane. They were from Iowa and Nebraska. Their daddies were grocery-store managers and shit like that. How did Charles Manson control them? With drugs. My advice to you is to stay the fuck away from them.

I was hanging out with dealers and users. Wearing a bad-ass three-piece Armani suit, gold chains around my neck, a Rolex and pinky rings, packing a five-shot Smith & Wesson .38. I was a high roller, the owner of the first discotheque in Alaska. Everybody who's anybody was drinking there.

"I've got this guy, Carlos, a coke dealer," Blake said.

"What're you paying?" I asked.

"I'm buying it by the pound. Delivered to Tucson for $17,500."

"Let me see what I can do."

I told Jett that I had a connection in Tucson and I could get a pound delivered to his house in Anchorage for $20,000. He said the quality had to be superb. I guaranteed the quality. I'd make $2,500 per pound, but I had to transport it, which in those days wasn't hard 'cause you just threw a pound in your suitcase and flew with it. It was nothing back then, and everyone was doing coke. Football players. Basketball players. Movie stars. Politicians. Lawyers. Prosecutors. Judges. Hookers. Pimps. Construction workers. One time, I went to my barber to get my hair styled, and he said, "Do you want a line?" and pulled a vial out of his pocket. Jett liked the quality of my shit, so it became a regular thing. After six months of my club being open, I started getting out of control on coke, basically putting Bogotá up my fucking nose.

At first Linda was OK with me tooting coke 'cause I hadn't self-destructed. We went on lots of trips. In Hawaii, we stayed at the Poipu Sheraton, brand fucking new in Kauai, and the Hilton Hawaiian Village Waikiki Beach Resort in Honolulu for a few days. We travelled to Acapulco, Mexico, and stayed at the Princess Hotel, where Howard Hughes was on the top fucking floor in reclusion. I didn't blow all of the money on luxuries. I tried to put some to good use. Blake said he was struggling to pay the medical bills for his little girl, who'd been diagnosed with Jacobsen Syndrome.

"What the fuck's that?" I asked in the club.

"It's very rare, and it only got discovered a few years ago," Blake said, his face aged by stress. "The doctor put it this way: we have twenty-three chromosomes and for the eleventh one there's a piece missing. In Mary's case, there's a very large piece missing. The doctor said she's a worst-case scenario. But I think that's bullshit 'cause she does all kinds of things they told us she couldn't possibly do. Our insurance company is refusing to pay all the costs."

I could tell the prognosis was fucked up and Blake was reaching. He'd backed me up in a number of situations and he'd never asked for much. He was always so fucking humble. I paid the medical bills the insurance didn't cover. If the kid lived, maybe the devil would take it into account when I ended up in hell for all of the fucked-up shit I'd done.

I was with Linda, eating crab legs and prime rib, when I got a call from Nogales Alice: "Jett shot one of The Brothers outside. Shot him five times, but the dude didn't die. There's a lot of shit going on. Jett's in jail."

The bikers were starting shit again. The Brothers had merged with another biker outfit and were expanding. I was wary 'cause there were even more of the motherfuckers. They'd opened a gambling joint and were distributing coke. They were extorting club owners for protection money they called insurance. A strip-club owner had refused to pay. They broke into his home, shot to death his wife and son-in-law and set fire to his house. Not long after that, one of The Brothers suspected of a dozen murders was found dead along the highway with a shotgun blast to the heart.

I bailed Jett out of jail. The next night, I went to his house on his two acres. Getting out of the car, hearing rustling, I wondered what the fuck was going on. A guy with a shotgun appeared out of the shadows. "The bikers have beefed up. They keep driving by taking potshots, but they don't have the balls to go in the house."

Inside was like a scene from *The Godfather*. There were two or three guys over here with guns, two or three guys over there with guns, pistoleros all over the fucking place. "Hey, if you wanna spend the night, stay here with us," Jett said. "You haven't got to go out in the cold though. Stay in the house in case they try to come in."

I ate moose steak with the twelve troops in the house. One handed me a raw piece of meat. "That's the heart. You gotta eat it."

"What? Raw!"

"C'mon. Are you gonna be a cheechako all your life?" A cheechako is a newcomer to Alaska, a tenderfoot. "Until you eat raw heart, piss in the Yukon River, fuck an Eskimo and fight a grizzly, you're a cheechako."

I didn't want to eat it. I had on my wolf overcoat, Bally Italy boots, and I was all done up, but I had to do it, so I did. It wasn't exactly tender, but I chomped the motherfucker down to keep my machismo intact.

The bikers never came back that night. With heat on Jett for the shooting, he decided to make himself scarce by going out into the woods. Days later, I took a rough road to visit Jett at his spread in the woods, twelve miles out of Chitna. Three groups of people were staying there: Jett and his crew, including Fred, a pistolero, second-in-command to Jett; Jett's old lady and her crew; and a group of overseers. Jett's cabin had a potbelly stove and no water. We had to go to the lake with a bucket. Someone heated up spaghetti. I didn't want any spaghetti and lake water, but I ate some to be polite, and I had to run out to the woods to shit as there was no latrine. A dude was reading a novel when Jett walked in from another room. Jett grabbed it. "Give me that! I told you I don't want no books at this camp!" To make it clear that he was the lord and master of the camp, he tore the book up. "Let's go into town. We'll take the trucks."

Armed to the teeth, the men got in two trucks. The pistoleros in the back had AR-15s with the stocks off them, shotguns sawn down and bandoliers of ammunition across their chests. It felt like I had gone back in time one hundred years. In the town, Jett's guys got out of the trucks with their guns. Hippies – all headbands and bearded down – had invaded Chitna. They'd brought generators, opened a store and were selling beer. Apprehensively, they gazed at Jett's crew. I was Jett's buddy in the middle of his assemblage, but even I was fucking apprehensive. We bought some beers and Jett took us on a tour of Chitna. We visited abandoned places and a mortuary. We came across a big safe that weighed a ton and an old ore cart that ran on railroad tracks. After that excursion, I headed back to Anchorage, convinced Jett was a cold fucking killer.

In 1977, I was at the club when Jett called. "Come and help me, man."

"What's the problem?"

"I'll explain when I see you. Come and help me. It's important. I'm at Jimmy O's gambling house." Jett explained that The Brothers' expansion into the coke business was stepping on our toes. Jett was moving coke for me. Grabbing pounds cheap at

$15,000, I was now selling them for up to $22,000, or sometimes even $25,000 if I caught a motherfucker right. One of Jett's customers was moving a pound every now and then. The Brothers wanted the guy's business. He'd said no 'cause he was already doing business with Jett. Gunner, who I'd shot in the foot, had told the customer, "Hey, fuck Jett. He shot one of our guys. I'll blow Jett's head off and you can be our customer." No way was I gonna let Gunner get the jump on us like this.

Gunner had a girlfriend at a whorehouse run by a classy money-making madam. The madam didn't like The Brothers going out with a few of her girls. Gunner ran his mouth off to his girlfriend that he was gonna kill Jett and come to my house and do some fucked-up shit to my wife and the kids. My daughter had just come to stay. I was enraged. There was no way I was gonna let that motherfucking Neanderthal fuck with my family. I checked around to make sure that Gunner wasn't just talking smack when he was drunk. After the madam confirmed that Gunner was preparing to follow through on what he'd said, I decided I was gonna get that motherfucker and do it right.

Jimmy O's gambling house had green felt tables, dealers and a bouncer. The cops knew about it, but had been paid off. I was there one night with fifteen associates from Arizona, including Sal. After we left, I got a call from Jimmy O, saying that Gunner, Happy Jack and their two girlfriends had stopped by. Drunk on whiskey and fucked up on Secanols, Gunner had argued with Jimmy O, who was ready to leave. "C'mon, you've gotta rest," Happy Jack had said, steering Gunner towards a back room. "Get in here and lay down, motherfucker." In the back room, Gunner had collapsed on a beanbag and passed out. Happy Jack and the others had abandoned him there. I told Jimmy O to leave, but not to lock the back door. I arrived at Jimmy O's, entered through the unlocked door and went into the back room. Gunner was on a beanbag snoring, his mouth wide open, revealing jagged teeth. Having been up for three days on coke, he'd crashed hard. I took out my gun.

When whacking a guy at close range, I preferred to shoot him in the head. A motherfucker is more likely to die from getting his brains blown out than from taking a hit to the body. The skull is like a helmet that protects the brain. It can slow a bullet down and sometimes even deflect it. To get around that you put the gun in his mouth if you're able to get that close. Aimed up, you can splatter his brains against a ceiling or produce a cloud of fine mist formed by brains and bone fragments. Aimed slightly down, you'll get a quick kill if you destroy the spinal column at the base of the skull. But the spinal column in that area is only slightly thicker than a pencil. That's why shooting someone in the neck is risky. You might get a good gargle out of the motherfucker, but the bullet will likely go through the neck and miss the spinal column. Two other nice spots are the temple and the side of the head under the ear, aiming up at the brain. Stay away from the chin. Some suicide nut-jobs shoot their chins off but completely miss their brains. Duh! The nose is good 'cause it's hollow, so it allows the bullet right into the brain, just like the eyes. The heart is a great target, but the chest is a large surface area, and the ribs can change a bullet's path. If a bullet doesn't cause fatal heart damage, you still might get a kill if the aorta or the largest veins into the heart or the major branches are destroyed. A shotgun is perfect to aim at the heart 'cause the pellets spread out, so even if you have a lousy aim, there's usually plenty of damage to cause a motherfucker to bleed out. A shotgun in the mouth will put someone to sleep fast. It might take a motherfucker's head off. Nirvana's Kurt Cobain chose that 'cause it's the deadliest form of suicide. If you're in the market for a gun to protect your home, get a shotgun.

I put my gun in Gunner's mouth at an upright angle. *Pop!* I put another in the side of his head, under the ear. *Pop!*

Unlike when I'd shot the motherfucker in the foot, this was a quick, clean whack. Watching his head slowly bleeding out, I was proud of my work. In the movies, they sometimes show someone shot in the head and it explodes like a watermelon and the shooter gets a face full of blood. In this case, there wasn't much splatter. One minute he was breathing, the next, there was no life in the motherfucker. Yes, this was During Drugs, but Gunner had a killing coming for threatening my family and my guys. If I had waited much longer to whack him, he might have got the best of me.

I called Jett to come and help. I drove over to a hardware store for a sleeping bag, a clothesline, blankets and Visqueen: a plastic sheet that catches paint drops. I went back to the club and traded my Eldorado for a partner's SUV. At Jimmy O's, I backed the SUV up to the rear door. The traffic was bumper-to-bumper on the street at 7 AM, but nobody could see me 'cause of a plywood fence.

We wrapped Gunner up real good with a clothesline, his hands at his sides like you would a mummy, so his hands wouldn't start doing the rigor-mortis thing. We put him in the sleeping bag. We cocooned him in more Visqueen, so there would be no blood stains in the SUV. We dragged him to the back door, went out, opened the back of the SUV, put him in, went back in, got the beanbag, threw it in and covered him up with a blanket and the beanbag in case we got stopped, so it didn't look like a body. "Let's take this motherfucker to the woods and burn him," Jett said.

"Let's go," I said.

We stopped at a hardware store for two five-gallon tanks and filled them up at the gas station. Jett drove by Eagle Creek and found an empty place in the woods, where we could douse him good with the gas. "Fuck burning this motherfucker," Jett said, "let's take him to Chitna and throw him off the bridge."

"That's 300 fucking miles. Why we gotta go to Chitna?"

"We're better off out there. There's a town, Cordova, where the bears will eat the motherfucker real quick. The bears are hungry 'cause the ice is thawing. They're waiting for the ice to break so they can eat the salmon."

"OK. Fuck it. Let's go!" We stopped at KFC and bought a bucket of chicken. It still seems surreal: driving along the Alaskan highway, packing pistols, eating chicken, with a stiff in the back. Jett was chomping on a drumstick. I had a gram of coke, my end-of-the-night stash. I tooted a bit.

"Look, if we get stopped by a cop," Jett said, "there ain't no way I'm gonna let the motherfucker take us down."

"Well, let's not get stopped. Let's not give them any reason to stop us. Let's stay at the speed limit."

We stopped for gas and coffee in Glennallen at a truck stop by a snow-capped mountain. At night, we arrived at Chitna. It was snowing like a motherfucker. There was no traffic or hippies out. We cruised right through. Jett took a road with a sign: Travel this road at your own risk. The state does not take care of this road. We went out to an old railroad-trestle bridge. Right in the middle, Jett parked. We looked down through the grating at the Copper River, twenty feet of water in the middle running fast, its sides ice. "Let's take this motherfucker downriver, about half a mile, and we'll take him out on the ice and throw him in."

I didn't want to do it as much as I didn't want to argue. It was cold and the body was stinking in the SUV. "OK. Let's go." Jett did a U-turn onto a road and got stuck in the fucking snow. "What the fuck are we gonna do now?" I asked, worried about the moose patrol, the motherfuckers who stopped people poaching. "Just our luck if the Alaska Department of Fish and Game catch us with a stiff in the back." We dug and pushed and eventually got out. I was so fucking relieved.

Jett drove back to the middle of the bridge. We dropped the tailgate, threw the beanbag over, heard it hit the water in the dark and pulled the motherfucker out. Jett took a knife to the Visqueen – *bam-bam-bam-bam!* – so air and water would get to the corpse. He threw the knife in and said, "Let's get rid of this motherfucker now." We threw him over. He hit the water and drifted off into the darkness, disappeared, the fucking scumbag. If there is a god in heaven, I hope he forgives me, but I still feel no remorse. We threw the blankets in, everything.

"The Brothers won't be rolling this motherfucker's ashes up and smoking him in a joint," Jett said.

I took the SUV back to the club. My guys asked where the fuck I'd been. "I had to take care of something. Don't worry about it."

"Heat?"

"No cop heat."

The heat was from The Brothers, who came over the next day, when I was with Toto and Blake. I had Jett hanging outside with an AR-15 in case anything popped off. Koot and Big Jim came in, followed by Happy Jack with a racoon cap over his long red hair. In situations like this, I had to train my eyes to watch everyone simultaneously to catch the first signs of anyone reaching for a weapon. Figuring they were gonna start some shit, I was ready to draw my .38.

"Hey, have you seen Gunner around?" Big Jim asked.

"No. I ain't seen him around."

"He always checks in with me or Koot. This ain't like him."

"He's probably with some hooker."

"Don't talk no goddam shit about my brother!" There was a look in Koot's eyes that said he suspected that I had played a role in the disappearance of Gunner, and it was on between us.

"Cool it, man," I said. "How the fuck am I supposed to know where he is? Am I his fucking babysitter?" I drew my gun on Koot.

Jett burst in with the AR-15. "None of you motherfuckers move!"

Koot didn't try anything stupid. "If I find out that you had something to do with whatever's happened to my brother, I'll hunt you down to the ends of the fucking earth."

"Let's go," Big Jim said, pulling Koot towards the door. They left.

A few hours later, I got a call from the house: Niki was missing. Linda said the kids had been playing in the treehouse in our backyard. Niki had come down from the treehouse and gone off into the woods with a neighbour's kid. The neighbour's kid had resurfaced, but not Niki. I rode home full-throttle, so fucking freaked I was ready to rip someone's fucking head off. After questioning the neighbour's kid, I had all of my guys meet me there and we scoured those fucking woods. I wasn't just worried about The Brothers. There'd been a recent child abduction in the area. Coming back from the woods without Niki, I had no choice but to call the goddam fucking useless cops and tell Niki's mom. What the fuck! But before I could call, a lady showed up at the house with Niki in her car.

"Where did you find her?" I asked, running from the house. I scooped Niki up and hugged her.

"My son was out on his bike and he drove by her in the woods. I came out and asked if she was lost, but she couldn't even talk. I drove her around and asked her to point out which house she was at."

A few hours later in the house after everyone had left, Niki said something that freaked me out again. "Daddy, I have to tell you something that that kid did in the woods that's supposed to be a secret."

"What did he do to you?" I asked, ready to smash the kid's door down and lynch the fucker.

"He was lighting matches." Fucking relieved, I picked Niki up and kissed her.

Ten days later, I was feeling a little fucking heat over Gunner. A teamster came to see me. "I gotta talk to you."

"What's up?"

"I was at the gym, working out and a cop asked me if I knew a dude called Gunner. I said, 'Yeah, I've come across the guy.' He said, 'We pulled a body out of the inlet with two tattoos: GUNNER and MOTORPSYCHO.'"

The cop was fishing, but how he'd figured out the body was in the water, I still don't know. Somebody had talked. Jett had a big mouth. I know he told some of his guys. I figured I'd better get out of town until things calmed down.

With Niki on the passenger side of my silver 1974 Jaguar XKE, a sleek hardtop with chrome spoked wheels, I headed for

Anchorage airport. There was little traffic. The sky was pale and cloudy as I passed the odd diner and convenience store. Cruising along, I noticed bikers in the lane behind. *I'll kill these motherfuckers if they fuck with me with Niki in the car.* Turning to smile at Niki, I took a gun from my ankle holster and discreetly placed it at my side. With their engines revving, they were closing in. The next traffic light was red. A truck with industrial equipment had stopped in the slow lane at the light. The fast lane was open, so I could haul ass and run the red light if I had to. I started to slow down, but the light changed, so I put my foot down and accelerated past the truck. The bikers maintained their speed.

The growling of their engines was freaking Niki out. "What's that?" Niki asked, raising her hands over her ears.

"Just some guys on bikes making noise. It's nothing to worry about."

They came up behind and signalled for me to get out the way like they wanted to overtake. To check out who the fuck they were, I moved into the slow lane. Approaching a red light, I passed a used-car lot. I hit the brakes, grabbed the gun and held it to the opposite side of Niki, so she couldn't see it. If shit was gonna pop off, it was gonna happen now at the light. The first biker arrived at the junction and screeched to a stop slightly ahead of my car. He was on a streamlined Harley-Davidson with its front extended to a skinny wheel. The patch on the back of his leather jacket was a death head: a skull facing sideways, wearing an aviator cap attached to a big golden wing. Above the skull, the top rocker embroidered in red said, HELLS ANGELS. I just watched the motherfucker. His buddies stopped behind him. The instant the light turned green, they roared off. I flew with Niki to Arizona and stayed until the first week of May.

Gunner's mother and sister came to Anchorage to visit him, but there was no Gunner. Staying at the Hilton, they put an ad in the paper along with his picture: Has anyone seen this man? The Brothers were driving around, looking for Gunner.

I got a call from Jimmy O. "Listen, man, there's a lot of shit going on up here."

"What's up?"

"The Brothers are real mad."

"About?"

"One of their partners. They're hearing things. They wanna kill you guys. They heard that you killed Gunner and Jett helped you throw him away."

"How the fuck did you learn that?" I asked.

"Happy Jack came to me drunk and said, 'Do you know what your guys did to our guy?' I played it cool and said, 'Yeah, I heard about it.' He said, 'Then you know what we're gonna do. Do you wanna help us?' I acted like I would help them."

Blake's kid with Jacobsen Syndrome died at only two years of age. Blake asked me to be a pallbearer at the funeral. Linda and I went to the church. I gathered with the fellas by the hearse, who all looked like gangsters dressed in black. The pallbearers wore ties and had white carnations on their lapels. The tiny white coffin was the saddest thing I ever saw. When the head dude from the funeral parlour extracted it from the hearse, we picked it up and stationed it at the front of the church. A bouquet was put on it and several more around it. Blake and his wife – a petite woman with long brown hair – were so distraught they looked like meth-heads who hadn't slept properly in six months. When everyone had parked their asses on the pews, Blake got up and thanked people for coming and for the outpouring of love and support.

"Mary was a lovely child. Precious," Blake said, choking up, his big steel-blue eyes full of pain. "How great it was just to have her. For fourteen months – actually, for the first two months, Mary was in the hospital – so, for, I'd say twelve months, my wife would drag an air mattress into the living room, 'cause Mary didn't sleep in a crib, she slept on a little beanbag 'cause that's where she was most comfortable in the living room, where we set up the feeding thing and all that stuff, and my wife literally stayed at the foot of Mary every single night, ready to provide feedings and give oxygen, just in case ..."

Listening to Blake and imagining something like that happening to my daughter made me misty-eyed. When Blake's wife got up and talked about giving Mary sponge baths and kissing her little fingers, nearly everyone was crying. You'd have to have been a fucking animal not to.

"Our days are numbered," the pastor said. "Only God knows the specific day you're going to die, and the way you're going to die. That's very current in God's mind, but he loves you throughout it all. It's up to you to respond to the call from God, and give your heart to Jesus. If you trust in God, he'll forgive you for all your sins. All of us have done things that are not right, but all of your lives are just as precious to God as Mary's life. If you don't give yourself up to God, you'll never know what good he's gonna do in your life and that would be a tragedy. God doesn't want to see you go astray. It says in the Bible, if the shepherd has a hundred sheep and one of them goes astray, the shepherd will go and find that sheep, even if it involves searching hills at night in the rain or rocky cliffs in a storm, the shepherd will leave all ninety-nine sheep to go get that one sheep, just like Jesus as the Good Shepherd comes to help you during your darkest times, if you open your heart to him and don't try to run away. Don't let Mary's life be in vain for you by turning away from God."

My coke-addled mind was zoning in and out of the motherfucker's droney voice. When I snapped back to reality, it seemed like he was preaching to me individually as if he knew how far off a stormy fucking cliff I'd gone. *Not even fucking JC can save me now.*

A few weeks later, I took Linda out to dinner. We had sauteed veal medallions with crab and asparagus, topped with a cheese sauce. We went to the club at 1 AM. There was a long line outside. In the line, I noticed Big Jim, Happy Jack and Koot. Big Jim waved as if everything was cool. Wondering what the fuck they were up to, I waved back. I had two bouncers on the door, Toto and Blake, and two bouncers roving around. My guys looked at me as if asking whether to let them in or not. I figured they'd be less suspicious about me whacking Gunner if I let them in. Toto sat them at the balcony over the dance floor, which had herringbone timber walls.

I was having a drink when Toto said, "You didn't want me to charge them, right?"

"What do you mean?" I asked.

"You told them it was on the house."

"No! I never said shit! Everybody pays, Toto. Go get $9 from the motherfuckers. Tell them to pay or get the fuck out!" I was beginning to think that letting them in was a mistake – they could have taken me by surprise at any time – so I was glad they'd provided a reason to kick them out. I was at the bar with Linda, Sal and twenty hangers-on ready as a standing army.

Toto bent over the table to talk to Big Jim, who got up and came towards me. I was holding a .38 – hammerless, lightweight, five shots – inside a holster on the right-hand side of my three-piece-suit pants. Big Jim made it to me, the others behind him. "Why did you send Toto down on me?" he asked in a hostile voice. He knew I had my hand on my gun.

"Everybody pays who comes through the fucking door and then you sit down and order a drink like everybody else."

Big Jim said to his guys, "Get your shit out," meaning weapons.

Koot came at me with an ice pick. Sal grabbed Koot. Big Jim grabbed me. We started wrestling. In two seconds, I heard *pop-pop-pop*. One of them was shooting. I ended up out in the foyer, struggling with Big Jim. Wielding a flashlight, the kind the cops used, Toto jumped on Big Jim's back and went crazy hitting his head. I was surprised he wasn't knocked out cold. He was dazed. My bouncers and some of the hangers-on threw The Brothers out, past the line, into the snow.

I went inside to see if Linda was OK. The music had stopped. People were stood in a circle around Sal, his head gushing blood. Nogales Alice handed him a towel. He was in a bad shape after Koot had stabbed him in the head with an ice pick while I was wrestling with Big Jim. Blake was lying there unconscious, his arm and chest bleeding. I checked his neck for a pulse. I thanked fuck he was alive. We called an ambulance and the police. Linda was crying, screaming, having never seen anything like that. The cops came. I rode in the ambulance with Blake in a coma. He'd been stood there with his big biceps, when Happy Jack had pulled out a bulldog, a .44, which shot him through his arm and into his lungs. At the hospital, I waited with Blake's wife, assuring her that everything was being done that could possibly be done to revive Blake. He lingered on for several hours. When the doctor confirmed Blake was dead, Blake's wife was hysterical. I tried to hug her, but she pulled back and screamed at me. Leaving the hospital, I vowed to get Big Jim, Happy Jack and Koot.

CHAPTER 8

"I'm still in shock from seeing Blake get shot," Linda said – a few days after the mêlée – in our living room after the kids had gone to bed. Tears were falling. "What if those bikers come here? Have you thought about me and the kids or are you too coked-up to give a shit?"

Yes, all of the values and the decision-making processes I'd acquired along the road of life, I'd thrown out the fucking window on drugs. Linda didn't want to be dragged down with me. "You're right, but if guys come in the club starting shit, what am I supposed to do about it?"

"I know those bikers are the guys who killed Jimmy Sumpter's wife and stepson." Sumpter was the club owner who'd refused to pay The Brothers' insurance. Linda had seen the murders on the news. "You can do whatever you want about the bikers, but me and the kids can't live with that kind of risk anymore."

"What are you trying to say?" I asked, my heart jumping – not just from the coke.

"I'm not asking for a divorce, but I think we need to live separately, at least until things calm down."

"OK. I'll rent an apartment until things calm down," I said, relieved that she hadn't broken us up. Somehow I'd restore our relationship. On coke, anything was possible. Thinking I was Genghis fucking Khan, I told Jett we needed to snuff out the bikers.

After moving into an apartment, I made arrangements to take my estranged wife to dinner at my bartender Joey's house, with him and his wife. I remember exactly what I wore 'cause I had to burn all of the clothes even though I loved the outfit. I put on a green gabardine suit. Out of my ten coats, I didn't choose my beautiful ankle-length wolf or my buffalo, but a $500 brown leather that complemented my green patent-leather shoes. We found Joey making corned beef and cabbage. The house reeked like balsamic vinegar. We sat around.

"Is that your secret Irish recipe?" Linda asked.

"Yes, and it includes Guinness." Joey smiled. "The trick is to cook the brisket for a long time in low heat, so the connective tissue dissolves."

"Do you stick a fork in it to tell when it's done?" I asked.

"No, it just falls apart. I use lots of red wine and onions. This will have you whimpering it's so succulent."

Just as Joey served a platter of corned beef and cabbage, the phone rang. Joey's wife answered it. "It's Jett for you."

I grabbed the phone. "Come and help me, man," Jett said.

"What's wrong?"

"I've got Crash wrapped up downstairs. I can't get this motherfucker out of the basement."

"Who's there?"

"Nobody. I run them all off."

"How did you get him?"

"I kidnapped the motherfucker from a whorehouse."

"I'll be there in twenty minutes." I hung up. "Hey, listen, I've got business I've gotta go take care of."

"Do you want us to put the food on hold until you get back?" Joey asked.

"No, you guys go ahead. I'll eat when I get back in an hour."

The lights were on at Jett's. "Where is everybody?"

"I told them to go eat pizza, to get the fuck out of here." We walked through the house. A campervan was backed up to the back door. Down the basement stairs, a corpse was tied to a piece of plywood wrapped in Visqueen. Jett had tied a clothesline to the plywood and tried to pull the motherfucker up the stairs.

Have you ever picked up a dead body? There is a reason for the terminology dead weight. If you weigh 200 pounds or less, I can lift you, but if you're dead weight lying on the floor, you'd be fucking hard to lift. Believe me, I know.

"I've got to get back over to Joey's," I said. "Let's get this motherfucker out of here. I'll get the bottom. On the count of three, I'm gonna push and you're gonna pull. One, two, three …" I pushed. The corpse scooted about two feet. "One, two, three …" The corpse scooted another two feet. It was working. The corpse was scooting up the stairs at a 45° angle, but on the third push, the Visqueen came open and a foot popped out. Blood stained from my chest to my knees. *My suit, my suit, every fucking thing!* I was still high on the coke I'd done earlier. I got mad. "Let's get this motherfucker out of here. One, two, three …" We got the corpse to the top of the stairs and threw him in the camper. I looked at Jett. "Hey, Jett, listen to me for a minute. You do what you gotta do with this motherfucker. I'm not going with you this time. I've gotta get back otherwise I'm gonna end up divorced."

"I've got him from here."

In my badass Eldorado, I had to sit really carefully, so as not to get blood on the upholstery. I couldn't go back to Joey's. In my one-bedroom apartment, I stepped on a padded cushion. I took off my fucking coat, suit, socks, shoes, everything. I got off that pad naked. I was good – professional: it took the cops twenty years to get me for one whacking. I got in the shower. Blood went down the drain like in that movie *Psycho*.

After changing clothes, I jumped in the car and went back to Joey's. I took the trash baggie in the trunk of the car. I went inside. My hair was wet and I'd changed my clothes, but nobody asked me a fucking thing. After food and a little glass of wine, I took Linda home and went to the club.

There was a friend at my club who owned five acres on the outskirts of town. "Look, I gotta go out to your land," I said. "I've gotta do some things."

"What's up?"

"I've gotta get rid of some things, burn them up."

On the way, we bought charcoal lighter and a fifty-five-gallon drum. On his land, I put the whole bag in the drum. I sprayed and lit it and stirred it with a stick. He saw the shoes and shit, but he didn't ask. There are certain things you just don't ask. There are things that you don't wanna know. And if he had asked, I couldn't tell him that Jett had killed a motherfucker 'cause I didn't wanna get killed. Do you understand?

The cops were still fishing around about Gunner and now investigating the disappearance of Crash. Homicide detectives wanted to speak to me about Blake's death. To avoid the heat, I went back to Tucson. I spent time with my daughter. We shopped at the recently opened Metrocenter Mall in Phoenix.

I got a call from Jett: "The Brothers are hearing things."

"What the fuck are they hearing?"

"I don't wanna go into detail, but pretty bad shit."

"Look, I'm on a flight tomorrow night. Pick me up at the fucking airport."

I flew to Alaska with two suitcases of clothes and a camera. I got off the plane and went down a ramp to Jett and his second-in-command, Fred.

"C'mon, we're going over to Fred's house in the city," Jett said. "My place ain't safe. The Brothers wanna kill us. They know we killed their guys."

Paranoid like a motherfucker, I didn't even go to my club. I got my .38 out of my suitcase and strapped it on.

"We've got a pound of coke," Jett said. "We're going to Valdez on the other side of Chitna. We've got business up there. Come with us. We'll take your car and deal with the silly shit when we get back."

"That sounds good," I said.

At Fred's, we grabbed baby laxative to cut the coke. We got two pounds ready to ounce out to the 2,000 construction workers at the pipeline. The three of us took off for Valdez with Fred's big mean Doberman. We were snorting coke like motherfuckers. In case there was a shootout with The Brothers, I needed these guys now.

We arrived at a trailer park in Valdez. The snow was starting to melt. Jett went into the trailer, took a big mirror down, put it on the kitchen table and put a pound of coke on it. I took some uncut for personal use. We didn't wanna fuck the coke up with too much laxative. It's like making a cake. You can't put too much sugar in 'cause you can't take it out. Fred and I didn't know how to do it. Jett mixed in the cut. I told them I knew some people in Valdez that I'd like to go and see.

"Jett's in serious trouble with The Brothers," Fred said. "He's gotta get out of town. We're scraping all the money together we can get our hands on to send him to San Diego. That's what this trip is for. Can you help us?"

"Yeah. I can throw in five grand." Immediately, I detected that I'd said the wrong thing. They were pissed at my response. I assumed they wanted me to pitch in more than five grand. After seeing my old friends in Valdez, I came back.

Jett seemed agitated. He'd been mixing coke at the table for two days and tooting coke with workers buying ounces to take to the pipeline. "Where the fuck did you go?" Jett asked.

"I went down to see the old bartender at the Chef's Inn."

"What did you talk about?"

"What the fuck do you mean? What the fuck do you want? A written fucking statement of what I've been doing." I had my .38. He had a 9mm Browning.

Jett grabbed me, swung me around and threw me in a big chair. He got in my face. "Listen, motherfucker, I've got my shit on the line for you with The Brothers, and you're disrespecting me big time."

I knew in my heart and soul that they were looking to kill me. All animals have a part in their brain that says fight or flight. I don't care if it's a white rhino or a bull elephant. My brain said flight, so I back-pedalled. "Relax, Jett. It's all good, man. What're you getting all uptight about?"

Fred was sat down, snorting coke, his eyes massive. He had a big old .45 right by his hand. They were riding together. I was outgunned.

"Where's your piece at?" Jett yelled. "Let me see your fucking piece!"

"I've got it right here. What's the problem, Jett?"

"There ain't no problem and there ain't gonna be one. Let me see that, motherfucker."

I had to give up my gun, but at the same time, I had a plan. Number one: they were doing business out there. Number two: they thought I had a lot of money in my safe in Anchorage, even though I only had ten grand at the most. Jett put my gun in a back room. "What the fuck's wrong with him? He's real uptight."

"He just has to get out of town," Fred said. Jett returned.

In my conniving mind, I had to give them a reason not to whack me. In *The Prince*, Machiavelli said the lion cannot protect himself from traps, and the fox cannot defend himself from wolves. You must be a fox to recognise traps, and a lion to frighten wolves. It was time to be a fox. "Look, Jett, I know you're uptight. I know you've gotta get out of town. I'm gonna help you get out of town. Look, I've got money in my safe, but The Brothers are staking out the club. On Sunday night, we close at midnight. The janitor comes at 5 AM. From midnight to 5 AM, there's nobody there. On Sunday night, I can go in after midnight to help get you out of town." They liked that, but I was still apprehensive 'cause I knew on the way back we'd go by the Chitna road.

Jett stood up and stretched. "I think I'm gonna take a shower." He did a strange thing: he reached and pulled out his 9mm and put it on the coffee table right in front of me. Perhaps he was testing me, but I didn't know for sure. He went for a shower. Fred was sitting there, mixing coke, acting like he was my buddy. It was the good-guy-bad-guy routine.

I imagined grabbing the gun and nailing both of the motherfuckers. *Did he take the bullets out? Did he really take a shower?* I was as high as Ike Turner on coke, and that's a motherfucker who grew a moustache just so he could catch the coke rocks falling from his fucking nose. I gazed at the gun. *Grabbing the gun is a bad idea. You've gotta finesse your way out of this.*

More Valdez workers bought coke. Jett and Fred decided to go back to Anchorage. They hadn't sold all the coke, but they had fifteen grand wrapped in rubber bands, stashed in black socks. Fred put the rest of the coke in a briefcase. We loaded the car, and the four of us, including the big black Doberman, got in, Fred in the back with the dog, me riding shotgun with Jett driving.

One hundred miles out of Valdez, we'd be at the road to Chitna. *Man,* I thought, *if they turn right on the Chitna road, I'm gonna jump out of the car 'cause they're gonna kill me.* They had even more guns going back 'cause they'd traded coke for guns. They had a Remington shotgun, side arms, three .45s, Jett's 9mm, which he had on him, and two more 9mms.

Driving by mountains, Jett said, "Hey, you know what, bro? I got a little excited back there. Forgive me."

I was on edge. *Are these motherfuckers setting me up before they whack me?* "That's OK. I don't mind you venting on me. That's what friends are for, bro." When Jett drove past the Chitna Road, I figured they were gonna whack me in Anchorage after I'd paid them. It was Mother's Day, too!

At 6 PM, we arrived at Fred's house on the outskirts of town. He parked at the front and left the keys and guns in the car. Jett took the briefcase into the house. His girlfriend was inside.

The bathroom window had an eight-foot drop I knew I could escape from. "I've gotta use the can."

"Go ahead," Jett said.

In the bathroom, I closed the door, so they'd think I was taking a crap. I opened a window and dropped out. I ran to the front, got in the car and took off like a motherfucker. I even had their guns.

I drove to Big Phil's massage parlour. At 6-foot-5, Big Phil was a tough motherfucker from San Francisco. He knew Jett but didn't like him. I told him what had happened. We decided to set a trap for them at the massage parlour. Toto joined us there. We put all their guns in the back room of the massage parlour, and we sat, armed, waiting for them, but they didn't show up.

I called Jett. "You fucked up, you cocksucker. You're dead now. I'm gonna kill you."

"Hey, I don't know what the fuck you're talking about. I want those things back we left in the car."

I called the guy I owned the club with. "Look, I'm gonna leave town. Buy me out."

"What do you want for it?"

"Fifty grand."

"But there's three-hundred grand owed and it's got escrows coming out of its ass. Look, I can't even send you pay no more."

"What do you mean?"

"You're never here. You're never working."

"Hey, motherfucker, you don't understand. I'm coming up there in a few days to get my money."

With so many enemies in Alaska, I flew to Phoenix to regroup. I put all my jewellery in a safe, including a Rolex and a pinky diamond. If I died, it would all go to my daughter. Before going back to Anchorage, I called Toto to bring my car to the airport. With shit flying, I wanted him in my corner. I flew first-class. Going down the ramp, I saw Toto with his crew. I looked over and saw another crew with Fred. "You got my car?" I asked Toto.

"Yeah. But before we go anywhere, you need to know the cops are here right now."

I felt a tap on my shoulder. It was Lieutenant Manning, from the Department of Public Safety, a big dumb motherfucker who'd harassed me in my club. "Hey, Lieutenant, do you want to arrest me for anything?"

"We don't want no trouble here."

"If you want to arrest me, go ahead and read me my rights, and let me call a lawyer. Otherwise, I'm here on business, talking to my partner, so stay away from us. I've got nothing to say to you." At the side of the terminal, I spoke to my partner from the club.

"Listen, I've got your money, but it won't be here until next week," he said.

"Are you telling me you've got all fifty grand?"

"My uncle's sending it from Portland, but I don't want you going in the club. The Brothers have been all over the joint. I don't want no shootout."

"Until I get my money, I'm your partner. I'm heading for the club right fucking now. Let's go, Toto." I had my baggage, but my shotgun hadn't come through. It had been misplaced. I had guns, including Jett's Remington 12-gauge shotgun, which I took inside the club and started to screw together. One in the chamber accidentally went off and shot through the roof. My business partner thought I'd shot a customer. I put the gun away, but I was strapped with a .38 on the small of my back.

Two big grubby dudes walked into the club and stood there gazing my way. They had purses on them. In those days men carried purses if they thought they were cool, purses with guns in them. They sat down and called me over. I told my guys to watch my back in case the dudes were with The Brothers.

"Let me go to the car to get my gun," Toto said.

"OK. Go."

I joined the dudes. "We heard you were back in town," one said.

"C'mon outside and talk," I said. "It's not safe in here 'cause the cops have bugged the joint." They got up and followed me. I was walking out of the door with a sports coat on when I saw Toto coming with his gun. I turned around and pulled my gun.

The dudes threw their hands up high. "Hold on, man. We ain't got guns. We're just businessmen. We came to talk to you about getting coke."

"Open those fucking purses!" I yelled. Toto opened their purses. They were empty. I figured they were trying to lure me to a coke deal to set me up for The Brothers. "Look, let me give you a piece of advice. Before you come looking for a motherfucker in this town, you'd better check out who he is. Anybody would have told you, 'Don't go down there looking for him 'cause he'll shoot your ass.' What are you guys driving?"

"A Lincoln." They still had their hands up.

"If I see you motherfuckers around where you ain't supposed to be or if I see that car, I'm gonna open up on it. Now get the fuck out of here and don't come back."

I figured by now The Brothers knew I was at the club and

they were gonna ambush me. I got high on coke with my boys, including Sal, who was glad to see me. About 3 AM, Toto said he'd spotted bikers driving around outside. From the entrance, I couldn't see anyone, but I could smell gasoline. "Let's take a look around," I said.

Holding guns, we walked along the perimeter. The gasoline smell got stronger as we approached the club's dumpster. Hearing rustling behind the dumpster, we drew our guns and approached cautiously in case it was a trap. We were too late to bust them. The motherfuckers had fled. We found the makings of a bomb: dynamite, gasoline and wires. It had to be Koot, the demolition expert, trying to blow me to kingdom fucking come. I stationed a few guys on the roof with guns and instructions to shoot any of The Brothers.

When it was time to leave, we formed a motorcade. I handed out Jett's guns, so there were guns in every car. About a quarter of a mile from the club, I spotted the silhouettes of bikers up the road. It was light outside 'cause in summer Anchorage never goes dark. They were probably hoping to ambush me on my own. I put my arm out of the window, signalling for the motorcade to stop. My crew got out with guns. With Toto and Sal next to me behind my car, I aimed an AR-15 and fired some rounds up the road. The motherfuckers took off. High on coke and adrenaline, I spent the night at Toto's, more worried about The Brothers than Jett, who was laying low 'cause the cops were on his ass.

The next night, I went back to the club and told my partner, "I don't wanna hang out here anymore than you want me to. I just want my money."

"It'll be here in a few days."

I left right away, but some of The Brothers must have been staking out the joint. Two on bikes followed my car. I U-turned back to the club, parked and got out, yelling for Toto and Sal. Out of nowhere came Koot with his ice pick. The motherfucker was on me fast. He swung. I stepped to the side and grabbed his arm. We ended up wrestling on the dirt. Toto smashed Koot in the head with an iron club, knocking the motherfucker out. Cops showed up. Hiding inside the club, I watched them arrest Koot with his ice pick. More bikers arrived and demanded the cops let Koot go. The cops told the bikers to get the fuck off my property. The cops were asking my bouncers where I was 'cause they wanted to question me. I disappeared.

Driving by my apartment in a taxi – as a disguise from the cops and The Brothers – I noticed the door had been busted open. My place had been trashed. It wasn't safe for me there, so I went to Toto's. From there, I arranged to have my car shipped to Seattle. I flew to Phoenix, where I received a certified cheque a few days later for my share of the club. In Seattle, friends picked me up in a limo. I partied for three days, and drove to Tucson in my Eldorado.

In May 1977, the snow started melting. Crash's body was found wrapped in Visqueen and wire. A hooker had ratted out Jett. They questioned him. He said nothing, but the cops noticed that a section of his wire clothesline was missing. Imagine if I killed you right now and took a cord, cut it, wrapped you up with it and put your body in the desert. If the cops found your body and compared the cord to my cord, I'd be busted. That's what got Jett busted. While he was in jail, The Brothers torched his house.

Jett was found guilty. Someone told the cops they'd seen me at Jett's house around the time of Crash's disappearance. The problem with a lot of motherfuckers who get arrested is they run their mouths to the cops. Whatever you tell the cops, they'll use it against you, even if you try to bullshit them. They'll twist and throw your words back at you in court to get a conviction. If you ever get arrested, keep your fucking mouth shut. Never rat out your associates. Omertà. Jett got a new trial. In the interim, someone put me at the death scene. By keeping shtum, Jett ended up beating the murder rap. But a few weeks after his release, he disappeared. The Brothers were obviously smarter than him at getting rid of bodies.

CHAPTER 9

With too many enemies in Alaska, I had no choice but to split, which ended any chance I had of saving my relationship with Linda. My lifestyle was such that staying would have exposed her family to danger. If anything had happened to them, I wouldn't have been able to look at myself in the fucking mirror. 'Cause I was doing so much coke, the split didn't rip my heart out like it did with Katy. When I got sad thinking about what I was losing, I just shoved more coke up my schnoz. My priority was staying alive, so I decided to stay on the down low in Tucson at the Sahara Hotel on North Stone Avenue, which Sherman – who I'd moved to Alaska with – ran for his parents, who were as senile as hell and owned a couple of big hotels in Tucson.

The Sahara was a mix of Hotel California and the Bates Motel. It had dope cliques out of its ass, living in it and doing deals out of it, not the actual transfers, but the business end of things. I was staying there carte blanche. I had a big room to lounge in on the fourth floor. I was eating great food at the restaurant, prime rib and lobster, drinking cocktails and doing plenty of coke. I'd breakfast in the coffee shop, drink beers by the pool, snort coke, take Valium before having a nap, shower, go out at night in a Louis Roth sport coat and hit a few clubs. I had no job and didn't answer to nobody.

Driving around with Sal in my Eldorado with the top down, I spotted a yellow cab following us. I could always detect a tail. I made a U-turn. As I passed by the cab, I got a good look at the motherfucker. He made a U-turn. I pulled up at a stop sign. The cab stopped behind us.

"Let's go back and talk to this motherfucker," I said, jumping out of the car. Sal followed me. I knocked on the cab driver's window. He was wearing a cowboy hat and looked like a rancher. "Hey, man, if you're a cop, show me your badge. If you're not, why the fuck are you cold-trailing me like this?"

"Relax, I'm a cop. I'm gonna show you my badge. Here, does this make you happy?" His badge said, DIRK TAYLOR HOMICIDE DETECTIVE. "Listen, a guy just broke out of the penitentiary, Jack Watson. He thinks you're responsible for killing his buddies in Alaska. I got word he's on his way down here to kill you."

Is this for fucking real? "Why didn't you let me know earlier?"

"I'm letting you know now."

"I'm telling you this: if the motherfucker goes for me, I'm gonna protect myself. You got a picture of the guy?"

"I'll bring one by the hotel," Dirk said politely. "I don't have one on me."

"I'm just letting you know if the motherfucker shows up at my hotel, I'm gonna waste his fucking ass if I think he's gonna mess with me."

"No, no, no. He'll never get in the hotel. We've got the Sahara surrounded."

I put all my guys on alert to watch out for any bikers showing up at the hotel. The next morning, I was in the coffee shop at the Sahara when Dirk showed up with a photo. Jack Watson was none other than the vice president of The Brothers: Koot. "OK. I see what he looks like now."

"Look, he'll never get in here. The place is surrounded."

Sherman only rented out the first three floors of the Sahara. The twenty rooms on the fourth floor were just for a few of us regulars. His aunt worked in the dining room and the coffee shop on the other end of the floor. A lush lived on the fourth floor. He worked for a rental car agency, so we got all the cars we wanted for free.

A guy called Dan was living up there, a big fucking bald dude just out of prison. Dan hung out poolside at the Sahara with the weed and coke dealers, doing coke together, laughing and joking.

Some were staying at the hotel, giving Sherman coke to get a good hotel rate.

I was out by the pool one morning, taking in the sun, gun on hand under a newspaper in case I spotted that bearded mother-fucker, Koot, ready to blast his ass. A guy showed up, not a guest, white as can be, who tried to swim with us. We figured he was a cop. There was a drugs task force in town. The 1970s was the first decade of the War on Drugs, kicked off by Nixon. So many people were doing coke, Nixon jacked up prison sentences. The coke added to our paranoia. Sherman paged me to the lobby. I was wondering what was up. We were also on edge 'cause of all the undercover cops posted around the hotel. *Are they waiting for Koot to come or was that just some bullshit to spy on us?* We were ready and not taking any chances.

Sherman met me in the mezzanine of the lobby. We went up to the poker room where we ran a few games a week, which took my mind off Koot and the cop heat. Dan was at a table with Ezio, a big Mexican, who was staying on the first floor. He spoke little English. We'd done coke together in Sherman's suite. "What's up?" I asked.

"You know Ezio," Dan said. "Listen, here's the deal. Ezio can go into Mexico and bring in some high-quality coke, but you've got to pay upfront."

The feds had busted my coke supplier, so I no longer had a Mexican connection. Now, I was the bull with the horns – short for I had the cash. In fact, I had just lent Sherman $10,000 to make his payroll. But I was no lame. My rule was: no fronting cash – dollars and dope on the table. Coke was eighty per cent pure at that time. Dan was talking about buying pounds. Sick of buying grams from nobodies, I said, "Look, why don't we send him down there and let him charge us for a quarter pound of good coke on a trial basis." *Wah-wah-wah* ... Ezio wanted $5,000. I decided to hedge 'cause I hardly knew him. "We gotta think about this." *Wah-wah-wah* ...

Dan started a sales pitch about how big Ezio was in Sinaloa.

How they were connected to the cartel. Sherman jumped in, trying to put the close on me 'cause he wanted coke. "Look, to show you his good faith," Dan said, "he'll bring back a half pound for $5,000. He'll even front you a quarter pound."

I decided to test this asshole out. "We'll go for that. When will he be back?" I said, thinking, *If it's good and all goes well, we'll place a bigger order next time. It's a test run to see how everybody acts.*

"If he leaves in the morning, he'll be back on Sunday." It was Wednesday afternoon. "He needs a ride to Nogales. He's walking across the border and catching the train. He's an official with the train company." Ezio was from Costa Rica, Mexico, a little town about fifty miles out of Culiacán. There were big-time gangsters down there.

"I'll take you to the border," I said. Sherman and I had rented a Bronco that we used when we went shooting. We had every gun imaginable. Two AR-15s. A Smith & Wesson .44. A Magnum .44, the *Dirty Harry* gun. Bookoo .38s. A high-standard 12-gauge pump. A couple of .22s. Sherman was a gun freak, and I was at war with The Brothers. I looked at Dan and said in my most serious tone, "Are you co-signing this deal 'cause we don't know Ezio from Adam?"

"Yes, I'm co-signing. I have no doubts. He's good. I've known him for years." In the drugs business, when you co-sign a motherfucker, you're saying you'll pay his bill. You're responsible if something goes wrong.

"OK. Let's do this deal." I shook their hands and left.

That night, I went out to party and eat. It was 1977, and women were wearing turbans, capes, puffy skirts and shirts with billowing sleeves. Flares were going out, but slim European suits were in. With Tucson being so close to the Mexican border, everyone was high on coke that hadn't been cut to fuck. Tucson was wild. Figuring Koot would show up in a bar while I was doing the ABBA thing, I was strapped and on alert. When I went clubbing, I got up and boogied. Yeah, I was a disco duck. If you wanted a woman, you couldn't just sit around and talk out of the side of your neck, you needed to dance and the coke helped, too. Every time I saw a grubby dude through the haze of the bar, I took the safety off my gun and got ready to waste the motherfucker.

Back at the hotel, I didn't go to bed. I snorted coke. I got $5,000 from my stash in Sherman's safe, and went down to Ezio's room on the first floor, ready to go to Nogales in the Bronco. If the cops pulled us over with the five grand, I had proof that it was from my investment in the Alaskan club, so the motherfuckers couldn't confiscate it. Besides, they usually only fucked with you about carrying cash if you had over ten grand. They used newly introduced asset-forfeiture laws. They'd jack your cash and you had to prove that it wasn't drug money. Ezio was snorting a brown liquid that smelled like dirty fucking socks. He offered it to me, but I didn't want it. In the Bronco, after we got on the road, he was sniffing that shit and pidgin-talking all the way to Nogales. At the pedestrian gate in Nogales, I handed Ezio $5,000, all of it my money, not Sherman's. Sherman was just my business partner in this deal. In pidgin Spanish, I wished Ezio good luck. He waved at me with a look that I translated to mean, *See you, you sucker motherfucker.*

On Saturday, there was a party by the pool. Weed buyers were in town hanging out with Dan. The hotel was jumping, women galore, drug deals being worked out by the pool. Coke and weed were kings. I was staying in Room 417, Dan was in 415, but we didn't chum together. His little clique was having a watermelon and vodka party by the pool on Sunday. I stopped by.

"Hey, I got a little blow," Dan said. "Let's go up to my room and have a toot." So I went with a couple of his pals to Room 415. Inside was a shotgun in the corner and a pistol on the nightstand.

"What you got there?" I asked.

He showed me his arsenal: a machete along with a sleeping bag, a canteen of water, a .44 Bulldog pistol next to his bed and an AR-15 fully auto. He was doing blow and his tongue was wagging, trying to impress me in front of his weed-head crew, so I gave him a few oohs and ahhs and no-shits as he explained that if they had to land and run from the Drug Enforcement Administration, they could survive in the desert. Real fucking cowboy shit. I kept expecting John Wayne to come in for a line of blow, wearing leather chaps, and to beg Dan for his fucking autograph. I asked Dan to step out in the hall, away from his lames, where I whispered, "Hey, your guy will be in tonight. Have you heard from him yet?"

He said Ezio would be there, arriving in a produce truck. Now I know we have all been in a situation, whether buying a car or even a washing machine, where the seller was saying things like, "Oh this is great. Don't worry. Just call me," but immediately after the sale, you pick up a tone in the guy's voice or his actions, and a little voice inside you tells you that you fucked up. Well, that's what I picked up from Dan. But I tried my best to shake it off.

On Sunday, Ezio didn't show. I stayed at the hotel bar hanging out with Sherman. We sat in a little corner with our backs against the wall, where we could see people coming into the bar before they could see us. No Ezio. No Dan. He was out somewhere.

On Monday morning, I got up and went to Dan's room. No Dan. I went to Ezio's room. No Ezio. About noon, Dan showed up. I was at the pool as he walked by. I stopped him. "Hey, the guy didn't show, eh?"

"No, but he'll be here. No problem."

"OK."

"Maybe tonight." Dan had picked up a little bit of an attitude towards me, which increased my gut feeling.

On Monday night, I went out drinking with Sal. A coke dealer started his sales pitch on us, so I burnt his arm. I was in a mean mood. I was calling Sherman every hour, but he kept saying no show on Ezio. At 1 AM, I took Sal to his car. We went for coffee. He dropped me off at my rental car. Coked-up from doing grams, I had a .38 snub-nose five-shot in an inside holster in the small of my back, real James Bond shit, hard for people to see, but easy to get to and real secure. I drove back to the hotel in a red 1977 Monte Carlo. Aggravated, I was jonesing for more coke and wanting to get the Ezio deal over with. On the fourth floor, Sherman was in his suite, coked-up. "Nothing yet, eh?" I said. "Is that motherfucker, Dan, in his room?"

"Yeah, I heard him come in."

I went down and hammered on Room 415. It was 2 AM on Tuesday, June 10th. The door opened. It was a hot month in Tucson, so he had a pair of cut-off shorts on, no shirt. "Let me talk to you." Dan lay back on the bed and turned on his night-stand light. All of the guns were still in the room that I'd seen before. He kept an AR-15 under his bed, a 12-gauge shotgun in the corner, a .44 Bulldog in the nightstand and there was a bayonet lying around, too. I sat down about eight feet away from him in an armrest chair. Dan was on his bed, he had one foot on the floor and one propped up on the bed. The bathroom was on the other side of the wall behind him. The only light on was in the bathroom. The bathroom door was open so it was shining in. I got right to it. I said to this cowboy, "Hey, man, where's Ezio?"

Now Dan was grumpy. He'd been partying all weekend, probably with my money or at least half of it. Plus, he'd just gotten to sleep and here I was waking him up at 2 AM with twenty questions. So he actually replied in a shitty tone, "I don't know." He'd acquired a little bit of an attitude 'cause I'd been bugging him since Sunday night.

"Well, when's he gonna be here, man?"

"I don't know. You know Ezio just as good as I do." As I rose from the chair, Dan reached for the drawer with the Bulldog. He'd done the stupidest fucking thing he could have done to me. It cost him his life. Just that one fucking thing: reaching for his gun. And he'd talked to me like he was spitting on my face. Basically, he'd said to me, *What the fuck's wrong with you, asking that question?*

I saw red – a red fucking flash. "You sorry motherfucker! Where's my dope?" I yelled, going for the gun in the small of my back. I put one in his mouth – *bam!* As I pulled the trigger, I felt a fine spray of wet sand shoot up in my face. The little fragments hitting me and ricocheting were his teeth. I don't know if it was the second shot that killed him. I've always been a two-shot guy. You're better off with two than one 'cause you don't want to leave a motherfucker alive. One guy, I put four in. I know someone who put one in a guy's head and the motherfucker didn't die and witnessed against him. Few can recover from two in the head. God rest Dan's soul. I've gotta ask God for forgiveness for this, but I feel I did the right thing 'cause he was reaching for his gun. Upon the second shot, more red mist flew up, bone and teeth fragments. There was stuff on the ceiling.

On TV crime shows like *Kojak* or *The Rockford Files*, you see a motherfucker get shot and he falls down, crying, "Oh, I've got shot." In real life, it's a little traumatic for the average person. I never had a problem with it, but I've been sick like that since I was a kid. After putting two in him, I decided to leave immediately. I figured the drunk down the hall or Sherman's aunt had heard the shots. I opened the door and went down the hall. I was doing what killers do: getting the fuck away from the scene of the crime. Sherman had stuck his head out of his door, gazing like an owl, his hair standing up like Groucho Marx, fucking high on coke.

"Get back in. See you later." Going by, I was thinking, *I've gotta get rid of the gun.* I took the stairs, not the elevator. In the hotel lobby, I saw the janitor vacuuming. Nobody saw me. I had a way to get to my car by going around the pool that avoided the undercover cops in the Cox Cable van at the front of the hotel. I got the fuck out of there. Only Sherman saw me. He was the only one who could get me busted on this. Driving to Sal's, I took the shells out of the .38 and threw them on Broadway. At the front door, I told Sal, "I just whacked Dan. I've gotta change my clothes."

"Come on in." Sal – still coked up – was with his wife and kids, making chocolate-chip cookies. It was a weird fucking night. They were putting eggs and flour and sugar in a mixing bowl. It smelt good.

"You wanna try mixing these together." Sal's wife handed a kid a whisk. "Use it gently, so the dough gets thick, but is still a little wet and soft. Good job! Now who wants to put the chocolate chips into the dough?"

"Me, Mom!"

"I do!"

"After you put the chocolate chips in, we'll be able to do a taste test."

"Save me some cookies," I said to the kids.

In the bathroom, I took a shower and changed into Sal's clothes as we wore the same size, now that his body had filled out a bit. I put my clothes in a baggie, which I was used to doing, my shoes and everything. I found Sal rolling cookie dough into balls.

We drove to Houghton Road, stopped next to a bridge and threw my clothes out along the highway. At Davidson Canyon, we parked and opened the hood of the car, so that anyone driving by would only see a car with its hood up. I hid the .38 in loose dirt under a cactus by a milepost marker, so I could retrieve it. I went back two weeks later and found it just like that. After hiding the gun, we went back to Sal's and I called Sherman at the hotel. "What's up?"

"Nothing."

"Nobody been there?"

"Nobody heard a thing."

"What about our friends in the van out front?"

"The van's gone. I think the Cox Cable guys have taken the night off."

"Good. I'll be back down." Preoccupied by the murder, I was starting to let my guard down about The Brothers. It was beginning to get a little light when I arrived at the Sahara at dawn. I knew the cops would be all over the place when they found the body. "Look, we've gotta clean up here," I told Sherman. We'd bought powder from a University of Arizona kid to blend into our cocaine for sale. "We've gotta flush the cut."

"We can keep these guns," Sherman said. "You didn't shoot him with these guns and I'm entitled to them."

"I've gotta go back to that room and wipe the motherfucker

down." With Sherman's master key and a damp towel, I returned to the death chamber and started wiping anything I might have touched. Dan was slobbering so much blood that he should have had a Red Lobster bib on. *C'est la vie. C'est la vie. Fuck him.* I took nothing. I left his guns and knives. I didn't even look for money. It wasn't about money or dope. It was about judging who you're fucking with. A human life is worth more than $5,000, but since then I've seen guys killed for $50. So it's not about money. Coke has a way of making you think you're all that and a roll of print toilet paper. After I'd left, a maid knocked on Room 415. No answer. She opened the door, but she couldn't see his face. She figured he was asleep and left.

That night, with a clean gun under my pillowcase, I slept deep. Coming down off coke, I had crazy dreams about The Brothers kidnapping my daughter. I woke with my pulse racing as if something was up. *Maybe the cops have found Dan.* I stuck my head out of my door to see if Dan's room had been disturbed. All was quiet. I strapped my piece to my ankle. I looked out of the back window to see what was going on by the pool. Nothing happening: mostly empty chairs other than a dude sat under a sunshade, reading a newspaper. With the weekend over and it being one of the hottest months in Tucson, the hotel guests had thinned out.

I turned on the TV, which said the temperature was gonna hit 100° today. After doing so much coke, my appetite was coming back, so I went down for some pancakes. Back in my room, I freshened up a bit. I wanted to see Sal to get our stories straight in case any heat came down.

Around nine o'clock, I left the hotel. The bright sun was blinding as I tried to scan the area, so I put shades on. Two undercover-cop vans, one Cox Cable, the other plain white, were parked down the street on the opposite side of the road, but nobody was out on the sidewalk. *In those vans, they must be sweating their nuts off today.* Ignoring the motherfuckers, I strolled by some tall palm trees.

Bam-bam-bam!

Shots came at me. Bullets bounced off the asphalt. One ricocheted off the hotel wall. I dropped down and drew my gun from its ankle holster. *Is someone trying to kill me or am I getting busted?* I saw a dude striding closer from down the street who looked like he was on fire. But it wasn't a flame. It was his long red hair glowing in the Arizona sun. It was Koot. He must have come from behind the undercover van that he was now in front of. I didn't wanna accidentally hit any of the cops in the van, but I had no choice but to pop some rounds back at Koot 'cause the motherfucker was trying to kill me. Shots were fired from behind Koot. It was hard to tell whether they were shooting at me or him, until Koot fell, shot in the leg. Cops jumped out of the vans. Using the vans as cover, they yelled at Koot to drop his gun. As if for a few seconds he didn't know what to do, Koot looked at them. I thought he was gonna open up on the motherfuckers and they'd do me a favour by wasting his ass, but instead, he threw his gun towards them. The gun skimmed the road and stopped in front of a white van. The cops told him to roll over, belly down and to put his arms above his head. After he'd assumed the position, they swarmed onto him. He was pinned down and cuffed.

Homicide Detective, Dirk Taylor, approached, but I said that I didn't wanna make a statement, they could do whatever the fuck they wanted to Koot. They tried to get me to talk, but I just wanted them to get the fuck away from the Sahara before they started sniffing around and found Dan. *Maybe they'll think Koot whacked Dan. This could work in my favour.* As they had nothing to charge me with, they let me go. From inside the hotel, I watched an ambulance arrive, which the cops escorted Koot into. As they'd witnessed him shooting at me in an unprovoked attack, he'd be charged with attempted murder and put in the state penitentiary. I wouldn't have to worry about Koot for now, just the rest of The Brothers. They must have known I was staying at the Sahara.

Later that morning, the maid went to Dan's room, realised he was dead and told Sherman, who called the cops. Ezio never returned.

I believe that death carries its own aura. Back in 1973, when I'd just married Linda, I took her son camping in the tundra, where the frozen ground makes it impossible for trees to grow. It's all wind and mosquitoes and bogs. The day before the hunting season began, we came across a herd of caribou. They were completely calm. The next morning, we strapped on our hunting bows and arrows. The herd took one look at us and bolted across the barren land. Do you attribute that to an awareness of the harm we intended to do? It's the same with dogs. Some like you, some don't. Some cower and growl. Others smile and wag their tails. I've met people whereby from the fucking beginning, the computer in my head, developed since cavemen over thousands of years, said, "Watch this motherfucker." With others, I'd have slept around a campfire with them anytime. Most of my victims, including Dan, had no concept of aura. In the realm of fist fights and spitting contests, Dan probably would have excelled. Death was in Room 415 that night. I sensed it. Dan was too lax. First of all, if my computer has been registering a sense of danger and I'm asleep in a hotel room, my gun ain't gonna be in no drawer. It would be right there on the stand next to me. The same goes for my house. I'm not saying I'm a bad motherfucker, but I am aware of the cosmic aura. The human computer has death perception. When I was with murderers who I knew were thinking about whacking me, I knew death was there and I had to think my way out. I didn't try to go Wild Bill Hickok on the motherfuckers.

The afternoon of the discovery of Dan's body, I went to have a pizza. I drove around to see my friends and came back to the hotel around 4 PM. Sherman was there. The cops upstairs questioned me: *wah-wah-wah* ... I told them, "Hey, I thought you guys were watching out for The Brothers. How the fuck could something like this happen?" *Wah-wah-wah* ...

I entered Room 415. Dan was gone. There was a collage of blood stains on the ceiling and walls. The closeness of the gun to his mouth had caused a lot of splatter. The cops had dusted everything in the room: light sockets, toilet seat ... It opened my eyes to their procedures. After that, I always wiped the toilet seat. Even if they'd found my prints, I had an answer for the cops. Sherman said Dirk Taylor, the homicide detective, wanted me to call him, so I did.

"We need you to come down here," Dirk Taylor said. "We wanna talk to you about the homicide at the Sahara. Maybe you can help us. We know you knew the guy."

I didn't panic in the least 'cause I knew my rights, and I had a good attorney. "I'd really like to come down and help you with this, but right now I'm suing the newspapers for slandering me." The media heat was on us at that time 'cause in June 1976, Don Bolles – a journalist investigating Mafia ties to business and politics – had been whacked. I told Dirk Taylor, "Second of all, I hardly know Dan. You are welcome to call my attorney. I need to run this all by him."

Dirk's tone got shitty: "We're working on a homicide. You need to help the community."

"I've got nothing to say to you other than call my attorney." Sherman and I went to Room 415. I'll never forget the blood.

Do you think I'm a complete fucking animal 'cause I've got no conscience about whacking people? I can hear you saying that I did it for business, not pleasure. But it was more than business. I felt slighted. I didn't want anyone to get one over on me. I didn't go in there to whack him that night, but shit happens like people have flat tyres. Years later, I even told the jury that I went in there to jam him up and enquire about my motherfucking investment, just as you would if a business didn't deliver a washing machine to your door. After it had happened, I had no conscience whatsoever. I was glad the motherfucker was dead.

After the cops got through with their investigation of the crime scene, Sherman and I took Dan's mattress to the dump. It was a bloody mess. Carrying it made me recall an incident when I was a shoeshine kid. A gangster sat down to have his shoes shined. Noticing the dog crap on them, I hesitated.

"Clean it up, kid," he said.

I picked up a rag.

"If that's the only shit you ever have to clean up, you're gonna have an easy life." Those words the hood spoke were right on. Believe me, I've cleaned up a lot of shit.

CHAPTER 10

By now you must be wondering how I got the nickname Two Tonys. Well, it came about as an inside joke between me and some of the fellas. Back in the early fifties, Charlie "Batts" Battaglia and Jimmy the Weasel, a made man working for the Dragnas, were assigned to clip two shakedown artists both named Tony, whose crime spree included several murders, numerous robberies and a rape. They fucked up by robbing the wrong people, including $3,500 from a mob-run gambling operation out of the Flamingo Hotel in Las Vegas. The Weasel, an enforcer out of LA, lured the two Tonys by asking them to join him on a bank robbery. In his book, *The Last Mafioso*, the Weasel describes what went down on August 6, 1951.

Batts was young and up-and-coming. It was his first whack, so he was nervous. "Relax. It'll be over in five seconds," the Weasel said. "Remember, when they pull up, you slide into the back seat and wait until I'm in and the door's closed. Then cut loose. Hit the guy in front of you. Empty your gun. Then get out fast, walk across the street and Angelo will be there to pick us up." With a smile, the Weasel said, "Is the safety off? Just don't shoot yourself in the balls."

The Weasel wanted Batts to put some bullets in the two Tonys, so Batts could never rat him out. A two-car assassination team took the Weasel and Batts to the spot. The two Tonys pulled up near Hollywood Boulevard, but Batts couldn't open the door, so the Weasel opened it. Batts got in first, and sat behind the driver, but he shit himself and couldn't draw his gun. The Weasel pulled a .38 from his waistband, put it to the back of the passenger's head, and fired twice. With Batts still sat frozen, the Weasel unloaded on the driver, and yelled at Batts to get in on the action. Batts

THE MAFIA PHILOSOPHER

finally got his shit together and blasted the driver once. They made it to the getaway car and took off. In the following days, the cops rounded up most of the assassination team, but they all walked after a waitress told a grand jury that the cops had burned her with cigarettes to make her change her testimony.

Twelve years later in 1963, Batts had multiple whacks to his name, and credibility. "Charlie wants to talk to you at the Hilton Coffee Shop," Sal told me at his house. "He's gonna ask you to do something. Tell him you don't wanna do it."

"What's he gonna ask me to do?" I asked.

"He's gonna ask you to whack a guy. I already told him I would, but I don't want to."

"Who the fuck's he want us to whack?"

"He wants us to whack his prosecutor, Norman Greene."

Batts had an extortion case pending. He'd sent us on a mission for the Bonannos to bust up some pool tables with bowling balls. After we did it, Batts went and told the owner that it would never happen again if they installed machines from Tucson Vending, which the Bonannos owned.

"It's up to you to get us out of this mess," Sal said. He wanted to be a made man. He thought he was on his way, but his nuts shrunk to the size of mothballs in tough situations.

We went to the fucking coffee shop. We sat down. A waitress brought coffee and Danish sweet rolls. Batts started out small-talking us. He stuck a cigar into his mouth, where it took on a life of its own, rolling from side to side, occasionally slipping out, so he could examine how soggy it was getting. After lighting it, he blew smoke at us and said to me, "Hey, I wanna ask you a question. I need a favour, but I want you to be real honest if you think you can do this. I'll still have respect for you if you can't do it. I'd rather you tell me than the moment of truth comes and you can't do it, and we all get in trouble."

Gazing hard, he removed his sunglasses. "Take off your glasses and look in my eyes."

I put my shades on the table and looked him square in the eyes to give him all of my fucking attention.

121

"I've gotta guy in my way that I want out of my way. I've already asked Sal and Sal says it's a go. I don't want your answer now. I want you to think about it, and I'm gonna ask you again in a couple of days to give you time to think about it. I don't want you to find religion or to start wanting to blab your mouth all over town to some holy-rolling pricks or to be having nightmares." Batts took a lengthy draw on the cigar and exhaled a funnel of smoke.

I already knew the question and our fucking answer. So far I hadn't done any whacks. I'd only done some bombings, buried bodies and busted a few heads open for the Bonannos. "OK, Charlie, let me kick it around in my head."

Two days later, we were back at the coffee shop. "Did you think about that problem we have?" Batts said.

"Yeah, Charlie, I don't think I can do anything that heavy. I think I might have nightmares or something. That's pretty heavy."

"OK. No problem," Batts said. "It's over. Forget about it." He changed the subject immediately.

Now let's roll the clock forward to where I am presently in my story. By 1977, the situation had changed. Sal and I were young Turks. I'd earned my spurs. I had fresh whacks to my name. I wasn't the kid Batts had tried to recruit over ten years ago. I was a formidable person. I had fucking Rolex watches, chains around my neck, three rings on one hand and pockets full of C-notes. I was driving my Eldorado and living in a fucking hotel for free. People suspected me of whacks, but didn't know for sure that I'd done them except for the in-crowd.

Batts had just done six years for extortion. Using the same routine as in 1963, he set up a meeting with us at 8:30 AM Sunday at the Village Inn. The Saturday before the meeting, I was up all night at the disco, doing the hustle, putting shit up my nose.

The next morning, Sal called my hotel room. "Are you up?"

"Yeah, I'm getting up, but I'm all fucked up."

"I'll meet you there at 8:30."

The Village Inn was full of church-going motherfuckers 'cause mass was down the street. Tall and chunky Batts was now in his mid-fifties. Wearing a black suit and shirt with a white tie, he had slicked grey hair, a dago's hooked nose, alligator shoes, dress slacks and pinky rings. At the meeting, he kept blowing cigar smoke and throwing out the name Lilo, who was Carmine Galante, a boss involved in over eighty whacks, who'd embraced the heroin business.

I realised Batts was full of shit. He was washed up. He had no power 'cause his old boss, Joe Bonanno Sr, who'd had a heart attack in 1968, had been forced into retirement by his rivals, who said they'd whack him if he ever interfered with the New York Mafia families again. Even Batts was mad at the Tucson Bonannos 'cause they'd fucked him while he was in prison. "I'm not with those piece-of-shit Bonannos anymore. I'm with Lilo."

In my mind, Batts had lost himself. I was as mad as hell. I had a hangover. I was so high on coke, my nostrils looked like the rims of margarita glasses. And right in front of my fucked-up nose, I had this motherfucker acting the part, when he'd shrunk down to scuzz. I was getting more and more pissed off at him. He was playing the big shot, throwing out Lilo's name, trying to give the impression of a crime family that didn't exist. I didn't even believe he was with Lilo.

"What about this guy who's supposed to be coming in and out of town from Phoenix, representing himself as part of the Genovese group?" Batts said, trying to get us to jam up some guy. He was telling us to find the guy and let him know that there were other people down here in Tucson whose toes he was stepping on.

Wound tightly, I didn't want any part of it. There was too much heat on, including a task force following me around. Batts' loud talking increased my bad mood. *This isn't a good time of the day for a meeting*, I thought. *This isn't a good location.*

Batts started on about my cocaine business partner, Sherman. "Fuck Sherman, too. We'll grab his ass and shake him down."

Slowly, I removed my glasses and looked him square in the eyes. "Look at me. Look at my fucking eyes. Let me tell you something right now. If you or anyone else makes a move on Sherman, I'm gonna take it as a personal attack on me."

I could tell by his eyes that he thought I was an umbatz – a crazy. Strapped with a .38 in a Velcro holster on my ankle, I was ready to turn the table over and whack the motherfucker right there in the Village Inn if he'd pushed the envelope any further. I was sick of listening to the fat grease-ball motherfucker, who had no fucking troops, who'd been trying to muscle in on my scores for the last two decades except for when he was in the joint. He was the kind of guy who woke up in the morning, thinking up ways to get guys like me to do his dirty work. Batts backed way down. Even his cigar drooped. He started talking about us forming our own group with Lilo's approval. He knew we knew he was a nobody and the tables had turned.

When we left the fucking coffee shop, Sal said, "You know when you got in that motherfucker's face, I could feel the spirits of those Two Tonys at the table." That's how I earned the nickname, Two Tonys. Batts never tried to recruit us after that.

CHAPTER 11

In 1977, man, I can't begin to tell you how much of a good summer I was having. It was non-stop pool parties and coke in Tucson. I was only being trailed by drug cops, not homicide. The Brothers still wanted to kill me, but they were too chickenshit to try after Koot's train wreck of an attempt. Koot was doing hard time in the Arizona joint. I was subpoenaed to testify at a grand jury, but they shit-canned it and that was the last I heard of the motherfucker. There was a rumour around Tucson that I'd whacked Dan, so motherfuckers were wary of me. But let's not forget, this was DD: During Drugs. Coke had scrambled my decision-making processes. I almost whacked a couple of guys over silly shit. I've never been as dangerous before or ever since. It was like the coke was eating up my fucking brain, but I kept doing more 'cause my habit was insatiable.

A buddy of mine owned the Jumping Jacks bar. A dude in there gave me the heads-up on The Brothers. The word was that with Koot in the big house, The Brothers figured a local biker gang stood a better chance of whacking me, so they'd reached out to the Dirty Dozen, who were strong in Tucson.

"Well, if they come at me," I said, "I'm always strapped and ready to deal with them. Fuck them!"

I spent plenty of time in the Jumping Jacks, drinking Mumm Cordon Rouge Champagne, big-shotting it, buying everybody drinks. I always walked around with $7,000 or $8,000 at that time. In the Jumping Jacks, Sal said that if he didn't get $3,000, his wife was gonna leave him. I reached in my pocket and gave him three grand.

As I got more insane on coke, my circumstances deteriorated. I sold my Eldorado and went into partnership with a lame, but the business went belly up. I was running out of money, so when a guy approached me with an ounce of cocaine, who wanted $2,000 for it, I told him to let me have it, that I'd sell it for him. I sold it and didn't pay him. I needed the cash to keep my lifestyle going. He didn't want no trouble. I had a nasty reputation.

Desperate for cash to pay for coke, I asked Sal to pay me back. When he refused, I got crazy with him. "Look, motherfucker, you've gotta pay me."

"I ain't got it."

I made him scratch up $2,000. He had a silencer with a gun that had an interchangeable barrel. I figured the silencer was worth $1,000, so I took it. It was as illegal as hell. When I took the barrel and put the silencer on, it made a sound like a gentle clap when I shot it.

After drinking at the Jumping Jacks one night, I stopped at a barbecue joint, where I knew the owners, a couple of dago kids. The place was as wide as a jail cell, but really long. There were booths on one side, and on the other, a long bench. I sat at the bench.

The waitress brought my ribs, Miami baby embers, a beautiful slab that I'll never forget. I was admiring the ribs when a gush of fresh air from the front door opening hit my face. I looked towards the door. In came a biker, wearing a baseball cap backwards, a sleeveless denim jacket over a dark sweater, dark jeans and combat boots, with a baseball bat on his fucking shoulder. He was staring as if he was gonna peel my fucking cap.

I knew this was coming. This instinct I've got is why I'm still alive. I didn't want to whack the motherfucker in front of all of the witnesses in there with my gun with the illegal silencer on it that carried a ten-year sentence. I knew it was time for flight – to get the fuck out of there – so I turned the table over. The ribs and dish and coffee cup flew in the air. I took off to the end of the restaurant.

On my right-hand side was the restroom, on the left, the entrance to the kitchen. The biker was chasing me, so I went into the kitchen, which was as long as the restaurant. After running that length again, I got to a rotisserie in the window with slabs of beef in rotation. As the biker closed in, I spotted skewers the size of big spears in the corner. I thought, *Man, I hope those motherfuckers aren't hot.* I grabbed a skewer. The biker came with the bat. The owner and his brother grabbed the biker from behind.

I raised the skewer. I was about to stick it through his chest and into his heart when the owner yelled, "What's wrong with you? Put that fucking thing down!" I saw they had the biker under control, and had the bat, so I dropped the skewer and got the fuck out of there.

After driving away, I came across cop cars blocking the road. I figured I was as good as busted with the silencer under my seat. I stopped at the blockade, consisting of fifteen cops with shotguns. A cop wearing a Smokey Bear hat looked in my car. "Picked up any hitchhikers?"

"No, sir."

"We're looking for some killers. They've killed and they'll kill again." Three Tison Brothers had helped their dad and his cellmate escape from Florence prison, where the dad was serving life for murdering a guard. They'd broken down in their getaway car and a Marine sergeant had stopped to help them. They'd killed the Marine, his wife, his fifteen-year-old niece and twenty-two-month-old son. They also killed a couple on their honeymoon. "For the next ten miles, don't pick up any hitchhikers. You wanna open your trunk?" I was glad I only had clothes in my trunk and no dead bikers.

Wanting to put a stop to the local biker shit before it got out of hand like in Alaska, I found out that the leader of the Dirty Dozen in Tucson called himself a warlord and had an auto-repair joint. Figuring the motherfuckers wouldn't expect me to just show up there, I got a crew of six associates together, including Toto and Sal, all strapped and ready to blast the motherfuckers if they started any shit. We went in two cars.

We parked and rushed inside like it was a SWAT-team raid.

SHAUN ATTWOOD

The motherfuckers polishing their bikes didn't know what the fuck was up. Dudes with big oil-stained hands put their beers down, picked up spanners and wrenches and expanded their chests like they were gonna do something. I drew my gun, and so did the rest of my guys. The bikers looked at each other as if they didn't know what to do.

Not knowing who the fuck the warlord was, I said, "Look, I'm gonna be right up front with you. A biker came into a barbecue joint last night with a baseball bat looking to fuck me up, and I almost had to fuck him up. I don't need no one coming to wherever the fuck I am trying to harass me no more than you do. Now, I'm told you guys want to fuck me up over some beef I had in Alaska, with some dudes who ain't even from your club. I wanted to come down to see you face-to-face and find out what's on your mind."

"Look, let me tell you something," said the oldest biker, in a sleeveless vest and jeans, his hair in a ponytail and his beard grey. "What those Alaska dudes got themselves into, they can get themselves out of. We don't run in the same circles. But I'll tell you something right now: if you, or any of these guys you've brought come back to our place of business or fuck with any of us, we'll all come at you and it won't be no little ol' fist fight."

"Fine. I'm glad we understand each other," I said. "Tell your dude with the baseball bat to stay the fuck away from me." We got the fuck out of there.

I figured it would be wise to get out of Tucson. I knew a guy who owned Dirty Dave's, a club in San Diego, which ranged from rock 'n' roll to topless. He said I could run the club 'cause he was moving to marry a rich Denver girl. I took the job and cleaned my act up for a bit, but then – *bam!* – I was right back into it. I was back on coke and – I'm ashamed to say – robbing the owner blind. I was fired, so in 1978, I went back to Arizona to see Niki.

In Tucson, I met up with Zane, a guy who owned a construction company. He got a $2 million insulation installation contract from IBM. He paid me $150 a week to be his fucking timekeeper and more money to handle certain things. Zane was a coke dealer, a boozer, a drunkard and a whoremonger, with a mansion on a mountain in Tucson. He couldn't control his wild side. He liked to fuck around.

Zane called: "Hey, can you get a crew together?"

"What kind of crew?" I asked.

"I need some guys to do insulation."

"My guys don't know anything about insulation."

"They don't gotta know."

Zane had twenty guys working for him on the IBM project. They were slowing the job down to squeeze money out of Zane. He knew how much work they were supposed to be doing. He fired one. The guy got mad and went to the union.

"You can't fire him. He belongs to the union," the union man said.

"I'll fire anyone who works for me," Zane said.

"I'll shut the job down. I'll pull out all the union workers."

Zane offered me $100 a day in cash to teach the union guys a lesson. I rounded up three tough bar fighters, including Toto. We met Zane. I had a .38 in my ankle holster and a sawed-off shotgun. We rode to the picket line and crossed it. We tried our best to put the insulation in. The union guy was pointing at me, so I came down off my ladder. "Hey, buddy, me and my boys here wanna join your union," I said. "We wanna be good union men."

"Well, you gotta come down to the union hall and get on the D list."

"Maybe you don't understand. We've got this job. The man's paying us. If you want us on your union, you put us on your union list." I got shitty with him. I was about to hit him over the head with my .38.

Zane intervened. "Go back to work. I'll handle this." Forty-five minutes later, Zane came over. "Get your crew. We're through for the day."

"I've gotta pay them."

"I've got your money at my office." Zane fetched $1,000. "Listen, me and the union guy took a walk. I told him I had the right to fire whoever I wanted. He agreed." Zane really appreciated what I'd done for him.

As it hadn't been two years since I'd whacked Dan, I was still hot in Tucson. Outside of RadioShack, I ran into some cops, including Dirk Taylor.

"Back in town, eh?" Dirk said.

"Am I?"

"Yeah, you're back in town. Where you staying at?"

"I'm staying around."

"Hey, asshole, do you want us to tell you where you live? Don't for one second think we're not doing our job."

"You've gotta good town here. A guy can get away with murder in this town."

Dirk squinted.

"I don't mean it literally though." Enjoying fencing him, I smiled.

"I know Koot arrived in town after Dan was murdered."

He obviously didn't have a case. If the cops have got you, they come for you. My first three weeks in Tucson, I sweated it, but Dirk had no witnesses. Hearing that some of The Brothers were in town, I figured I'd breathe easier if I returned to California.

With $1,000 and a 1978 Ford from Zane, I went to San Diego and moved in with an old buddy of mine, a nightclub bouncer who'd just got out of prison in California. We'd get up early and go to the beach. It was sunny, but not hot enough to fry your balls like in Arizona. There were always lots of yachts and boats on the harbour, and sometimes warships. We'd steal a boogie board from the back of a truck and surf for a few hours.

I got a job tending bar at Machos Mexican Restaurant and Nightclub, located across from the US Navy base. I was living a good life. I started work at 6 PM or 9 PM until 2 AM. I'd wash glasses and go to eat at a breakfast joint. Sometimes I'd go to Anthony's Shrimp Boat for shrimp and scallops. To begin with, my coke consumption wasn't as bad. I'd do coke with my co-workers and steal $50 to $100 a shift. Two waitresses were filching with me. The owner of the bar was a lush. He was drunk every night, the fucking jabroni.

When I was drinking on a night off, I met a Palestinian. Some dudes were on his ass talking about the fucking Iranians 'cause in the news, Iran was raising hell with America. I said to them, "Why don't you leave him alone? He ain't bothering you guys."

"He's a fucking sand nigger," one said.

In San Diego, I always carried a Buck 110 Folding Hunter Knife. I grabbed my Buck and nailed the motherfucker. I went to work on him real good. He went to the hospital to get sewed up. I took off.

Next night at work, I was fired for beating up a customer. Well, what the fuck! The jerk had fucking deserved it. I had the hots for the singer of a band that played at Machos. She had short reddish-brown hair, flicked to one side. I bought a quarter ounce of coke and went to see her perform. The club was packed by midnight. I was by myself in a sweater, waiting for her to take a break.

Two guys at the bar were glaring at me. I had no pistol, only the Buck. One of them approached. "What happened the other night? What did you hit him with?"

"My fist."

"No way, man. He had 110 stitches."

"His head must have hit a sharp pole."

"You're gonna help him with his doctor's bill: $200."

"I don't do doctors' bills."

"You're not gonna help him?"

"No."

"OK."

I watched them leave and approached the singer on her break. "Let me pick you up tonight. Go powder your nose." I slid her a vial of coke.

"OK. Pick me up after work."

I exited down a wooden boat ramp. Two guys were down there. I got my Buck open real quick: *pft*. I thought it was the lames from the bar. By the time I saw it was Big Jim and Happy Jack from The Brothers, it was too late to back away. As I got closer, I saw they had gloves with no fingers on them, ready to whup some ass, and were holding weapons. Once again, I knew I'd end up dead if I didn't act really quickly. I dropped my hand to my side. The Buck handle slid right into my hand.

If you're ever cornered down a dark alley, what I'm about to tell you might just save your life. In a deadly situation like this – with no gun – you need to nail a motherfucker as quickly and violently as possible. When motherfuckers are coming to kill you the main thing you have going for you is that you're equally capable of killing them. A good target to go for is an eye and you don't need a weapon either. There's a guy in prison here who was getting gang-raped by the Aryan Brotherhood. They were going in on him like a pack of wolves. He stopped it by plucking out two of the motherfuckers' eyeballs. Their eyeballs were dangling out. A guy who's had his eye pulled out may never see through it again. It might cause a brain haemorrhage or the fluid that cushions the brain might leak out through the hole. A popped-out eyeball doesn't exactly fit back in snugly either. There's no instruction manual for that. After the guy in here started plucking eyeballs out, the Aryan Brotherhood left him alone. Throwing dirt or sand in a motherfucker's eyes works, too. Sand is great 'cause it damages the tissue and scratches the cornea. Eyes are easy targets. They'll put a motherfucker out of action fast.

With that in mind, I caught Happy Jack up high in the eye with my Buck. He let off a banshee howl that half-assed scared me. I slit his throat deep and with blood gushing from his neck, he jumped back, so the third stroke only got him in the arm.

To this day, I don't know what Big Jim blindsided me with, but it knocked the living shit out of me. I have a scar on my face that looks like a wrinkle that took three layers of stitches. I went down on the ground hard and rolled under a truck. The only thing that saved my life was fear of death. I should have been knocked out and killed. I rolled out of the other side of the truck and ran and ran and ran … I abandoned my car and everything.

At a shopping centre, I called my bouncer friend. He took me to his house, where we examined my wounds. My face was swollen and opened up bad. My neck and upper body were caked in blood. I rubbed coffee onto my facial wound to try to stop the bleeding. But considering the stakes, I'd gotten away lightly.

"You've gotta go hospital."

"I can't. I think I killed one of the motherfuckers."

"You've gotta get sewed up."

I put on an old jogging suit and tennis shoes. He drove me to Escondido, fifty miles north of San Diego. With blood all over my clothes, I told the hospital that I was out jogging and I slipped on a FOR SALE sign in somebody's front yard. They sewed me up.

I went and stayed with the singer. I was terrible looking, with two black eyes. The way I looked must have brought out her nurturing instinct 'cause she took real good care of me. Having got word that more of The Brothers were on their way to San Diego, I packed the Ford and drove to Tucson.

In Tucson, I went to Zane for money. "Let me tell you something," Zane said, "you saved me a lot of money with that union guy. I ain't forgetting it. You don't gotta go nowhere. Get yourself a restaurant, a hamburger joint, and I'll pay for it with $20,000." I knew I had twenty grand right there. I lived in the guesthouse at Zane's mansion.

Buying coke, I met Vic Vanderhoof, fresh out of Florence prison on parole, a big ol' motherfucker, 6-foot-4, 250 pounds, a blond-haired, blue-eyed warrior, who belonged to the Aryan Brotherhood prison gang. Just as shit attracts, we took a liking and hung out at bars.

Zane contacted me. "Hey, listen, I just fired Carl."

"Oh, yeah."

"He was stealing materials and selling them to my competition. He got real shitty and started talking bad about my wife and daughter. That he'd fucked them and all that. Why don't you tighten him up a little bit when you see him?"

"Yeah. That'll be done." He wanted me to ass-whup him, not kill him.

"If you run across Scott, he owes $3,500. He was talking bad. He said I was nothing. Tell him I want my fucking money. He owes me." Scott was a half-assed gangster I'd tooted coke with. "Also, Darryl owes $2,000, too."

"Yeah. No problem. I'll tell them all what time it is."

On Saint Patrick's Day at 10 PM, I finished eating some meatball sandwiches, picked up Vic and went straight to Carl's house. His roommate answered. "Is Carl here?"

"No, he's not."

"When's he coming in?"

"Later."

"Listen, you know me. I know your dad well. I'm gonna tell you something. Don't tell Carl we came looking for him. If we come back, and Carl's here, stay in your room."

I'm gonna stop here for a second 'cause I have a question for you. Are you anticipating more violence in my story? Does that repulse or excite you? Is there a slight tingle of some sort? You've probably never whacked a piece of shit who had it coming, but you need to ask yourself: what does that tingle say about you? At some point on the road of life you've probably fantasised about fucking up someone. Maybe you even have. Maybe back when you were young and didn't give a fuck. My point is that the potential for violence is inside all of us. Some people join the military out of a pure desire to kill. My problem is I take what we've all got inside of us to the fucking maniac level. What happens next we called The Night of the Long Knives for a long time. *Ha ha ha ...*

We went downtown, drinking. Every bar was full. At the Living Room, I saw Scott with a woman. I bought them drinks. Scott had seen me in action before, when I'd grabbed a guy from a party who'd tried to fuck Peter Licavoli Jr's wife. I'd put a gun to the guy's head and said, "I'm gonna blow your fucking brains out." He started crying. "Please don't kill me. I'm gonna stay at home with my wife and kids."

I said to Scott, "Hey, come outside a minute. I wanna talk to you in private."

At the door to the parking lot, Vic grabbed Scott and carried him outside. They started scuffling. Scott pulled out a .357 and tried to shoot me. Vic put him in a bear hug. Scott couldn't get his hands up. I pulled out my Buck knife and started stabbing. I stabbed Scott eleven times in the neck and once in the thigh when he tried to kick me. Vic spun Scott around, grabbed his gun and shot Scott in the fucking back, right outside of the front door of the bar. Scott arrived at St Joseph's Hospital on Wilmot Road, just in time for them to save his life.

We went straight to Carl's and kicked in his door. We found him sat up in his bed. I grabbed him and pistol-whipped him. I hit his fucking head over and over. When his face was all busted up, I said, "Get on a Greyhound bus tomorrow and get the fuck out of here and never come back. Do you understand me, motherfucker?"

We found Darryl at a bar, the Red Carpet, and kidnapped him. He claimed he didn't owe Zane any money. We took him to a payphone. Vic put a gun to Darryl's head. I called Zane. "Hey, Zane, I've got Darryl here. How much does he owe you? You want us to take this motherfucker out to the desert or what?"

"Don't do nothing to him. This ain't what I had in mind." Zane had lost his nerve.

Two nights later, I saw two guys in a parked car at a closed gas station. Plain-clothes cops. I could smell them a mile away. As I approached the car, they jumped out with guns drawn. "Hold it right there!"

Throwing up my arms, I said, "Hey, take it easy, guys. I was just coming over to see who you guys are."

"You know who I am, asshole," Dirk Taylor said.

His partner pulled a badge out, pushed me over the hood of his car and handcuffed me. "Where's Vic?"

"Vic who? Aren't you forgetting something here? Why don't you read me my rights, and then we'll start?" Dirk read my rights. "I've got nothing to say other than that I want a lawyer."

CHAPTER 12

Getting strip-searched in the old Pima County jail intake, I had to run my fingers through my hair, flap my ears and spread my ass cheeks. I ended up in a brutal bullpen, crammed with addicts, drunken Native Americans, goofy motherfuckers from all over the world and bums and hobos sleeping on the floor next to a pool of puke. With all the crazies around, I couldn't sleep. *When am I gonna get before a judge and get bonded out?* From the intake, I was moved to a twenty-man tank in the jailhouse. From there, I was handcuffed to a chain gang and taken to court. The prosecutor asked for no bail. My attorney asked for bail 'cause nobody had died and I was a businessman in Tucson, so I wasn't a flight risk.

"This man stabbed another man eleven times in the neck," the prosecutor said. "He shot him in the back while another man held him. He doesn't deserve bail. He's a threat to the community." The judge set bail at $100,000. I winked at Zane in the courtroom. Vic was still on the run.

I was escorted back to the jailhouse, where my attorney showed up. "Listen, Zane is doing your bail bond."

"Great. I'm glad to hear that."

"But Zane's attorney is angry. He told Zane, 'Don't post his bail. He'll run on you.'"

"I ain't gonna run."

Hours later, a guard came. "Pack your shit up. You're leaving."

Outside the jailhouse, Zane was waiting. He said to rest up in his guesthouse.

Vic called from a mobile home, where he was shacked up with his girlfriend. "Look, I'm on parole and my parole officer is looking for me. I've gotta turn myself in."

"Go for it. We'll beat this fucking case. We took that punk's gun and shot him with his own gun. That proves he pulled a gun on us."

I picked up the gun and took it to my attorney. He said we didn't need it and to not let the cops get it. I sold the gun to a guy who sold it to an undercover cop, but he didn't rat.

Two weeks later, Dirk busted me at the guesthouse. With his cop buddy, he took me to and from court. I was charged with trafficking in stolen property. No bail.

Guards pulled me out to Visitation for a meeting with my attorney. "Listen, I just had a talk with the prosecutor. I can get you out of here right now on your own recognizance."

"What's the catch?"

"You've gotta help him get the big man."

"Who's the big man?"

"You know – Zane. They wanna know about his financing and coke deals." To make his job easier, he wanted me to rat.

"Tell the prosecutor, I don't know no big man."

"If you don't cooperate, I can probably get you five years."

"I wanna fight it. Let's take it to trial."

My attorney kicked me to the curb, so I fired him. I got a public defender who was even worse, John Witherspoon, a fucking punk. Can you visualise a Witherspoon? Really geeky. The prosecutor came at me for pistol-whipping Carl. Vic took a plea bargain for ten years. He'd be eligible for parole in seven years. My public pretender advised me to take a plea bargain, which I did. It was a set-up. I was sentenced to the super-aggravated maximum, seven-and-a-half years. Oh well, I should have been serving life for whacking motherfuckers, burying stiffs and blowing shit up with dynamite.

On the bus to the big house, I was no fish as I'd been in and out of jail throughout my life. I spent thirty days in the Arizona Department of Corrections' Alhambra Diagnostic Center, where prisoners' security levels are still calculated. The bunks in the thirty-man dorms were all taken, so motherfuckers had to sleep on the floor. Someone was always getting killed or stabbed or raped or their head getting busted open 'cause prisoners of all levels were jammed into unsupervised dorms. To see if I was a psycho, they gave me tests to fill out.

These stupid fucking personality tests originated from the work of a sick chauvinist who down deep inside wanted to fuck his mamma. If Freud were doing time in this day and age, they'd probably classify the schmuck to the nutward. He specialised in telling you why you'd pick your nose, piss the bed or what your dreams meant. Psychoanalysts – just like the pope, the preacher, the car salesman – don't want to lift or plough the fields. They want to mesmerise the sheep and live off their wool. It's called hustle. Freud was great at that shit, getting seriously rich big-shot people to apply for his huge hourly rate. He didn't want beggars with fetishes for stray dogs to take up his time. Only people who fucked their poodles. He should have been called Fraud instead of Freud. I've been sent to these psychoanalyst punks. They never got to me. They thought they were gonna sit with me for half an hour and tell me why I whacked motherfuckers. I don't think so. Balderdash. Fuck them!

After thirty days at Alhambra, I was put on a chain bus, a 1950s vintage school bus with a lead vehicle in front and a tail gunner behind, ready to mow down anyone involved in escape attempts. Two hours later, the bus stopped at a giant steel-barred electric gate, the entrance to Central Unit, Florence, famous for being the bloodiest half acre in the Sonoran Desert, also known as The Walls by prisoners and staff due to its ancient thirty-foot concrete perimeter. Most prisons now – including where I'm at – are surrounded by cyclone fences and coils of razor wire. Back then in Florence, wild camels roamed in herds, and wolves, mountain lions, coyotes and dogs hunted for goats and cattle. Warden Cardwell was a mean son of a bitch, who rode around the prison on a little golf cart and carried a .38 on his side.

We were put in holding cages in 115-degree heat, our chains so hot they burned us and the guards when they unlocked us. After an hour, a slot opened and we were told to take our jumpsuits off and put them out of the trap. A fishnet bag full of boxers of all sizes was shoved in for us. In a room, I was strip-searched and given the finger wave: two rubber-gloved fingers in the ass, poking around for contraband. During those searches, some guards were busted and fired for sodomising youngsters. They took a mugshot and I had to answer yes or no to a shitload of questions. I was given prison blues, socks, boots, T-shirts, and a fishnet sack with my bedding, shower gear and hygiene supplies. Outside of the yard office, a sergeant gave us our block assignments. Mine was CB1. I went through a hall and electronically activated steel doors to a pod with cells.

After orientation at CB1, I was classified to South Unit, next to where my crime partner, Vic, was. Around 1978–1980, Arizona had the most dangerous prisons in the country as far as stabbings and killings went. The main prisons were in Florence, and there was Fort Grant, a gladiator school in Tucson for under twenty-fives.

Nowadays, they're churning out prisons like GM manufactures Chevrolets. The politicos have turned Arizona into a prison economy. Towns like Safford, a mining and farming community, have the politicians vie for prisons 'cause they create employment and bring income to the town. The locals can get off their tractors and lay down their picks at the mines and become prison guards. And it's not only the men who work for the state, but their ol' ladies, too. If you're the mayor of Bumfuck Arizona, and the mine just shut down and the cotton crop went bad 'cause of the drought, you go to the governor and say, "We'll vote for you, governor, if we can have a prison. It'll employ cooks and guards and nurses." The president of Iran said to Mike Wallace on CBS's *60 Minutes*, "One per cent of the US adult population is in prison and it's growing all the time." Prison is an industry. There are probably thirty prisons in Arizona now, but back then, motherfuckers had nowhere to hide, so they were getting punked-out every day. Stabbings and head-bustings were always going on.

The gang running the white race was and still is the Aryan Brotherhood. The old and new members of the Aryan Brotherhood had a conflict going on, and had been shooting each other with zip guns. The Mexican Mafia were big. The black gang was the Mau Maus. Each gang was set up on the principle of looking out for its own race. If someone in your race was in trouble, you had to go to his rescue or else there would be consequences.

Nobody rolled on – stabbed or murdered – anyone without permission from the shot-caller running the yard. In the case of the Aryan Brotherhood, they had a three-man council voted in by other members. You had to be a probate for a year before they'd take a vote on you for regular membership. A probate would be asked to do certain things like punching, stabbing or killing, and if they got caught, they had to keep their mouths shut while they served their punishment time in the hole. Probates were observed. For them to become full members, the vote of the three-man council had to be unanimous.

Vic was already an Aryan Brother in high standing. On the streets, he was a big, dumb fucking German ten years my junior, but in here he had penitentiary savvy like I had street smarts. We basically reversed roles. He'd been under my wing on the streets. Now I was under his. Vic had been raised in the joints. He was a veteran of federal and state time. He knew how to conduct himself. His size and nature had helped him excel into a shot-caller with the white-boy clique. I was low-profile, and he knew we'd both be back on the streets someday.

Vic gave me the heads up on Koot. After getting busted trying to whack me in Tucson, Koot was sentenced to Florence prison. Biker gangs didn't have much pull in the prison system. The Aryan Brotherhood had power over the entire white race. They decided who lived and died.

Vic said, "In the chow hall, when you get your tray, make sure you sit near the back on the left. That's the Aryan Brotherhood's section and for whites they don't have any beefs with. The back right-hand corner and along the wall, about two-thirds of the hall, belongs to the Mexican Mafia. The last third of the right wall and across the front of the hall belongs to the Mau Maus. The centre row is where convicts and inmates who aren't clicked up with the gangs sit. The few Native Americans are at the back left, along the railing that divides the hall from the chow line. Don't go into any of the other areas. Most stabbings and killings happen in the chow hall. Overhead near the thirty-foot ceiling is a gun tower and guards with tear gas and automatic rifles." The Aryan Brotherhood accepted me due to Vic.

Do you wonder why guys join gangs? I guess it stretches back to the cave-dwelling days. If you're a hunter gatherer making your way through the tall grass of the Serengeti plains, and you hear some sabretooth tigers getting nearer, and you know there's a cave nearby with fifteen motherfuckers armed with clubs, you're heading for the fucking cave. It's the same with baboons travelling in packs forty to fifty strong.

Vic got me a primo job cooking in the kitchen. I made and stole what I wanted, while hooking up the whites. The kitchen was next to lockdown in CB6. Part of my job was to put food in canisters, put them on a cart, wheel them over to the sally port, come back to the kitchen, go to the office, pick up a phone, dial 222, and say some shit like, "Hello, CB6, this is South Unit kitchen. Your carts are in the sally port." Then I'd hang up. An inmate trustie out of lockdown would feed the guys in CB6.

After doing that one Saturday morning, I was at the salad compartment in the kitchen. A clerk, a big guy, 6-foot-1, had his laundry in the bins we washed the salad in. I raised hell with him 'cause it was unsanitary. He called me a fish 'cause I had a new Department of Corrections number. Everyone coming into prison gets assigned a number, which you keep for life.

Five days later, I was about to call CB6. The clerk was in the office talking to Koot, who was now out of the infirmary with a steel rod in his leg from where he'd been shot by the cops, and with his long hair in a ponytail. Koot saw me. I've never seen eyes fill with so much hate. He lunged. I clocked him and run a good fucking set on him 'cause I was in shape. He fell on a chair and rolled around dazed. I saw a prison worker, a white shirt coming in. It was his last day on the job, so he told me to just get the fuck out.

I went and stood on a stool and stirred a big pot of corn with a long aluminium ladle, a Viking's sword with a paddle on the end. This wasn't my first rodeo. My eyes were peeled, watching the office, which was all glass.

Koot came out with a puffy red eye, humiliated 'cause I ran a set on him. He thought he was being sly by grabbing an industrial can opener with a retractable bar, a solid foot of steel. With the bar at his side, he started walking with a slight limp. I was calmly stirring corn. I extracted the Viking's sword and got off the stool. Seeing my face, he showed his weapon. His crazy expression and evil eyes made him look possessed.

I stared at him. "Don't come near me with that, motherfucker."

"I'm gonna kill you."

"No, you ain't." I was in the zone that you get in before violence. The way I swung the sword, I must have looked like Prince Valiant. The fool put his bar up to block it. When he did that, I brought the sword down on the motherfucker, and by accident, I caught his hand. In my life, I've done a lot of harm by accident. I severed his finger, but it didn't quite fall off. It was hanging by a thread and blood spurted everywhere.

A lieutenant arrived. "Put that down now!" I was cuffed and put in a little room, not a cell, where I awaited the captain.

When the captain finally arrived, he asked, "What happened? They've got his hand in an ice chest. They're taking him to hospital."

"Hey, captain, I've got five years of doing time in this fucking place," I said. "With all due respect, you've gotta ask him what happened." The captain seemed to like that. He didn't press me after I said that. It was all part of a day's work.

I was sent to the hole at the back of CB4. I've been in a lot of holes, but this one was a fucking dungeon. To get there, I had to go through death row. I was assigned cell 9. Nine is my lucky number. I was born on February 9th, 1941. My Department of Corrections number ends with the number nine. I always bet on nine.

A porter stopped outside my cell, a one-eyed Norse-warrior-looking motherfucker covered in blue tats with a bald head. He had cleaning supplies. He said that when I got up in the morning, I needed to bang my shoes against the wall to get rid of scorpions, black widows, spiders, centipedes, millipedes or any other poisonous shit that might have crawled into them. He said I needed to shake my sheets and blankets before bedtime and my clothes before putting them on otherwise I'd get bitten or stung. He gave me some matches and newspaper. I rolled some paper up, lit it at one end and swiped it under my bunk, setting fire to scorpions and spiders. With a broom, sponge, bleach and disinfectant from the porter, I spent hours cleaning the cell.

For six days, I was waiting for my disciplinary action to come. I hadn't been to prison-court yet, and I intended to fight it, but no disciplinary officer came. Then, all at once, I was rolled-up and put back in the general population of CB4, where I didn't know anybody.

A Mexican porter was mopping outside of my cell. "Hey, partner," I said. "I've just got outta the hole. I'm really thirsty. Can you trade me a soda for a pack of Camels?"

"Sure." He left with my cigarettes, but didn't come back. I yelled for him, but got no answer.

The next morning, I didn't go to breakfast. I put on body armour: *National Geographic* magazines, which I wrapped around my back and torso, with my belt and pants holding them in place. I put a T-shirt and a blue cambric shirt over them. I went to the recreation-field fence, which separated us from The Walls, and sent for Vic, who I told about the Mexican punking me out. I hated getting ignorant, but stealing the Camels was one of many prison tests. The porter was out there with seven Mexicans, including the boss of the Old Mexican Mafia, short dudes, but muscular and covered in tats.

Vic called over some Aryan Brothers. "Hey, listen up, this is my crime partner. You've gotta watch his back. He's gonna confront that Mexican dude. If anything happens, it's a one-on-one."

Seeing me coming, the porter said something in Spanish to his comrades.

"Hey, man, where's my cigarettes?"

"I smoked them."

"Where's my soda pop?"

"I drank it."

The motherfucker had the advantage, but then again, I was a fish to these guys. They didn't know that behind me, fifteen Aryan Brothers just got instructions. By now there were ten Mexicans. Their leader was no dummy. He saw the makings of a confrontation.

"You know what, I guess 'cause I've got a fish number that you think I'm some kind of lame, and you can just take my shit, and not bring it back. So I guess it's me and you in the handball court."

"Hey, did you take the man's cigarettes?" the Mexican Mafia boss asked.

"Yeah."

"Did you take him a soda?"

"I got locked-down. I couldn't get out."

"Get the man his fucking soda! What's wrong with you?"

The porter's whole attitude changed. "Hey, man. I got locked-down. Your soda will be there this afternoon." The arrival of the soda squashed my beef with the porter.

At disciplinary court, I was found guilty. I lost eighteen days' good time, all that I had built, and I was sent to the hole for five days in a stripped cell, brutal, just a dungeon room with scorpions and a Bible. The room had a steel door, a shitter and a sink that hadn't been cleaned in decades. After getting strip-searched, I spent five days looking at the walls.

An Aryan Brother, Skull, had smuggled in psych medication, which he kept wrapped in the finger of a rubber glove stored in his ass. Skull was an extremely fucking dangerous buddy of Vic's, a scary motherfucker with a scrunched-up face, and slanted eyes that gave him a Cossack look as if he were a nomadic herdsman from the Russian fucking Steppe, the eyes of someone who killed easily. He was a stabbing, shooting motherfucker with a lot of tats. He'd even shot a rival Aryan Brother in the chow hall with a zip gun. Skull gave me ten of the psych meds. I went dizzy, bouncing off the walls, but I eventually slept.

When I woke up, there was nothing else to do but push-ups and sit-ups. I even reached for the Bible. Believe it or not, I'm from a religious family. We went to church on Sundays. I see nothing wrong with that to the degree that it's a social outlet.

Reading the Bible in my bare cell, I couldn't help but wonder that if I sat down for coffee with a fucking guy and he started talking about Adam and Eve and the fucking snake in the garden and Jonah being swallowed by a whale and the Immaculate Conception of Jesus as if it were all happening in this day and age, I'd look at him like he was from fucking Mars. If he said to me, "Do you believe in the God of the Bible?" I'd probably say, "Look, man, I believe in something, but it ain't what you believe in if you're referring to God as He, an old-ass grey-haired man up in heaven, sitting on a gold throne looking down directing the play of humans like we're all on a fucking chessboard with some getting cancer and some winning the lottery. Most of the major religions – Christianity, Islam and the Jews – claim God is a man, recruiting men to be His top dogs, and has treated women as second-class citizens or worse for centuries."

We all know God didn't write the Bible, and the stories are more metaphorical than literal. But for motherfuckers with eighty-year sentences, coming through the prison gate, shattered motherfuckers, especially young ones, the Bible gives them something to lean on. I don't think for one second that Pope Benedict XVI goes to bed believing God wrote the Bible or that the Walls of Jericho tumbled down or that Moses turned the Nile into blood and had it rain fucking frogs. Of course the Pope doesn't believe that 'cause he's in de bizness. The Bible's a hormone-releasing remedy for the blues. Yes, the Bible is full of good, sound advice, but there's also a lot of fucked-up shit, too.

When I read, "But I tell you not to resist an evil person. But whoever slaps you on your right cheek, turn the other to him also," I thought, *For use in prison, this scripture is a complete fucking joke. So if a guy shanks me in the right kidney, am I to offer the motherfucker my left? C'mon now!* There are lots of weakies who can't fight, who won't fight, who hide behind their Bibles when confronted. They claim they walk with Christ – which we all know is bullshit. I'm talking about fucks who rape, steal, molest, lie, testify, and as soon as they hit the county jail they grab a Bible and look for a good plea deal. If I slap a fool and he turns the other cheek, I'm gonna knock the shit out of him regardless of his goddam beliefs. And he's losing my respect. But if he fights back and shows heart – win or lose – he's earned my respect, and everyone else's.

Contemplating quotes helped time pass in the hole:

"Give to him who asks you, and from him who wants to borrow from you do not turn away."

Well, that would be fucking nice, but it's just not practical in prison. Imagine an army of mooches knowing that you'll give shit up upon request. Forget about it! That's not even practical on the streets. Who the fuck does that? A guy in here would never have any coffee, zoo-zoos or wham-whams. There'd just be a line of mooches at your cell.

"Which of you by worrying can add one cubit to his stature?"

Listen, you have to worry. You have to contemplate your situation. Worry is good to the extent it can keep you alive. But you've gotta worry about the real shit, not if the laundry grunts put too much starch in your underwear, or if it's five minutes past recreation and your cell door isn't open. But if some fool wants you X'd out in the chow hall, or if some motherfucker who owes you money is trying to blindside you, then worrying may keep you on your toes in those situations.

"But I say to you, love your enemies, bless those who curse you."

How the fuck can a guy love his enemies or bless them in prison? I mean think about it. You've gotta bloke over here lying awake at night, sharpening his shiv, planning on harming you or robbing you or raping you or taking what's yours. How can you love him or bless him? C'mon! You've gotta take care of business. You've gotta do what needs to be done. Do you honestly think that motherfuckers claiming Christianity – like George Dubya Bush and Tony Blair – are loving and blessing Osama bin Laden? Or even that the pope is doing that? Are they fuck! Love is easy to say, but really hard to do. Perhaps the popes and kings in charge of the monks demanded their subjects love their neighbours and enemies for the purpose of controlling the masses. Love love love! Fuck that! Watch your back back back!

"For where your treasure is, there your heart will be also."

I wasn't sure about this quote for a while, but it's definitely the best of the bunch. JC's speaking in metaphors, so, by treasure he's not referring to gold, a Mercedes or hedge funds. What is treasure? Think about it. It could be sitting down at teatime with Mom and Pops, and enjoying the conversation, everyone's good health and overall well-being. That's treasure that you feel inside – where your heart is. Do you think some guy driving down the Vegas Strip in his five-grand Armani suit, coked-up, with a $500-an-hour hooker next to him in his Caddy with the top down is rich in the treasure JC's talking about? Do you think his heart is there? No! His dick is there. His ego is there. His lust is there. He's having fun and enjoying the moment, but his heart ain't there. This scripture can be reversed to read: where your heart is, there your treasure will be also.

"Judge not, that you not be judged."

Fuck that! I judged and still do so. I don't wanna hang out with any pieces of shit who've harmed kids, beat their wives, raped old ladies or done any shit like that. I knew of a prisoner who was in for fucking a calf to death and one who bludgeoned a granny with a hammer and raped her. And I'm not supposed to judge them! No. I judge and I can be judged. I can handle my judgement. I'm not perfect, but who the fuck is? Are you? I've done bad things. But I can sleep at night and I can look any motherfucker alive in the eye – yeah!

"For everyone who asks receives, and he who seeks finds, and to him who knocks it will be opened."

This is a silly one. For most of us, especially in here, who the fuck receives what they ask for? We get shit on so much in prison, there's a saying, "You ain't got nothing coming." Do you get everything you ask for? Who does? Does Billy Graham? This quote was put together for control of the masses – the great unwashed – years ago, by the priests, the monks, the kings. I've read about it. They had what was called scriptoriums, rooms in monasteries where they had scribes and monks who wrote shit to keep the mooches and masses in line. It's nothing new. And it's not gonna end as long as people exist. The strong will take from the weak, but the smart will take from the strong, and the poor unwashed will get fucked over. But it don't matter. Let's enjoy this ol' life. I laugh every day. Make the most of it 'cause you're not here for but a quick minute – and then you die.

That's the kind of shit you ruminate on when you're locked in a cell with only a Bible and a couple of scorpions.

In November 1980, I got out of the hole. Fresh from studying the word of God, I was in the right frame of mind to kill Koot. Vic said that Koot was on a mission to shank me. I had to take Koot out first. We decided to do the hit in Koot's cell. Vic recruited Skull and two probates. The probates dug up shanks buried on the recreation field. I told Vic I didn't want the probates in on the hit 'cause if the prison started threatening them with the death penalty, they might rat us out. So it was just me, Skull and Vic tooled up with shanks.

Let me tell you about shanks. A shank is a blade or stabbing instrument. It's the most common and efficient method of killing staff and prisoners. One of the best to use is what we call an Arkansas toothpick – an old-style Bowie knife, a long, thin, double-edged blade, usually six to nine inches, with a handle on it, so the whole thing is about twelve to eighteen inches long.

The metal to make a shank is obtained from pieces of table or chair or anywhere there's metal. Back then, we used dental floss, Ajax and a little water to cut sections from metal bunks. You get the Ajax wet, make a paste out of it, apply it to the metal, and hold the dental floss and go back and forth with it on the Ajax, and it goes through the metal like a saw. It's a slow process, but it's not like you've got anything other than time on your hands in here.

You can make a shank from the perimeter fence. You just straighten the metal out, sharpen the end and make it into an ice pick. A variation is the slicing shank, which is made out of any kind of flat metal or round metal. You can use it on the neck to kill someone. If you can slice either the jugular or the carotid, odds are the victim's gonna die. You may go for the inner thigh. If the femoral artery is cut with a slicing blade, it'll cause the victim to bleed out. Anyone shanked there should put pressure on it and get to the hospital.

I've even seen shanks made out of toilet paper and glue, or newspaper and glue, or notepaper and glue. They have metal tips purely for stabbing. To make a paper shank, you soak the paper in glue, roll it up real tight and make a long, thin, pointed stabbing implement. Some put a needle at the point of it, or some kind of pushpin, so it has a sharp metal point. Once the metal point breaks the skin it goes right in with one hit.

The quickest way to kill someone with a shank is to go for the heart. You aim just below the breast bone, and the shank goes in and up. Once it's in, you move it from side to side, and either break it off or pull it out. Going in, it makes such a small-diameter wound, that when you pull it out there's not a lot of blood. With a small diameter the skin will close in, but by wiggling it, it does a lot of damage to the heart or aorta. The victim bleeds internally, and dies a long time before the prison can get him to a hospital. If they life-flight him out, it's usually at least half an hour. It takes time for them to figure out what's going on. Then they gotta call for the helicopter. The helicopter has to fly in, land, pick you up, fly out. If they wait for an ambulance it takes a lot longer. Plenty leave on the helicopter and don't come back. I've seen guards leave on the helicopter and not come back, and they get the helicopter here a whole lot quicker for the guards.

Prisoners get shanked over drug debts, plain stupidity, disrespect or trying to get in the mix with the gangs. My advice to new prisoners is: do your best to stay out of the gangs and anything that brings problems, especially drugs.

To protect you from shanks, you make body armour. You take magazines – preferably *National Geographic*, that's the best one – and strap them around your waist using either Saran Wrap or garbage bags. You tie them on with clothes or whatever works. Saran Wrap out of the kitchen is best. You have to tie it up to cover your middle-torso area. Then, if you haven't got a shank or big fists, get a big stick, a rock, batteries or a padlock in a sock or anything else like that you can lay your hands on to combat your opponent.

Shankings are common and taken for granted in prison. I saw a guy get stuck in the chow hall. He was hit three times in the back before he even realised what was happening. He got up, ran out of the door and the guy with the blade was chasing him. As the guy ran away, the guy that was sitting across from him reached over to his chow tray, said, "I guess he's not gonna be eating that," picked up his burger and ate it.

There's no disposing of bodies in prison 'cause everybody's accounted for. You can hide a body for a little while, but come headcount time, they realise something's wrong. There was a body they didn't find right away. The reason they found it was he was in the bathroom and the blood ran out from under the door.

Disposing of shanks, you can try to throw them on a roof or bury them or throw them over a fence. Sometimes, you'll leave the shank inside the victim, especially if it's made out of Plexiglas and the blade part of it breaks off.

I had to take all of that into account as I prepared to whack Koot. When we got the signal that Koot was in his cell, I entered fast, followed by Skull. By the time he saw death had arrived, it was too late. The motherfucker was cornered. He barely had a chance to yell, which no one paid any attention to 'cause prison is so fucking noisy.

Vic guarded the door. Facing me, Koot retreated to the back of the cell. Approaching him, I feinted a punch with my hand that wasn't holding the shank. Koot moved to block that hand, exposing his chest. Lunging forward with my shank, an Arkansas toothpick, I used my free hand to grab the side of Koot's neck, so that I had just enough of a grip on him to pull him forward. As the shank went up, Koot folded into a V shape, dropping his chest, which enabled me to stick him below his breastbone into his heart. He made a sound like *uhhhh* as if air was coming out of him. As I wiggled the shank, Koot growled and twisted his body to my side. He almost fell down. Skull approached Koot from the opposite side. He sliced Koot's throat. Blood spurted. Collapsing down, Koot tried to kick us away. Standing on his right thigh, I used my left leg to shield kicks from his foot, and leaned forward to stab him again in the heart. Skull was hacking so frantically at Koot's neck, I thought his head would come off. Koot was jerking around. When his body went limp, I knew he was as done as a Christmas turkey. We shoved his body under the bunk to give us time before the guards noticed his disappearance. We went back to our cells and gave our shanks and clothes to the probates. While we took showers, our clothes were washed in bleach water and the shanks were reburied on the rec field.

It was hours before the guards saw the corpse and the prison was locked down. The guards swarmed into Koot's cell like a tribe of monkeys trying to fuck a football. Nobody squealed 'cause they knew they'd be next. It was one of many professional jobs I got away with in prison. Skull had killed a lot of motherfuckers in the joint and he was as good at not getting caught as Charlie "Batts" Battaglia. Skull and Vic would never rat me out even if they were busted.

A few days later, walking to the chow hall in the sunshine, I was feeling great about how we'd handled Koot. I met a kid, Pete, twenty, a well-natured youngster. As a kind of mentor, I took a liking to him. He was running errands for the Aryan Brotherhood, carrying shanks and beating up guys. I saw in his admiration for the Aryan Brotherhood the extent that I wanted to get involved with mobsters as a youngster. Pete was near the end of his term as a probate. The Aryan Brotherhood council voted him in as a member. He was really proud to be part of that shit.

Pete jumped on a guy and was sent to lockdown. A white guy in lockdown had broken the gang rules by siding with a black guy over the whites, and he'd also tried to stab a white gang member. The Aryan Brotherhood sent Pete a shank, with instructions to do a number on the white guy. That's known as a kamikaze move. Pete only had less than a year left to serve. It's kamikaze 'cause you can't come back from a mission like that without getting caught. Back then, if you drew blood in prison, you got twenty-five to life added to your sentence. Pete got out of his cell to work as a porter, but dropped the shank in front of a guard 'cause he didn't wanna kill the dude. He made it look like an accident. The guards moved him to a lockdown within a lockdown.

While on his way, he heard an Aryan Brother yell, "Hey, motherfucker, you dropped that shank, you piece of shit."

The day Pete came back on the yard, I was sick, laying up on my bunk. When the 1 PM headcount cleared, I was told Vic wanted to talk to me at the fence. I went down there and as I approached the twenty-foot no-man's-land separating the two fences, I looked across the way, and there was Pete talking to Skull, the Aryan Brother he trusted the most.

"Hey, Two Tonys!" Pete yelled. "Can you clean me up over there with the fellas if you can? I didn't do nothing wrong."

"Yeah, sure," I said.

Skull said to Pete, "Take a lap, kid. I want to talk to Two Tonys in private." Confused, I looked at Skull.

"I'll be back." Pete took off for a lap. Skull got on his haunches. I squatted down. "What's up?"

He motioned with his right fist as if he were stabbing his left palm.

"When?" I asked.

"Right now." Looking around, I saw all the signals were there. Guys were throwing horseshoes that didn't play horseshoes. Guys were digging up shanks buried on the yard. Guys were doing things they didn't normally do, like grouping up. All routine was broken. "I'm running it," Skull said.

I knew then he was gonna have Pete killed. I tried to use my pull. "How much time has that kid got left?"

"Eight months."

"Do you have to do it like that? Can't you just bust his head open and put him in hospital?"

"It's gotta be done."

I'm not an animal. I'll kill a motherfucker in a minute and I have when I thought he was gonna harm me, or if he was trying to scheme on me, but these Aryan Brotherhood motherfuckers like Skull were cold.

Pete came back and stopped. I looked at little Pete for just maybe fifteen seconds and an inner voice told me to yell over at the kid, "Get off this fucking yard now. Get under that fucking gun tower now." But I didn't and I couldn't 'cause I'd have been killed.

"Don't forget to clean me up," Pete said.

"I'll get right on that, little bro." I walked about twenty yards and turned around.

Skull had his arm around Pete's shoulder, walking another lap. Three dudes grouped up were about to roll on Pete. They came up behind him and started stabbing him over and over, in the kidneys, neck, stomach and the femoral artery in the thigh. Pete dropped. To this day, I still think about little Pete, the poor motherfucker. He left in a pine box to be buried at Boot Hill with no gravestone marker.

A month later, I met a prisoner called BW out of Nevada. A hustler. Smart. At times too smart for his own good, as we shall see. I came out to recreation on a cold winter morning. As all the prisoners filed out, I noticed three young guys trying to be nonchalant as they dug up an area where shanks were buried. As they unearthed them, I strolled up to them and asked them what was up. Now they were young – maybe nineteen to twenty – and eager to make names for themselves. The Aryan Brotherhood was set up so the older members could send the youngsters on missions to evaluate how they performed, which factored into their acceptance in the pack. So these kids, with nostrils flaring, were ready for blood. They wanted to show what great killers they were, that their hearts were committed to murder. Now not to sound vain, but they knew who I was and that I deserved an answer.

"We're taking out BW this morning."

"Who says so?" I asked.

They said an Aryan Brother, Roy, had called the hit, so they could get their hands bloody. Not wanting a repeat of the Pete situation, I told them to hold off until I got back to them. I found Vic's overgrown ass in the shack we had for drinking coffee. I asked him to step over, so we could talk. "Hey, these fucking nutcakes are getting set up to kill BW. I'd like to know what he's done. Roy called the shot."

Well, upon that Vic's nostrils flared 'cause number one: no one was supposed to call a shot without several nods. Number two: Vic hated Roy as most did.

About that time, BW showed up. Vic asked BW to hang out in the shack for a few minutes, and then he asked a couple of guys to hang out with him while Vic and I looked for Roy, but he wasn't out yet. We approached the three would-be killers. Vic told them to put the shanks back in the soil and stand by. Roy walked out and we went up to him.

"Hey, Roy, you telling these youngsters to hit BW?" Vic said.

Roy started with some bullshit about a $50 debt for smack. The bill was three-months old. He was tired of BW's stories and wanted his money or his blood.

I jumped in with, "Excuse me," to Vic. I said to Roy, "Look, BW ain't perfect. There's a lot of snake in him. We can all see that a mile away. If he got to you for $50 or $500, that's on you. He's a friend of mine and that makes him a friend of Vic's, and he don't get stabbed on the prison yard, especially by a pack who don't even know what he's about. So rethink your plan of action."

Cutting in, Vic said in his hoarse frog voice, "Hey, if you feel he has to die, then go kill him. He's right over there by the shack. We'll dig two of these shanks up, and you go at it one on one, but don't even try to send a pack in on him." Roy backed up and said he didn't want to kill him, just scare him. "Oh, then go scare him," Vic said. We turned and walked away, leaving pooty-butt Roy to reflect on his cowardice.

I'm glad I saved BW's life. We had a few fun years together. We were even cellmates in supermax for a time. I never told him about that day. Why should I? It was over. Why put him on a paranoid trip or stir up more shit? Now did BW go on to discover a cure for cancer or some great gift for humanity? No. But he was a damn good legal eagle and smart as a whip. And I know he got a few guys' cases overturned and they were freed. And perhaps, just perhaps, out of those freed guys, one of their grandchildren might have discovered a cure for cancer that wouldn't have been possible without Two Tonys being on a prison yard one cold morning. Wild ain't it, how my fucked-up mind works? Am I actually trying to claim my exploits as a rogue were for a cause?

CHAPTER 13

My daughter laughed at the 1970s suit I left prison in. She could talk! Niki's pink hair and punk style freaked me out. Not to mention how much she'd grown now that she was in her late teens. To try and compensate for my absence in her life, I moved into a house in Phoenix, so I'd be near to where she lived with her mom. Even though I'd served five years, I'd gotten away with so much serious crime, it was time to retire from that lifestyle and become a worker ant. I got a job as a salesman at a dealership run by a Mexican. I hooked Niki up with a car from there. Niki came and hung out at the house a lot. We'd watch talk shows like *The Arsenio Hall Show*. I got a medium-sized brown dog, Dancer, a mix of chow and coyote. I loved Dancer. She was so loyal. If anyone came snooping around, she'd let me know. Things were fine that first year.

A guy I met at work, Pat, asked if I'd ride up to Tucson with him to auction a car. I was meeting my daughter that day, so I told him sure, as long as we could take Niki. Pat had gangsteritis, but he was a wannabe who didn't have no backbone.

In case you have gangsteritis, I'm gonna give you some advice. Most of the gangster groupies I knew were preyed on by real gangsters. One did a swan dive off the roof of the Pioneer Hotel without a parachute. Keep your day jobs, folks.

Pat drove. I was in the passenger seat, Niki in the back. We'd been on the freeway for about thirty minutes when I said, "Hey, Pat, I'm sure that car behind has been following us since Phoenix."

Niki looked back at the car. "Hey, Dad, I'm scared."

"Don't worry, honey. Everything's gonna be fine."

"Is this car stolen?" Niki asked.

"No," I said. "Ain't that right, Pat?" Pat glanced over with an expression that suggested something was wrong.

Near Casa Grande, the police had blocked off both sides of the freeway 'cause a cop had recently pulled someone over and got shot dead. A helicopter was out and news crews. All of the cars on the freeway had stopped.

"Holy shit!" Niki said.

As we approached the traffic, the car behind us put its police lights on.

"What's going on?" Niki asked. She looked terrified.

"Just do as they say," I said.

I knew something heavy was going down when the cop didn't approach the car and do the routine request for driver's license and registration. The cops opened their doors, got out and pulled guns, using their doors as cover. "Everybody put your hands where we can see them!" a cop said over a bullhorn.

Niki was so nervous, she started digging in her handbag for a hairbrush. "Stop fucking with your hands, Niki!" I yelled. "Put them up! That's how people get shot by the cops."

"Get out one at a time! Driver, you come first!" Pat got out. "Keep your hands up!" I got out next. Niki got out so scared she couldn't even turn around.

"It's gonna be OK, Niki," I said calmly.

"Dad!" Niki was crying.

"Don't worry, baby. It's nothing. Just do what they say. It's all gonna get worked out."

"Walk backwards on the asphalt! Now get on your knees!"

When we got on our knees, cops came up behind us, put guns to our heads and handcuffed us. Seeing Niki, weighing about ninety pounds and with a skirt on, kneeling down with a gun to her head, I lost it. "You motherfuckers! You don't fucking mess like this with my fucking daughter! You think you're big shots, you Casa Grande hick motherfuckers!" They told me to shut the fuck up as I called them every name in the book. "Leave her alone! She has nothing to do with this!"

"I'm his daughter," Niki said in-between gasps. "I don't know what's going on." They put Niki in the front seat of a car, which was a relief.

At the cop shop, they said they'd found stolen guns in the trunk. Pat didn't wanna cop to it. The pooty-butt was crying. I wasn't going down for this petty bullshit. I told Pat he needed to take the heat off me and Niki by copping to it, so he did. They released Niki the same day. On the jail phone, I called Niki. She said she was OK.

"How're you doing?" Niki asked without sounding angry.

"I'm fine. Somebody had sold the dealership a stolen car and we didn't know. Don't worry about me. This ain't no big thing. This ain't nothing for me. Pat's still crying like a baby."

Three days later, our Mexican boss bailed us out. Pat ended up found dead in the trunk of his car, and no, I hadn't whacked him. He was killed by his wife and the dude she was cheating on Pat with.

Figuring there was more to the dealership than fixing and selling cars, I checked around and found out that the dude running it was connected to the Mexican Mafia and weed importation. Pissed at him for getting my daughter arrested, I planned to kidnap him and hold him for ransom 'cause the motherfucker had a lot of cash. I was gonna stick him in the trunk of a car. But the cops raided the dealership and arrested him before I had a chance to kidnap him. Maybe the raid happened for a reason: going back to crime wasn't such a good idea. I got a job selling cars at Mel Clayton Ford.

Since our arrest in Casa Grande, Niki hadn't come around to my house in months. Her mom, Katy, kept her away. I didn't really talk much with Katy, so I was surprised when I got a call asking me to meet her at Coco's Restaurant to talk about Niki. Toto was visiting, so we headed to Coco's.

"This is what's going on," Katy said. "She quit high school and took off with some guitar player, Doug, who's twenty years older than her."

They were staying in some pay-by-the-week fleapit near Coco's. Toto and I went there. The guy who answered the door was tall, but looking like he weighed a whole 120 pounds. He was wearing a vintage cowboy shirt unbuttoned and Levi jeans. "Are you Doug?"

"Yeah."

I pushed him inside. Niki wasn't there. "Who the fuck are you?" I said to his buddy.

"Richard."

"Beat it, Richard." Toto opened the door. Richard disappeared. I grabbed a chair, put it in the middle of the room and told Doug to sit.

"What have I done?" Doug asked, his voice going up a few octaves.

"I'm Niki's Pop."

Whatever colour was left drained from Doug's face. With a big beard that made him look like some psycho wood chopper, Toto came up behind Doug, so close that his thighs were touching Doug's shoulders.

"Hey, pal, let me tell you how the cow ate the cabbage. If you know anything about Niki, you know who I am, and she's only a teenager. Listen, if we've gotta come back, you'll never see us coming. And I can guarantee you one thing: you'll never be able to tie your shoelaces again much less play the fucking guitar. I'm gonna tell you this right now." I pulled out my gun. "If you don't pack your bags and get out of here by six o'clock, you're dead."

The motherfucker started crying, opening drawers, rifling through them and packing his shit. We left.

An hour later, Niki called. "Why the fuck did you do that to me? Don't butt into my life and tell me what to do!"

"Listen. I told the guy to leave. He didn't have to. In fact, if he would have stood up for himself, I would have respected him a lot more, but he didn't."

"Of course not, Dad! He's not used to fucking gangsters coming to his room. You fucking terrified him. He's never been in a fight in his life and he's never even stolen. I'm so mad at you, Dad. I love Doug so much. I need him."

It took a few weeks for things to settle down with Niki. She went back to school. Unknown to me at that time, she stayed in touch with Doug, who kept out of my way for years, thinking I was gonna kill him. Eventually, I spoke to Doug. Niki was no longer seeing him. They were just friends. Everything was cool.

With things OK with Niki, my life was rocking along smoothly until Skull, fresh out of prison, showed up at my house with fifteen cents in his pocket. I let him move in, gave him $200 and hooked him up with a job at Mel Clayton Ford as a mechanic. At first, Skull kissed my ass and was respectful. But then he started getting out of control, slamming crystal meth every day.

Time went by. I came home one night to Skull and a chemist, a short, clean-cut guy with brown hair, a miserable slant to his mouth and bugged-out eyes from being up for days. They were moving my stuff into storage 'cause the chemist was gonna cook a batch of meth, so they were setting up a lab. It was too much. I told them, "Get the fuck out! This is my house!"

Skull flipped. "Don't disrespect me in front of my friend!"

At that point, I thought of *The Art of War*, the words of Sun fucking Tzu: never underestimate your opponent. Skull was so dangerous that if things had escalated, he would have killed me right there. I backed off, but I knew there was no other way to get him out of my house: I had to kill him.

I got a call from Niki. "Look, Dad, you know I don't keep secrets from you. Something happened last night that you need to know."

"What's up?"

"Skull called Mom's house and said to me, 'Hey, I really need to talk to you. Can I come by and pick you up?' He picked me up and took me to the Dirty Drummer. We were sitting there with beers, and I started to realise that this wasn't such a good idea. He was saying how much he loves you and how fantastic you are. He went on and on about you. So I was drinking a beer, and then he gave me some speed. He told me not to tell you."

"What did you do with the speed?" I said calmly, but inside

my body was tightening as I visualised putting a gun in Skull's mouth.

"I threw it away. I didn't do it. Please don't tell Skull I told you." Niki started crying.

"Honey, don't worry about it. It's OK. It's no big deal."

"There's more I gotta tell you. After he gave me the speed, I got the feeling that he liked me. You know, like I could tell he was gonna make a move. I got this weird feeling. He tried to put his hand on my leg. I moved out of the way. I stopped drinking. I didn't do the speed. I made it clear I wanted to go home. I don't know what he was thinking. He's insane. I only went there 'cause I was nervous and thought that I should do what he said. Look, Dad, don't do anything. Nothing happened. All he did was talk about you and how much he respects you and how great you are and how you've been so good to him …"

Messing with Niki, Skull had crossed a line. I told Skull I had a deal for us in Prescott, a store to rob. I had the perfect spot in Prescott to whack a motherfucker, right under the freeway on a one-way road that formed a U-turn. There'd be no flash of the gun. Skull wanted to take his chemist buddy with us to Prescott. "OK," I said, realising I was gonna have to whack them both. "No guns," I said. "We'll pick up guns when we get there." I had an extra gun stuck in the back of my pants.

We snorted crystal meth and went to the car. It was getting dark outside. The chemist got in the back seat behind me, emitting a strange vibe. Immediately, I knew something was up. As a killer living in a killer society, out-of-the-ordinary shit like that was a warning going *ding-ding-ding*. I was riding, sitting with my back to the door, watching these two motherfuckers, suspecting one of them had a gun. If my intuition was right, I'd catch one of them making a move for it.

We pulled in at a Walgreens store to get some drinks and shit. Skull reached to his side, pulled out a gun and put it under his seat. I asked why he'd brought a gun, and he said, "I just forgot to leave it behind." Something in his eyes warned me that he was imagining what my death would look like. When Skull was in the store, the chemist got panicky in the back of the car and ran out and joined Skull. I watched them argue. I later found out that the chemist was telling him, "Kill him. We need to kill him now." Skull got back in the car with a bag in his hand and passed the gun to the chemist under the bag. Skull opened a Coke, which fizzed – making me jump – and asked, "What's wrong?"

There are nerve endings in your nose that tingle when you're about to sneeze. Within seconds, the tingling intensifies. It peaks in the fraction of a second before the sneeze detonates. In terms of death perception, the tingle in my head had the intensity of that final fraction of a second.

"I gotta pee." It was dark, so as I got out, I left the door ajar, so the dome light would stay on. That way I could see the mother-fuckers. I stood behind a truck with a good view of them. It was an ideal position to shoot them from 'cause if they shot back, they were more likely to hit the truck. When I saw the chemist pass the gun to Skull, I knew it was on. I took the safety off my 9mm and I nailed Skull. *Bam!* I was relieved the gun had fired. He did a little twitch thing and looked at me. I savoured the moment. I felt the spirit of little Pete – the youngster he'd had whacked in prison – right beside me, even more satisfied than the spirits of the two Tonys on the day I turned the tables on Charlie "Batts" Battaglia. Skull only looked at me for a second, but when you're doing something like that a second is an eternity. I wanted to kill the motherfucker. It had been building up ever since he'd moved in, spending my money, disrespecting me and my daughter. He was out for himself. Then I put another three in his head. *Bam! Bam! Bam!* I knew in my heart of hearts they were gonna off me. I looked over at the chemist, aimed and pulled the trigger, but the gun jammed. He took off and lived to rat me out.

All of the neighbours were coming out to see what was going on. I tried to pull Skull out of the car, but ran into the problem of dead weight. One of his eyes had been shot out and his jaw was hanging off. People started yelling. My adrenaline kicked in more 'cause I didn't want to get caught. I found the strength to drag him out. I screeched off. Driving down the highway was a thrill. My mind was tripping. High on meth and adrenaline, I turned up 'Another Brick in the Wall' by Pink Floyd.

Skull had a killing coming. The first time I heard that expression, "He had it coming," was from Abe "Kid Twist" Reles from Murder Inc, an old Brownsville Jew mob back in the 1930s. Abe's preferred method of killing was by ice pick through the ear, which he rammed into the brain to cause a haemorrhage. They were questioning Abe Reles, and he said, "They all had it coming," which is true 'cause people like Skull do stuff to get themselves killed. If I get killed it's 'cause I have it coming. In the killing business, you don't just go out and kill someone for no reason. Who needs the fucking aggravation? If someone's getting killed, they've usually either killed someone, fucked someone's wife, stolen something or really pissed someone off. I must admit, though, that when you want to whack a guy it's a lot easier if you tell yourself, "The motherfucker has got this coming 'cause he did me wrong."

I've got a lot of regrets about my life, but I never whacked a motherfucker that I didn't feel good about afterwards. For the record: there were no working stiffs amongst those I whacked. None of them were on the way to the mill, lunchbox in hand. They were all in de bizness. And I didn't learn that expression from Elmore fucking Leonard. I'm sincere about that. The element I've been brought up and raised in didn't copy Elmore Leonard. He got his shit from people like me, unless you think Mr Leonard is a whacker of men. I'm not lying on my bunk at nights, tossing and turning, seeing this dead motherfucker's face or worrying if he had a wife or a daughter. I'm seeing the eyes of motherfuckers who had it coming. So what if I nailed Skull, put slugs in him? I've got no remorse for that piece of trash. He was one of the most murderous motherfuckers to walk the face of the earth.

It came out at trial that Skull had planned to kill me that night, which is what I feared was gonna happen. Yeah, I said fear. Everyone fears. Don't be bullshitted by those macho types who say, "I don't fear nothing or no one." Fear is natural. It's a survival thing. Animals fear going to the waterhole where predators hang out, but they must drink. Some animals sense fear and that's how they choose their victims. Just as some people do. If I hadn't feared what Skull was gonna do, and acted on it, I wouldn't be alive.

CHAPTER 14

After whacking Skull, I sped back to my house and packed up my shit. I had no choice but to abandon my dog. I figured Niki would take care of Dancer. With the cops and the Aryan Brotherhood after me, I fled to Sal's house in Tucson. He'd visited me at Florence prison.

By 1984, Sal had hung up his gangster spurs and was selling cars. I'll be damned if he hadn't turned into a born-again Christian. He was in the deep end of the religious pool, and so was his wife. Sal said that Charlie "Batts" Battaglia had died of a heart attack in 1983, at the age of sixty-six, in St Mary's Hospital, Tucson, struck down by God for his sins, and that I'd end up like Batts if I didn't get on the path to Christ.

Showing me his new house, Sal picked up an ocotillo cactus skeleton in the shape of a cross. He said, "Look what we found. This is God talking to me. We found it when we were looking to buy the house. It was a sign we should buy it." He was enthusiastic about me staying with them, but I was a little wary. He said he got up early every morning to go to a prayer meeting and he asked me to come.

He was so excited, I said, "Fuck it, let's go." Skull's murder was headline news, but I didn't let Sal know I'd done it 'cause that would have made him an accessory after the fact in the eyes of the law.

At 5 AM, we were up and on our way to the prayer meeting. Sal got a flat tyre. "See what Satan did?" Sal said.

"What?" I said.

"He gave me a flat tyre. He doesn't want us to help you get away from the work you're doing for him. Satan's always trying to upset me and mess up my schedule." He was as happy as can be fixing the flat. Carefree. Whistling like the flat was the best thing that ever happened to the motherfucker in the whole world. I was thinking of popping the motherfucker in the head for turning goofy, putting him to sleep and out of his misery, but then I felt bad as I remembered everything we'd been through, from us first setting off from Detroit in his 1958 Plymouth Fury convertible, speeding across the desert in New Mexico, to all of the shit that went down in Alaska, and Sal getting an ice pick in his head on the day Blake died.

Back on the road to the church, he said, "The reason I joined the Assemblies of God is 'cause a church member told me that the Lord had spoken to him and told him that I was being sent to join the congregation."

Ten guys were at the meeting. Hardware-store people. Chiropractors. Shit like that. I didn't know what to do. I sat down and they surrounded me in a circle. They started praying and putting their fucking hands on me. When they started talking in tongues – *skoobydawackeeballamackasallikodo* – I realised I was being exorcised. They were all talking in different tongues.

I was thinking, *What the fuck has Sal done? How the fuck did I get myself in this situation? Sal's house is a good hideout and the grub is good, but I've fucked myself coming here. It's six in the morning and I'm at the Assemblies of God Church surrounded by a bunch of holy-rolling motherfuckers praying for me to cast out the devil like I'm Attila the fucking Hun. But I can't hate them. They're not trying to pick my pocket or sell me nothing. They're just trying to bring me into their flock. I guess that's the bottom line with these motherfuckers: get a guy in your flock.* After ten minutes, I was getting pissed off. *Let's get this over with. I want to get the fuck out of here.* Sal had me trapped by a bunch of religious fanatics still talking in tongues out of the sides of their necks.

On the way home, I wanted to put Sal's head in a cholla cactus and to ensure that the needles stuck in his fucking eyeballs, but instead, I just said, "Hey, Sal, what the fuck's up with that? Why take me down that road? I didn't ask for that."

"Look, even if I'm wrong, it ain't hurting nothing. It's changed my life."

"Well, it ain't for me."

I imagine now that Sal's one of those sorry-asses who sends Jimmy Swaggart money. Swaggart's with Assemblies of God. He keeps getting caught with naked prostitutes, but his flock keep forgiving the sick motherfucker and sending him even more money. Swaggart's being kept rich by sad motherfuckers like Sal. When I turn on the TV and see a fucking asshole like Robert Schuller of the Cathedral of Tomorrow sitting there in his big glass palace in elaborate robes, taking people's money, telling his flock what is right and wrong, I see a high-class motherfucking flimflammer, a snake-oil salesman, no better than me. From Schuller to Billy Graham to the guy in Vatican City who used to ride with the Nazi Youth Group, they're all fucking scammers. They're not interested in the truth. They're interested in de bizness.

When the equivalent of *America's Most Wanted* broadcast my story, it was time to get the fuck out of Sal's. I called Niki, "I'm gonna be leaving Arizona. I've done something horrible, but don't believe what the police or the news say about me. You might not see me for a while. Never forget how much I love you." She said she had rescued Dancer before my house had been broken into and trashed. She said dudes with a lot of prison tattoos had been prowling my neighbourhood. I figured it was the Aryan Brotherhood hunting me down 'cause Skull was a member in such high standing. The gang had members and wannabes all over Arizona.

I met up with Toto at a bar. He gave me a fake ID. I asked him to drive me down to Hermosillo, Mexico, so if we got pulled over by the cops, his ID would be the only one they saw unless they grew suspicious. In Hermosillo, I checked into a hotel. Toto went back to Arizona. He called to say Sal's house had been SWAT-team raided. The next morning, I took a cab to the airport and flew to Cancún, where I partied at the clubs.

I had connections in Hawaii. Figuring the cops had assumed I'd fled to Mexico by now, I decided that Hawaii was the last place they'd search. With the fake ID, I flew there. I stayed in Maui and Waikiki. I lived in a house on the slopes of Mount Haleakalā by myself. It was time to create some memories that I could take to the grave. Trust me, if there was a chance of you being arrested tomorrow and sentenced to death, you'd start living differently. Imagine how much your life would improve.

I explored the Diamond Head crater, a 150,000-year-old ash cone with a view of the aquamarine Pacific Ocean. I hiked the crater of Haleakalā, with its exotic flora and barren hillsides, my shoes crunching volcanic popcorn, rocks that are ochre or rust or metallic green. For hours, I staggered over the crater floor, a landscape of mist, bottomless pits, bubble caves and lava tubes. Every now and then I stopped to smell the silvery ahinahina plant with its honey-sweet blossoms, which looked like a cactus exploding into a thousand swords, its hairy leaves reflecting the sunlight. I trekked through a rainforest and swam in natural pools. It was one of the most scenic places in the world, but I was lonely.

Every now and then, I visited my daughter at her grandma's house. I called her grandma the Duck Lady 'cause she made the best duck. Using my fake ID, I'd fly into Phoenix and Niki would pick me up. She'd drive me around to places where I could collect money from people, even up to Tucson. If the police were to pull us over, they'd ID Niki. If they ran her name, it would come back clean. Out of devotion, she drove me around, but I was a stupid motherfucker for involving her in that shit.

One night, Sal called the Duck Lady's house. "Can you come up here right away?" he asked.

"What's up, Sal?"

"Let's talk in person."

"OK. I'll be right up." Sal had sounded stressed out. *Maybe he's mad at me for the cops raiding his crib.* Feeling lousy about the way I'd treated Sal when I'd stayed at his house, I figured I could use this visit to make amends.

On the way to Tucson, Niki asked, "Where are we going?"

"Just to see my old buddy, Sal," I said, my eyes peeled for cop cars.

It took us almost two hours to get to Sal's. It was dusk. I told Niki to park down the street in case the cops drove by his house and noticed her car.

"Can I come in?" Niki asked.

If Sal had some heavy shit to lay on me, I didn't want Niki hearing it. Besides, no matter where the fuck I went, I always told Niki to wait outside. "Let me go inside and see what he wants first." Opening the little gate to Sal's, the usual sounds of the kids and stuff inside couldn't be heard. Walking the path to the front door, I scanned the windows for family life. Nothing was registering. The alarm in my brain went off. The hairs on my forearms and the back of my neck started to rise. Approaching the door, I knocked with one hand and grabbed my gun with the other.

The door opened. Sal was stood there with a fucked-up expression as if he were about to puke. Behind him was an Aryan Brother with a gun to Sal's head. The dude had short hair, a big moustache and viper eyes. His skin was all tatted down with neo-Nazi jailhouse shit. There was no time to think things through. If I got clipped, Niki might be next. I drew my gun and shot. The bullet hit the dude in the shoulder, spinning him around. Sal fell. I was about to go in and finish the motherfucker off, but more of the motherfuckers emerged from inside. I opened up on them: *bam-bam-bam!* I took off. From behind the gate, I crouched down and shot into the house to keep the fuckers there. The motherfuckers shot back. I sprinted to Niki's car. "Get ready to put your foot down, Niki!"

Having heard the fucking bullets, she was revving the engine. More shots were fired at me. The Aryan Brothers were through the gate. I fired back. They retreated a bit. I got in the car. "Go! Go! Go!"

As Niki screeched away, her back window was shot out. We both dropped our heads. "I'm fucking scared, Dad!" Niki almost lost control of the car. I grabbed the steering wheel. Turning a corner, the car almost flipped over. "I don't wanna die! Holy shit, Dad! Are they gonna kill us? Am I gonna die?"

"It's OK now. Just keep driving, so they can't catch up with us. Stay focused on the road." With the back window shot out, I figured the cops would pull us over on the way to Phoenix or the Aryan Brotherhood would know where we were going and catch up with us. There was a stink coming from the car engine like human hair on fire.

By the time we got to Phoenix, Niki was traumatised. Once we got off the freeway, I told her to pull over and get out. On the sidewalk, I said, "It's all over now. We made it. You drove really well under pressure. Good job, kid." She couldn't talk. I gave her a hug. She was sobbing and trembling. There was no way I could take her back to her mom with the window shot out. It would have caused too much shit. "Look, nothing bad's gonna happen now. We're gonna take the car to a friend of mine who'll fix the window. That'll give you an opportunity to chill out before I get you back to the Duck Lady's." We hung around the car for five or ten minutes until Niki was able to say that she was OK. I drove to the house of an associate from the dealership I used to work at who could replace the glass. He was surprised to see us, but he knew my history, so he didn't ask any fucking questions. Waiting for the glass to be fixed gave Niki time to shake off some of the shock.

"Are you sure they won't come looking for us down here, Dad?" Niki asked.

"Yes. No one knows about the Duck Lady's. Even the cops. If your mom's there, don't say anything about what happened otherwise she won't let us hang out no more." After it was fixed up, I drove the car to the Duck Lady's. Walking to the front door, I said, "Everything will be OK if we both act cool." Using my keys, I opened the door, distracted by what had happened at Sal's. At first, I was glad the Duck Lady and Niki's mom weren't there. Niki was still pale. They would have noticed something was up.

The TV was off. Niki went from room to room to find the Duck Lady. It clicked that something was wrong. *Where the fuck's the Duck Lady?* It was too late at night for her to be at Circle K or some shit.

The electricity in the house went off. I looked out of a window. The street lights were off. *Maybe a power outage.* Cars pulled up outside. My adrenaline kicked in. *Who are these motherfuckers?* With high-powered guns, dudes in SWAT outfits got behind the cars. Not only was I fucking trapped, Niki was fucking with me. *Motherfuckers!*

Niki was crying. "What's going on, Dad? What should we do?"

"Grab some pillows and lie down on the floor and stay down."

Next up, there was a helicopter above the house. My homicide detective nemesis, Dirk Taylor, got on the bullhorn. "We know you're in there. We've got the place completely surrounded. Come out now."

Outgunned, I knew it was over. My main instinct was to protect Niki. "Don't shoot!" I yelled, stood behind the front door. "There are people in here. My daughter, her mom and grandma."

"That's not true," Dirk said. "Her mom and grandma are out here with us."

"If that's the case, let me speak to them."

"I can arrange that. Give me a few minutes."

"Is Niki OK?" was the first thing her mom asked.

"She's fine," I said. "Trust me, I'd never let anyone hurt her. You have nothing to worry about."

"Nothing to worry about! You've got my daughter in there, you son of a bitch! They've got guns aimed on my mom's house and some sort of tank down the street ready to destroy the house with. They said if you come out right now, no one will get hurt. Please come out now. For Niki's sake, you must come out. Out of all the crazy shit you've ever done, now's the time to do the right thing for your daughter. The detective has given me his word that nothing will happen to Niki if you come out now."

"I'm gonna come out," I said. "Nothing's gonna happen to Niki. Put Dirk Taylor back on."

"We can do this the easy way," Dirk said, "with you coming out and no one getting hurt, or the hard way."

It was over, so I had to plan ahead. For whacking Skull, the Aryan Brotherhood would kill me as soon as I stepped foot in the jail. My crime partner, the Aryan Brother Vic, couldn't get me off the hook 'cause Skull had been in higher standing with the gang for being a bigger killer. My best chance of survival was for the jail to put me in a single cell in lockdown, but they had no reason to do that, so I had to give them one. I needed the TV news to film my arrest. If I declared war on the Aryan Brotherhood and they broadcast that across Phoenix, the jail would have no choice but to lock me down or else my death would be on their hands.

I told Dirk Taylor that I'd surrender only if the media were filming live. I wanted the electricity back on, so that I could turn on the TV to make sure they weren't bullshitting me. Dirk arranged those things. The TV showed the stand-off on headline news.

Grabbing a cowboy hat, I tried to raise Niki's spirits by saying, "Do you think I'll look good in this on TV?" Gawking like I was crazy, she shook her head as if she didn't know what to say. She was in shock.

"OK. We've arranged everything you requested," Dirk said. "You gave me your word that you'd come out now."

"Listen, Niki. You know I love you and I don't want anything bad to happen to you. I need you to stay down, even when I'm gone. They're gonna come in here with their guns and shit looking for trouble, so don't give them any reason to do any bad shit to you. When I open the front door, I need you to stay down, belly down and keep your hands on your head. I love you, Niki, and I always will." Trembling and huddled on the floor like a whipped dog, Niki still couldn't speak. Wearing the cowboy hat, I opened the front door. Seeing all of the cops and the guns and the camera crews and the lights was a rush. With my hands in the air, I said, "I'm unarmed and surrendering myself."

"Keep your hands up! Walk towards me!" Dirk said.

Treading slowly towards Dirk, I yelled at the camera crews, "Hey, Aryan Brotherhood. I know you want me dead. But guess what, I'm coming for you guys."

"Now kneel down and keep your hands up!"

"My daughter's in there. No one else. Don't you motherfuckers harm a single hair on her head!"

Determined to savour my final seconds of freedom, I smiled at Dirk as I dropped down. He cuffed me, read my rights and said I was under arrest for homicide. "I guess you finally got what you wanted."

"I just wish it had been sooner," Dirk said. "Then maybe a few folks would still be alive."

They threw me in the back of a cop car before they brought Niki out unhurt. After being on the lam for so long – I was forty-nine years old – getting busted brought on a strange sense of release.

After getting booked into the jail, I was separated from the general population of prisoners, just like I'd hoped for. The news had broadcast my threat to the Aryan Brotherhood. Due to the nature of my crimes, my case being high-profile and the risk to my life from the Aryan Brotherhood, I ended up in my own high-security cell in lockdown. The Aryan Brotherhood couldn't get me for now, but the State of Arizona wanted to give me a lethal injection.

PART 3

AFTER DRUGS

1990–2010

CHAPTER 15

I enjoy reading Tolstoy. *The Kreutzer Sonata*, with its love theme, is fucking dynamite. How many people think they love a woman 'cause she's beautiful, but the minute she gets smallpox, they're fucking ashamed of her? Reading Dostoevsky, I thought his pencil wasn't sharpened as finely as Tolstoy's, but I did enjoy reading about Dostoevsky ending up like me: facing the death penalty. His crime: he'd clicked up with some dudes calling for more freedom in 19th-century Russia. Word got back to Tsar Nicholas I, who was so pissed, he had Dostoevsky and his brainiac comrades rounded up. On the day they were gonna whack the motherfuckers, the Tsar's troops arrived with rifles and coffins. They told them to strip. They put hooded white gowns on them that they were gonna use as burial shrouds. They grouped them up. The command came down, "Ready! Aim!" Then silence. Right on cue, the Tsar's pardon was read. Now that's not so easy to forget. Dostoevsky credited that and his four years in a gulag for making him a great writer.

The Schop said death is what makes most motherfuckers philosophise in the first place:

"Death is the true inspiring genius, or the muse of philosophy … Indeed, without death man would scarcely philosophise." – Arthur Schopenhauer, *The World as Will and Idea* (1819)

In Arizona, they carry out the death penalty in Florence prison, where I've done plenty of time. From 1910, they hung motherfuckers using a scaffold and a trapdoor. In 1930, they took Eva Dugan – a serial killer of husbands who'd snuffed out her rancher boss – to the gallows. The rope snapped off her head. It rolled to the feet of the spectators and her body catapulted to the floor. In 1934, they started using lethal gas. The prisoner was strapped into a chair in the death chamber. One guy, Donald Eugene Harding, lasted ten minutes after the cyanide tablets had been dropped. In agony, he flopped like a fish and turned from red to purple. In 1992, they brought in lethal injection, which doesn't exactly kill you immediately either.

The penalty for crime in America depends on two things: who your lawyer is and how much money you have. If a guy with no money steals some property and he's a repeat offender, he might get twenty-five years to life. Under the three-strikes law, there are guys serving life for stealing chocolate-chip cookies and pizzas 'cause they were hungry. A politician who is molesting children may get a slap on the wrist 'cause he can afford a good lawyer. You purchase whatever level of justice you can afford.

To avoid lethal injection, I gave the money I'd been collecting from people in the last year to an attorney. I wanted my daughter to testify about Skull giving her alcohol and speed at a bar. My lawyer contacted Niki, but she was too scared to testify, not just of the Aryan Brotherhood, but of the whole court process. I left Niki out of it.

Death-penalty cases take forever to come to trial. In the Maricopa County jail, I was in cells for over two years. The place had a fucked-up smell that no amount of bleach could get rid of. It was as if someone had taken the rotten meat they served us and used it as wallpaper.

When the time came for my trial in 1993, I wasn't sweating it 'cause I hadn't exactly whacked anyone on the list for a Nobel Peace Prize. Skull's rap sheet was so long, I was convinced the jury would view my whacking that piece of shit as equivalent to cleaning up the gene pool. For court at 8 AM on a Monday, they got me on Sunday at twelve midnight. Eventually, I was escorted in chains to the old jail, downstairs in a dungeon. There were a bunch of prisoners squatted down in the holding tank, with old rotten apples and shit like that strewn on the floor and hardly any place for a motherfucker to sit.

In court, I shook my lawyer's hand, winked at Dirk Taylor and waited for the old motherfucking judge to come out and bang his gavel. As usual, the prosecutor portrayed me as a psycho. My lawyer portrayed Skull as an even bigger psycho, which was easy to do 'cause it was true. I was convicted of first-degree murder and sentenced to ninety-one years plus life. I gave Dirk Taylor a sly look, so that he would sense my satisfaction. The court started to empty.

Dirk stood and approached me. "You sure saved your ass this time," he said politely, "but we're still investigating the rest. The difference between me and you is that you need to beat every single murder trial to stay alive. I've only gotta win once to get you a lethal injection." Watching him leave, I imagined that with a .357 I shot the motherfucker in the back of the skull and his brains splattered over the prosecutor and all of the courthouse groupies in the gallery.

My sentence was so long, the guards wanted to put me on suicide watch. "What the fuck's wrong with you guys?" I said. "I just beat the death penalty. Let's stop at Bobby McGee's on the way back to my house, so I can have a cool beer to celebrate." They laughed. I wasn't put on suicide watch.

I went for almost fifty years out there breaking all of the so-called Ten Commandments and had always landed on my feet, but I knew that when I fucked up and got caught, I'd never be getting out. My attitude was: fuck the law. I'd chosen to roll like that. I'd whacked motherfuckers knowing I'd face the possibility of death or life in prison. So fuck it, I was done and ready to deal with it, to take responsibility and pay the price for my homicidal choices. No *wah-wah-wah* woe-is-me bullshit. After sentencing, I looked back with contentment at all of the years I'd gotten away with serious shit.

Sal visited. The Aryan Brotherhood had roughed him and his family up, but they'd scraped through it without anything too heavy happening. Niki's mom wouldn't let her come and see me after all the shit I'd put them through, which hurt. I wrote Niki letters, letting her know how much I loved her and how sorry I was for being such a fuck-up. Some members of the Aryan Brotherhood still wanted to whack me, mostly those closest to Skull. Another faction led by Vic had my back. Due to the general threat against my life, I was kept in the highest security level for years. I got in a few situations with motherfuckers, but I always held my own.

While I was in the joint, Dirk Taylor put together a collection of files on my outstanding homicides. With no witnesses coming forward or any physical evidence linking me to the crime scenes, Dirk attempted to get me to talk by showing up here with an Alaskan attorney and homicide detectives. Even though I had nothing to lose by talking to them – the death penalty was abolished in Alaska in 1957 – I don't know what the motherfucker was thinking. I wasn't gonna roll on myself. When the cops show up like that, word quickly gets back to the yard through the trusties. Ratting motherfuckers out gets you killed. I was glad when the motherfuckers had gone, so I could get back to my routine. They never tried to pull that shit again, but Dirk did get enough evidence to charge me for whacking Dan.

For that beef, I was brought to Tucson court in 1996. Again, I was confident of beating the death penalty, which had never deterred me from committing homicide 'cause on drugs I thought I'd never get caught. Knowing that whatever the verdict, I'd never get out, I decided to represent myself at the trial and enjoy being my own barrister of the Old Bailey, as the English put it. Yes, I had a ball. I really rubbed it in Dirk's face, which, as he'd gotten older, was starting to resemble dried apricot.

"I shot Dan 'cause he was reaching for his gun." I told the jury that Dan should have offered reassurance by saying something like, "Hey, look, Ezio will be here. He's coming. We'll get it right." If he was so worried, why did he respond so shitty to me in the room? He could have worked out the money with me. I'm not an animal – I saw something on CNN the other night: a little chunky Lebanese boy on a stretcher all full of shrapnel. I took off my glasses and got all teary-eyed.

The prosecutor – a bespectacled schmuck in a grey suit – told the jurors that even though I'd killed Dan in a dispute over drug money, I was generally a whacked-out serial killer. Now if that were true, I would have been imagining much more in court that day than taking a tyre iron to the prosecutor's teeth. Something more along the lines of taking a blowtorch to his nut sack while making him chow down on one of his eyeballs.

I said I'd like an acquittal 'cause I wanted to beat the prosecutor for being a lying hypocrite. I told them that as a man of integrity it was my duty to be honest about being a cold and cruel killer when it came to people fucking me over in the underworld. I admitted committing numerous murders of motherfuckers who had it coming, while adding that I'd never killed any women or kids. "I'm not bragging. I'm not boasting. I'm ashamed I've killed people," I said. "I've got no reason to really lie here."

In my closing argument, I told the jury that Dan should have made a sign and pasted it to his forehead, reading: KILL ME. I added that if I got an acquittal, I would sit there and smile at the prosecutor, who was basically wasting taxpayers' money by bringing the whole thing to trial. The prosecutor said I'd treated the trial as a game and he urged the jurors to hold me accountable for slaying Dan. Before the verdict, I thanked the judge for presiding over a nice trial. I ended up with another life sentence, which didn't mean shit. A life sentence is twenty-five years, so with my ninety-one years and two life sentences, I was now serving 141 years. Before I got a chance to smirk in his direction, Dirk Taylor left the courtroom as composed and unreadable as usual, but I instinctively felt that he'd gone as far as he could with me.

Where the fuck are all of the female philosophers? Aren't women lovers of truth just as much as men? There aren't many female philosophers 'cause most women weren't allowed to pen their thoughts back then. Well, one, Simone de Beauvoir, wrote that life imprisonment is the most horrible punishment 'cause it preserves your existence while preventing you from doing what you'd most like to be doing, but I reckon she was full of shit on that one. What about the motherfucker working for Intel in his cubicle? How's life imprisonment worse than being a corporate fucking slave? So what if he gets a lunch break. He's gotta punch in again at 12:30. So what if he gets to check out the women in business suits kicking it at Starbucks drinking their Frappuccinos. He's still just a fucking slave like I am. Instead of whipping him, they dangle him stock options. He's fucking his life off for the benefit of corporate slave drivers. It boils down to different degrees of slavehood, and there's motherfuckers whose minds put them through worse punishments than imprisonment – that's inner slavery.

I agree with Simone about encouraging people to put meaning into their lives, but I'm still wondering where she was coming from saying that if shit hits the fan then to commit suicide. No question about it. I've been down and gloomy, and spent lonely nights in dark places after doing terrible things, and I've thought, *Man, if this happens, here's what I'm gonna do. If I get cancer, am I gonna lay up in this cell, rotting away an inch at a time, with some quack Venezuelan doctor telling me to take two aspirins and to write a medical request in the morning? Fuck that!* There ain't many motherfuckers on this planet whose minds haven't thought about suicide.

When you're locked up for life, you learn that you have to adapt. Who do you think lasted the longest in concentration camps? People who put meaning in their lives, like Viktor Frankl. The ones who survived had adapted. Of course, we all have to put meaning into our own fucking lives 'cause each and every one of us values different things. What is important to you isn't important and meaningful to an ant. Finding a grasshopper's leg and dragging it down a hole in the ground may be meaningful to an ant. Winning an Academy Award may be meaningful to Dustin Hoffman. Going into the gutters of Calcutta to help the sickest people in the world, washing and cleaning and feeding them, was good for Mother Teresa's inner spirit. And I'm fucking sure that developing the polio vaccine put meaning in Jonas Salk's life. Serving 141 years left me no choice but to adapt and put meaning into my life.

Look, I'm a retiree who doesn't get out until the 23rd century, but at least I have a fucking life. I'm into what I'm doing. Tonight, I'm gonna play a casino card game. I'm gonna have some pasta with marinara sauce. I'm gonna sit down and watch Michigan kick the shit outta USC at the Rose Bowl. I'm gonna eat some chocolate-covered peanuts watching Detroit play Dallas. The last thing on my fucking mind is what kind of car Jay Leno is driving or Paris Hilton going to jail for forty-five days and if she's gonna be allowed Charmin toilet paper to wipe her hairless ass with or be forced to use state-issued sandpaper.

CHAPTER 16

In 2005, I arrived at Buckeye prison, where I had a good rep with the fellas in bright orange mobbing the chain-link fence, yelling banter, watching me cart my belongings in next to an armed guard under a sun so hot no fucking wildlife was out on the barren beige desert except for the odd scorpion.

"You old motherfucker! Where you been?"

"I've been in the hole for five months! I can't win them all!"

"I'm gonna fuck you up next!"

"The only thing you're gonna fuck up is a honey bun on store day, motherfucker! You fuck with this old man and you get a one-way ticket out of here on a chopper!"

"What cell block you going to?"

"I'm going over here to two dog. Give me two weeks and I'll be running the place. Now, who's gonna fix me a fucking peanut-butter sandwich?"

A few days later, I got a visit to my upper-tier cell from a young guy, Long Island, who I knew from another yard. He had a shaved head and tatted arms. "My cellie, Shaun, wants to play chess with you. He's from England. He's a good dude."

"Is this Brit gonna whup my ass?" I said. "You putting money on this guy?"

"No. I'd just like you to meet him. He's a writer. He might be interested in your life story. He's got quite a following on the net. Tell him about the old days."

"Is he really from England?"

"Yes, he was a stock-market trader who got caught up in the rave and Ecstasy scene. Him and Sammy the Bull Gravano were competitors in the Ecstasy market."

"Sammy the Bull was a killer for real. The Bull's son's cellmate don't like me 'cause I killed his Aryan Brotherhood friend. Him and Skull were partners."

"You should tell Shaun about that, too."

"I got way better shit than that. I can tell him stories about back East and in Tucson, when I worked for the Bonannos. You know I'm in a book about the Bonanno Crime Family. I'll show it to you sometime."

"You definitely need to talk to him. I told him you're serving all day for multiple homicides. He shit himself."

"OK. Let's go." We headed downstairs. "They've only got me for whacking some of the motherfuckers. The rest they still ain't found."

Hovering by a table in the dayroom was a gangly bald guy. Pale as a haemophiliac and with no tats, he obviously wasn't fucking hip to the latest convict fashions.

"This is Shaun from England," Long Island said.

"An Englishman, eh?" Picking up on his nervousness, I smiled.

"From near Liverpool," he said.

In my best British accent, I said, "Oh, the bloody Beatles! I do like their music and John Lennon's from when he went off on his own. I remember when Lennon got whacked by that fucking nut-cake, Mark Chapman. His fans were lined up outside his and Yoko Ono's New York crib singing 'Imagine,' 'Give Peace a Chance,' and all that shit. Did you ever get to have tea and crumpets with any famous Liverpudlians?"

"Unfortunately not," Shaun said, smiling.

"How about with Amy Winehouse or the Spice Girls?"

Shaun laughed and proceeded to beat my ass at chess, which was fine 'cause I'd only come down to size up the motherfucker. Offering me his hand, he said, "I won because you kept speaking your mind. It gave me an advantage."

"What do you mean?" I asked.

"You wouldn't show someone your hand in a game of poker, would you?" Long Island said.

"Me and my big mouth." I slapped my head. We laughed.

"Shaun writes stories for the Internet," Long Island said.

"What kind of stories?" I asked.

"About prison. What we take for granted is a completely different world to the public. They find it fascinating. If you like, I'll show you what an English newspaper published about my writing."

"Yeah, I'd like to check that out." After reading the article and probing Shaun a bit about his background, I said, "On the road of life, I've dealt with a lot of cut-throat motherfuckers. To stay alive, I became a quick judge of character. I like you, Shaun. You seem like a nice guy. I also think you've come into my life for a reason. Would you consider writing my story?"

"I'd be honoured. Perhaps we should start by putting some of your stories on the Internet."

"Let's go to my cell and I'll tell you a story."

Shaun fetched paper and a pen. In my cell, he sat at a stool with a tiny steel table above it bolted to the wall. Long Island sat on the bottom bunk.

Stood up, I began, "One spring morning in Tucson, me and Charlie Batts Battaglia have a body to bury in the desert. Batts was a big, loud-talking motherfucker with his hair slicked back. If I'm Francis Ford Coppola, and I'm making a gangster movie, I want a guy like the Batts in it. We take care of business and set off back to Tucson at about 7:45 AM. I'm riding shotgun in Batts' white Caddy Eldorado. The sunroof's down. I'm enjoying the smell of creosote in the air 'cause it's been raining. The sun's coming up through the mesquite trees and the Palo Verdes, which are turning a little yellow and are blooming. We're cruising along the roly-poly roads in the Catalina Foothills. The radio's playing, 'Get up America … we love you,' and all that shit. Earth, Wind & Fire's 'Fantasy' comes on. All at once we rise up a steep hill, hit a dip, and see a hen quail going across the road with little chicklets behind her, all of them in a straight line. Batts has got a big cigar in his face. He sees the quail family, slams on the fucking brakes, and my head almost goes through the windshield 'cause

I ain't wearing no seat belt. I thought somebody had shot Batts. I'm scared. I'm wondering, *What the fuck's going on?* The Caddy's spinning on the gravel, but somehow he regains control and we head for breakfast.

"At Sambo's on Miracle Mile, over bacon and eggs, I say to Batts, 'You know, you almost killed us back there for a fucking bird.' I'm looking in the eyes of a killer, a guy investigated for whacking motherfuckers, but knew how to get away with it.

"Batts looks at me and says, 'Hey, let me tell you something: it wouldn't have been the right thing to do. Somewhere out in the desert tonight,' – a smile came across his face – 'a mother quail and her little chickadees are gonna be all together at suppertime, and I'm not gonna be responsible for breaking up their little family and squashing them on the highway.'

"I'm salting my cantaloupe, and I get the impression that Batts is putting me on. But there's something in his eyes that tells me he's serious. This leads me to believe he justified doing the things he did as just something he had to do. Although I hadn't seen much of it, it was clear that Batts had a heart …"

Shaun mailed out some of my stories to his mom and pops across the pond, who posted them on the Internet, which I've never been on, but I've read about in books and mags. I'll never get online 'cause prisoners in Arizona are banned from accessing it. His mom and pops mailed us printouts of the blogs, and comments and questions from the readers, which was fucking cool, as I thought I'd never communicate with anyone outside of this motherfucker again. Some of the blog readers thought my phrases had come from Hollywood, but it's the other way round: characters in gangster movies are based on motherfuckers like me. Hollywood plagiarises what us real gangsters have said. And authors, too. Anyway, blogging was therapeutic. My thoughts of ripping a sex offender's face off with a claw hammer were replaced by answering blog readers' questions, like one from a schoolteacher in Singapore interested in my Mafia days.

Chow hall. A hundred hungry motherfuckers lined up at a rect-angular hole in the wall that the plastic-gloved hands of kitchen grunts were doling food trays from.

"Hey, you gonna eat your chicken patty?" a youngster, Little Wood, yelled as I got my tray.

"No, I'm not," I said.

"Can I get it?"

"Let me check with my dog here first," I said. "Hey, Cowboy, you want my chicken patty?"

"Yeah. Fuck, yeah," Cowboy said. "I want it if you're not gonna eat it."

"Hey, I asked first," Little Wood said in a raised voice. "I thought we were better than that, Two Tonys."

"Hey, Little Wood," I said. "You know Cowboy here's my road dog. He's gonna get food off my tray before you. You've gotta accept that."

"Fuck it," Little Wood said. "I ain't talking to you no more. I ain't got no rap for you."

"Awww," I said. "How the fuck am I gonna make it through life without you rapping to me. I'm sixty-five. I've killed six-ty-three of those years without you rapping to me. Do you think I can make it through another ten?" The shithead scowled. "What the fuck, Little Wood," I said. "Are we gonna have a beef over a chicken fucking patty that smells like something out of a fucking birdcage? If that's the way it is, fuck it, you ain't got nothing coming from me." I sat with Cowboy at a table. "Would you believe it? Here I am, a guy who's eaten abalone in Hawaii and lobster in Cancún, and I've got a jabroni over here who wants to argue with me over a thirty-nine-cent state-issue piece-of-shit chicken patty. Sometimes I think I'm better off checking out of this fucking place and seeing what's on the other side. Stupid shit like arguing over chicken patties makes my fucking blood boil. Motherfuckers should be happy that I share my state-issue when I can." Spotting two overgrown bikers, Ken and Cannonball, approaching the table, holding plastic chow trays, I said, "Then there are motherfuckers around here who just grab your chow. No names. Just a melon-headed motherfucker with a big moustache."

"Who you calling a melon-head?" Ken said.

"You're right. I was wrong," I said. "It's more like a fucking pumpkin."

"Room at your table?" Cannonball said.

"We'll make room," Ken said. "We'll knock some motherfucker out."

"Come and eat with us," I said.

The two fat, useless soap-opera-watching motherfuckers sat down. Long Island had given me a heads up that Ken had been sweating my English blogger friend. Ken had snuck up behind Shaun and punched him in the back when Shaun was going to see his mom and pops at Visitation. Sneaking up behind him was a chickenshit move. If you're calling a motherfucker out, go eyeball-to-eyeball. I was starting to get a protective feeling over Shaun like I've had over the years for certain people. Bored of listening to them arguing over dope, I put a question to them.

"If they cut your ass loose in Mall of fucking America what would you loot?"

"I'd hit the diamond stores," Cannonball said.

"Smart," I said. "Lots of small pricey shit: diamond rings and gold chains. What about you, Ken?"

"I'd go where the big money's at: the banks."

"Get out of here!" I said. "How the fuck would you get in a locked bank vault, motherfucker?"

"I dunno. I'd figure it out."

"You couldn't even break out of your own fucking cell. If they locked you in, you'd die in there. You know nothing about locks or robbing banks."

"What should I be looting then?"

"You'd do well looting Los Angeles."

"Why's that?"

"'Cause of all of the fucking porno stores. If Korean snipers didn't cap your ass, you'd be cleaning out the sex stores. I can see you running down Hollywood Boulevard with a backpack full of dildos."

"How come Cannonball gets to be a diamond looter, and I gotta be a fucking dildo looter? What are you trying to say?" Ken was giving me the stink eye.

"I'm saying you fit the dildo-looter profile. There's something about you that exudes fucking dildo looting. Cannonball would be grabbing diamonds, and you'd be grabbing big, black double dildos."

Taking me by surprise, Ken grabbed my neck.

"Hey, motherfucker, don't fuck with an old man doing fucking life sentences. You fucking fish number!"

Ken let go. "You fucker. I should have choked you out."

Coughing every few seconds, I said, "If you're gonna choke me for clowning you about dildos then we're not fucking playing anymore!"

Ken apologised, but he didn't know who he was fucking with. On the way out of the chow hall, I asked Long Island to get a shank. Back in my cell, I boiled water with a heating element called a stinger, ready to throw it in Ken's face if the motherfucker stepped inside. Long Island showed up without a shank. Shaun followed him in. I vented on Ken, but they steered me around to talking about my Mafia days and I calmed down.

In mid-2005, they moved nearly all of us from this yard to Tucson prison. I've always preferred Tucson. It's about 10° cooler than Buckeye and it ain't all snakes and scorpions. Prairie dogs scoot around and you see giant toads, which are so fat their bellies slap the floor when they land from hopping. I started to have problems with my eye – this growing old business ain't for wimps – so I put a request in for medical.

The guards who transported me to the doctor's office were real negative motherfuckers, trained to give us what we've got coming: chains, transportation and a cup of fucking water if there's a fountain around.

I arrived at the doctor's. There must have been twenty fucking people to see him, and I was at the bottom of the list 'cause I'm a state prisoner. I looked around and I had no one to talk to. The others wouldn't make eye contact. Sitting between two guards packing Glock pistols, I had belly and ankle chains on. The patients were frightened. So I was looking at them, studying them. There must have been six old couples. I was trying to figure them out in my brain 'cause I had nothing better to do. I was gonna be stuck there for a couple of hours.

I saw a couple about my age, probably married for forty fucking years. The guy in grey, knee-length shorts, a cotton shirt, argyle socks and Nike-swoosh shoes. You know, presentable. A typical retired suburbanite who probably got a gold watch when he quit working for the phone company or the insurance company or some other shit, where they gave him cake and donuts at the office cubicle party, and told him what a swell guy he'd been for the past twenty-five years, running from cubicle to cubicle, saying how much they were gonna miss him, till his ass hit the door.

And the guy was just sitting there, gazing at the wall, not saying anything to the old prune-faced lady next to him, who he had to be nice to, and would probably miss like hell when she died. And she was just sitting there looking at the wall as well. So I said to myself, *You know what? He's doing time. You think this motherfucker ain't doing time? He's gonna see the doctor, and his wife's gonna give him moral support after they squirt that shit in his eye* – after they squirted me, I couldn't see shit on the way home. I had to feel my way to the fuckin' chow hall – *and then he's gonna go home to his nice middle-income house, with a pool in the backyard, and the grandkids, who probably live in Cincinnati, are gonna come over and visit him once a year at Christmas, and his ol' lady knows just how he likes his coffee in the morning, and they might or might not still be fucking – forty years, come on now! How much can you fuck the same person for forty years? It's gotta get old. Put me with J.Lo or Salma Hayek or Teri Hatcher of* Desperate Housewives *and I'm gonna get fucking tired eventually.*

Here's the crux of my thoughts: the old guy wasn't happier than me. I could see it in his face. Yes, I was going back to the joint, but I was gonna clown with the youngsters and talk a lot of shit. I'd do a little walking and exercise. I'd enjoy my shows: *American Idol, Survivor*, and I watch a lot of PBS. So what if I have to get up four or five times to piss during the night due to my enlarged prostate, the old guy wasn't having as good a time as me. His food might have been more succulent. He might have been eating Waldorf salads and lamb cutlets with apple sauce or mint jelly, compared with my burrito mix and two tortillas. But I was going to the store the next day to get me some Milky Ways, Nutty Cones and a couple of Sprites. I was gonna plug up my arteries real good, but I deserve a good time every now and then. I can tell you this much: the old guy might have been eating better, but he wasn't laughing harder. He didn't have my sense of adventure 'cause anything can kick off in the joint at any time, and it often does. I ain't got it that bad. The old guy's gotta pay the bill for his life, whereas the State's picking up my tab. That's called PMA: positive mental attitude. Happiness is just a state of mind. If you could buy a fucking jar of happiness, Walmart would be having it mass-produced in Chinese suicide sweatshops with jumper nets and marketing it all over the world.

Eventually, the doctor squirted some shit in my eye and looked at my cataracts to determine whether to cut them out or not. But you know what? A lot of guys don't make it to my age. You might have heard of Achilles, the Greek warrior and hero of the Trojan War, who got whacked by Paris, who hit him in the heel with a poison arrow. Well, when Achilles was in hell or Hades, Odysseus asked him in so many words: is it better to die like a hero, young, in battle, or to grow old on your fucking farm feeding your goats? Achilles reply was: I'll take the goat feeding or even be a slave any fucking time.

"Do not speak soothingly to me of death, glorious Odysseus. I should choose to serve as the hireling of another, rather than to be lord over the dead that have perished."

—Achilles' soul to Odysseus. Homer, Odyssey 11.488

"What're you reading?" I asked Shaun in the chow hall, where we were sat eating.

"*Kolyma Tales*," he said. "About a prisoner in a Soviet labour camp. If you refused to work, you were thrown off a cliff or tied to a horse and dragged to death."

"Have you ever read *One Day in the Life of Ivan Denisovich*?" I asked.

"No. There's an Ivan Ivanovich in this book, who hung himself from a tree without a rope by placing his neck where the tree branches forked."

"I'm talking about *Ivan Denisovich* by Aleksandr Solzhenitsyn, a writer who fought in World War II and was sent to the gulag for criticising Stalin. The conditions were barely survivable. It was eat, keep warm and try to stay alive. That was the whole struggle. There was none of this shit, 'Chow's twenty minutes late!' or 'Why haven't they opened my door for recreation?' Those folks in the gulag were praying for a fish eyeball in their soup – a little protein. They weren't whining 'cause they couldn't wear beanie caps. They had to wrap old socks around their heads, so they wouldn't lose their noses and ears to frostbite in the Siberian weather. There were no grievances and lawsuits. Imagine standing next to Ivan Denisovich, whose fingertips are turning black with gangrene, and complaining that the store didn't have your favourite brand of toothpaste or the water's not hot enough or the razors are dull or you only got two rolls of toilet paper. It was a raw battle for survival. This was deep behind the Iron Curtain in the late forties, early fifties. Sheer communist totalitarianism. Most of the people they sent there were just political prisoners who hadn't committed crimes. They'd just criticised some commissar's old lady for having a fat, red ass."

"So you feel lucky being here?"

"Yeah. My predicament's a joke. I'm sixty-five. I'm gonna die in this motherfucker. But you've gotta die somewhere. Some get cancer. Some get their faces burnt off in car wrecks. Some kids get the flag waved at them in high school and hear, 'God Bless America,' and the next thing they know, they're in the back of a Humvee in Iraq driving over some IED, and all that's sent back to their parents are their nuts in body bags, folded in American flags, with letters from the draft-dodger George Dubya Bush saying, 'Thanks for the sacrifice.' So big deal I'm gonna die in here. It could be worse. That's what I've got coming 'cause I earned life in prison. I had to whack a few motherfuckers to get here. But at least I'm not in a Siberian gulag with some honky Polack, who eats pickles or fish-eye soup for breakfast, beating me down if I don't push enough wheelbarrows of iced dirt to meet Uncle fucking Joe Stalin's quotas. How the fuck can I get depressed in here? This is my retirement home. Not just any motherfucker qualifies to be in here, you know. You don't just hop on a bus and say, 'Driver, take me to the big house.' This is an exclusive club. You've got to put in some serious work to get here. And what's good about it is they can't ever kick me out 'cause I'm doing life. If things get shitty in here, I just tell myself, *Get a grip, man. What would Ivan Denisovich be thinking? Would he be raising hell about his waffles being cold in the morning? Would he fuck!* Life is nothing but a state of fucking mind. That's why you get rich motherfuckers living in mansions on Camelback Mountain blowing their brains out 'cause the stock market went down. Compare that to some Native American dude off the reservation at the bottom of a ditch who loves life 'cause he's got enough chump change to get himself a six-pack of Old Milwaukee and some green bologna. Why's he happy? 'Cause his mind tells him he's happy. Me? I'm having the time of my fucking life."

"How much Shakespeare you read?"

"Enough to know a few quotes. 'Hark, hark. Who knocks at yonder door.' 'Out, out damn spot.' That was when Macbeth and his wife had just whacked the king, and they were trying to wash the blood out of their clothes and hands. 'A horse. My kingdom for a horse.' That's Richard the Third."

Grim joined our table. "Did you see the ambulance outside of Building 2 last night? Some guy blew his asshole out while taking a shit." Like I wanted to hear that while slurping my fucking chicken noodle soup from this 6-foot-7 mutant with flames and skulls tatted on his elongated bald head, looking like he belonged in a Wes Craven horror like *The Hills Have Eyes*.

"I hope my eating my soup doesn't interfere with your discussion about assholes and taking fucking shits. Do you fucking mind?" I said, frowning at the motherfucker.

"What's wrong with talking about shits and assholes?" Grim said, digging his Spork into his chow.

"It's not just that. It seems like every time I sit down to eat my fucking chow, you come around, and the conversation goes straight to shits and assholes and nasty stuff that's unappetising to me. We don't have to talk about splitting the fucking atom here, but we could at least have a normal fucking conversation."

"You've been down plenty years. You've heard worse than shits and assholes."

"Yeah. And I was in the Navy for fucking years keeping the Red Chinese from snatching your fucking ass."

"That's before my time. If you'd fought on the Hồ Chí Minh trail, you'd get my respects."

"I was in fucking Blood Alley, Formosa. If Chairman Mao had of had his way, you'd be speaking Chinese and eating noodles with chopsticks, motherfucker."

"I like Chinese food."

"You would, you bizarre-looking motherfucker. When you get out, I'm gonna send you to the Coast for lunch with Francis Ford Coppola. But when you talk to him, don't mention people taking shits and blowing their assholes out, and you might get a bit part in one of his movies as a fucking monster."

"I can't go to California. I've done too many repetitive dangerous crimes there."

The next evening in the chow hall, I was having a chat with Shaun. "I appreciate you introducing me to Tom Wolfe," Shaun said. "*A Man in Full* is now my favourite work of contemporary fiction. There's not many contemporary authors who hold my interest."

"Average authors are churning out junk food," I said. "Compared to their hamburgers, Tom Wolfe's books are Beef Wellingtons."

"My parents sent me some Stephen King. I enjoyed *The Shawshank Redemption*."

"Stephen King's running a fucking McDonald's franchise. He's pumping out books like they make quarter pounders. It took Wolfe eleven years to write *A Man in Full*. Wolfe's so fucking good he's got a war going with those other authors: Updike, Irving and that fucking thug, Mailer. They're jealous of his skills."

"What do you think of Tom Robbins?"

"I'm not familiar with this Robbins guy, but I'll tell you something though: he's got to get up real early in the fucking morning to sharpen his pencil to be in the same league as Tom Wolfe."

Grim sat down at our table. "I saw She-Ra coming out of the shower. That girl's got a big-ass schlong. Ever notice that shit?"

"What is it with you?" I said, throwing my Spork down on the metal table. "We're over here trying to have an intellectual fucking conversation about books and you've gotta come along and talk about schlongs. Have you got some kind of fucking fetish for talking about schlongs and assholes when I'm eating?"

"But it's true," Grim said. "I've been down a long time and I've noticed that gay guys have bigger than average schlongs."

"Listen, I've been down twice as long as you and I'll be honest with you, I'm not in the habit of checking out men's schlongs. And the fact that you're bringing schlongs up while I'm trying to converse with my Brit friend, I'm finding insulting. You wanna talk about schlongs, sit at a fucking chomo or sex-pervert table. This table's for crimes of integrity, like homicides for motherfuckers who asked for it."

"How about asses? I saw She-Ra's ass as well," Grim said.

"Hey, Grim, you know my reputation. I don't look at men's asses. It's a case of each to his fucking own. I can imagine taking you to a fancy joint like the Four Seasons. The maître d' gives us a choice table, and you wanna talk about the Guatemalan bus boy's ass or the shape of the maître d's trouser trout. That's why I can't ever envisage taking you to a five-star restaurant, Grim. You're strictly McDonald's drive-thru material."

"This spaghetti sauce looks like some Marines took a shit in it. Straight fucking Panama water," Grim said, stirring the sauce with his Spork.

"That's 'cause of your sick fucking mind. It's stuck on schlongs and shits and assholes. Come hotdog day, you're gonna be seeing the hotdogs as schlongs and cockheads. You're stuck on phallic fucking symbols."

She-Ra – with long hair and as tall as Grim – approached our table. "Hey guys! Who wants a table dance?"

"Me and my Brit friend don't, but Grim'll take you in a private booth. He'll meet you at your cell later on."

"I was just telling them about your big-ass schlong," Grim said.

"Not that I asked for that info 'cause, to be real honest, I don't give a fuck if you're hung like the incredible fucking Hulk. All we're trying to do is have an intelligent conversation about literature."

"Two Tonys, are you sure you don't wanna see my swing set?" She-Ra said.

"No, I don't care to. But if the day ever comes when I do, I'm hoping you motherfuckers will snuff me out by smothering me with a pillow like at the end of *One Flew Over the Cuckoo's Nest*. After that I'll meet you motherfuckers in hell 'cause that's where we're all heading."

"Look at that motherfucker spreading his germs around on our clothes," I said to Shaun about the overgrown biker, Ken, handling our clothes with snot running down his face over his horseshoe moustache, which he kept wiping on his forearms. "Hey, Ken, that ain't your job. Why don't you let the laundry porters do that?"

"Don't worry about what I'm doing. You ain't no fucking cop!" Ken said, scowling.

"My fucking laundry is in there, and I don't want you touching it," I said. Ken swaggered over. "Back off, motherfucker! Don't get up on me," I said.

"I'll snap your neck and put you in hospital, motherfucker."

"Do it then, motherfucker!" I said.

We were gonna collide until prisoners split us up.

Later on, Ken approached me in the chow hall. "There's that old motherfucker who started shit just 'cause I was going through the laundry."

"This big-headed motherfucker," I said, pointing at Ken, "wanted to kill me over the laundry."

"You fucking started it!" Ken said, foaming at the corners of his mouth due to dehydration from all of the meth and medication he was on.

"And you insulted me by calling me a guard," I said calmly, "and threatening to put me somewhere there'd be tubes in my fucking nose."

"Why you gotta be acting like a cop around the laundry? What are you trying to do, earn parole? You ain't getting parole. This motherfucker's serving how many life sentences? He ain't ever getting out. He needs to stop acting like a fucking cop."

"Let me tell you something, motherfucker: if you'd wash your hands and face, and stop blowing snot all over the place, you could handle my fucking laundry."

"How about I just straight kill you and stick your laundry up your ass, you old motherfucker."

"You couldn't even kill a fly. We all know you ain't gonna kill nothing, motherfucker. The only thing you're gonna kill, motherfucker, is a fucking extra chicken wing if some motherfucking fool gives you one."

"You need to watch your back, motherfucker." Ken strutted away.

When I exited the chow hall, Ken was sweating Shaun again, threatening to move into his cell as his cellmate, Long Island, was about to be released. Ken punched Shaun, and Shaun kicked him back, just like I'd taught him. If someone disrespects you in this motherfucker, you smash them so other motherfuckers won't perceive you as weak. You must stick up for numero uno, otherwise all kinds of doors are opened. They'll be on you like wolves. I've personally taken severe ass-kickings, but I still fought. Figuring it was time to intervene, I said, "Hey, Ken. Have you looked under your nose lately?"

"No. Why?" Ken touched his top lip.

"Your moustache looks like a broom that you haven't washed since you've been down. I can see nits in it and lice crawling around your fucking head."

Everyone laughed. Ken puffed his chest out, marched over, snatched the ID that I'd clipped to my T-shirt – a piece of plastic we wear to the chow hall that shows our photo, name and Department Of Corrections number – and squeezed it in his hand, bending it in half.

If I'd had a rock in a sock, I would have smashed him in the temple. Instead, I stepped forward, hitched a leg behind Ken, and pushed his shoulders. Ken fell hard. The big dumb motherfucker stayed down. "Why'd you grab my ID? I warned you never to lay hands on me, motherfucker!" I threw my glasses down and raised my fists. "I'll kill you, motherfucker!"

"I told you a long time ago that I'd never hurt you," Ken said, getting up. "Well, fuck all that. Come on, motherfucker! Get some of this, old man!"

"Come on, motherfucker! Let's do this. I ain't scared of going to the hole. I've been in every hole in Arizona's state prisons." The whites pulled Ken away. Some Mexican Americans grabbed me.

Back in my cell, I said to Shaun, "I'm gonna get a shank and kill that motherfucker. I know what he's up to. He wants to get close to me, so he can give me a sucker punch …" After venting, I calmed down. "You know what though? Putting him down like that made me think about the sweetness of life." I sat on my bunk and rested my hands on my thighs.

"What do you mean?" Shaun asked, sat on the stool.

"There's people my age driving around Sun City in fucking golf carts right now, and here I am – sixty-five years old – putting down a thirty-five-year-old, a big motherfucker. That makes me feel fucking great."

"I'm glad you put him in check."

"The motherfucker had it coming."

The next day, Ken barged into my cell when I was in a better mood, doing blogs with Shaun. "I want words with you, you old bastard! Why are people on the yard saying you pulled a tae-kwondo move and threw my ass in the dirt?"

Sometimes I like to use wit to show a guy who's trying to submit me to his bullshit that it ain't shit. When people are out to make us suffer, it's important to make an extra effort to try not to suffer. Wit can be used as a safety valve, but it has to be controlled. I mean, how would you like to be in a line at Auschwitz, going in that so-called shower, and some smart-ass in front of you starts cracking jokes? No. There's a time and a place for wit. I enjoy being around men in orange who are witty. That's not a category I put Ken in.

Sat on my bunk, I raised a finger at Ken as if scolding a child. "Wait a minute, motherfucker. First of all, this is my fucking home. Don't ever barge in here again like that, motherfucker. And second of all, let me tell you something: when you're mad like this, you're a handsome devil. When you get out, I've got some connections in Hollywood I'm gonna send you to 'cause you remind me of an old actor called Lon Chaney who played some characters that look just like you when you get angry."

"Who the fuck is Lon Chaney, you old motherfucker? What the fuck's that got to do with you telling people on the yard that you threw my ass in the dirt?"

"Hey, relax, dude. It was what it was. Was your ass in the dirt? Did you have to get up and wipe the dirt off your ass? Was I still standing?"

Ken leaned forward as if to crush me. "That's 'cause I happened to slip, motherfucker. You know how it went down. You didn't throw me nowhere!"

"Bring one motherfucker in here who said that I said I threw your ass down. People saw what the fuck they saw. You've got so many enemies on the yard, they probably wanted me to throw your ass in the dirt, you big-headed motherfucker. Why you gotta come barging in here when I'm talking to my Brit friend? You'd better thank God I ain't got my pistols 'cause I'd have capped your sorry ass six fucking months ago. Outside of that: do you want a cup of coffee?"

"I'm telling you," Ken said, pointing at me, "you didn't throw my ass in the dirt, and I've got my own fucking coffee! I'm not drinking with you, you old motherfucker! I ought to just snap your neck and take your fucking coffee."

"God damn, bro. Can't we all just get along? What the fuck's the problem here? You wanna kill the Two Tonys, is that what you wanna do, you big-headed motherfucker?"

"That's exactly what I'm gonna do if you continue to make me look like a punk by telling people you threw me in the dirt." Ken stormed out, slamming the door.

"Ken's getting out of control," Shaun said. "Maybe it's time for the psych doctor to increase his meds again."

"Everybody's gotta vent." I smiled. "Let the motherfucker vent."

Reading the latest blog printouts sent in by Shaun's parents, I enjoyed the record number of comments and questions about my life. I dictated my answers to Shaun. When we were done, I was in the mood to keep going, so I suggested that Shaun start writing my autobiography. We discussed the logistics. Over months, Shaun would have to sneak into my cell and write for hours. I'd post a few friends outside my cell, so he wouldn't get busted for cell visiting.

The project got off to a strong start. Shaun even asked what method I'd use if I had to kill him right then. In case anyone ever tries to take me out in my cell, I'm always ready with the necessary tools. I figured I could practise on Shaun without doing him any harm. I grabbed a heating element, wrapped the electrical cord around Shaun's neck and tightened it. He was stunned, but he didn't panic. I refrained from double-wrapping the cord and squeezing it into a square knot. I kept the chokehold on just long enough to have him gasping without putting him to sleep. Shaun was a bit shook up, but at least I'd given him something to write about.

It was nice to have a person around like Shaun who I could sit down and kick it with in a refreshing way. Too many people here only want to talk about the great robberies they did, and how many kilos of coke they dealt, or how many showgirls they banged when they went to Vegas with $100 bills plastered all over their foreheads. It was good to be able to sit down and have a normal conversation. There are motherfuckers in here I've been around for years who I have to walk to the chow hall and sit with, and I don't even make eye contact with them. I don't ever wanna speak to them.

I saw Shaun as a good guy, a compassionate person. The cards turned on him and he wound up in this motherfucker 'cause he made bad decisions due to taking drugs. I went to him several times looking to vent about some motherfucker or other. I'd say something like, "Hey, Shaun, so and so is a piece of fucking shit," and in a roundabout way, he'd usually say, "Hey, Two Tonys, if that guy's no good why are you wasting so much mental energy on him right now? He doesn't even know you're hating on him like this. Why let him control your mind?" And I'd think about it, and realise what he said made sense. He was a bright light on a dark shore, who helped me several times when I was headed for the rocks and shoals, just by being around and helping me calm down.

Shaun said to read Viktor Frankl's *The Doctor and the Soul.* I found something profound in it. Frankl recommended that you find happiness in the simple things you do each day. I'm not physically free due to the razor wire, but I do have a degree of freedom that starts with the decisions I make each day. I can choose to stress myself out by hating on people and releasing negative hormones into my system, or I can relax, read some Wolfe or Updike, and make the most of my circumstances. Freedom's a state of mind. Look at all of the people choosing to live with husbands and wives they can't stand, and doing jobs they hate. The ex-gang member, Tookie Williams, one of the early leaders of the Crips, had the right idea. For over twenty years on death row, he did positive projects, writing kids' books about staying away from gangs. He made the most of his time before Arnie Schwarzenegger declined his appeal for clemency. I've been too much of a fatalist, sitting around and sweating myself over shit like getting some new motherfucker for a cellmate who I might have to get into it with and end up in the hole or in the hospital. Shit's just like that in here. It fucks up your plans. If Tookie Williams was able to put meaning into his life while awaiting a lethal injection, then shame on me for sweating the small shit.

CHAPTER 17

I never imagined putting blogs out there would lead to a request to solve a murder. The son of Joe Hootner, who was whacked, asked online at Jon's Jail Journal for me to fill him in on what went down with his old man. Putting myself in his shoes, I understood the interest of trying to find out what had happened, so I decided to put his mind to rest. I hadn't whacked the guy, but I knew the guys who did – they're all dead – and why he got taken out. I wanted to do the right thing without making a sport of the guy's missing father, so here's my reply:

Peter Licavoli, Joe Bonanno Sr, Bonanno lieutenant Charlie Batts Battaglia and his brother-in-law had formed a business venture developing a tract of land with homes. It was called Telesco Terrace. Peter Licavoli had to go to prison in Atlanta for refusing to appear before Congress investigating organised crime. So he had Joe Hootner, who was running a book (a bookie for him), designated as his guy while he was away to get his end of the money and to do with it as instructed. Well, the Bonannos started skimming while Peter Licavoli was in the joint, and they got Hootner, who Peter Licavoli told me with all sincerity was one of the nicest, gentlest guys around. Peter thought Hootner could handle this no-rough-stuff assignment. Well, they got his bookie money and the development money, and I guess they conned Hootner. But just before Peter Licavoli got out of the joint, they whacked Hootner, so he couldn't run the whole thing down to Peter Licavoli, who found out from Tony Telesco, after they fucked Tony Telesco's end of the money.

Peter Licavoli told me, "And you know who the cops think had Hootner killed? Me!" He was mad at having to ride the heat.

But you have to remember at one point the Bonannos were real strong. But by the 1970s, they became real weak. They had just got run out of New York. They were a real fucked-up crew. Peter Licavoli talked real good of Hootner, said he was a trustworthy guy, but that gang of thieves, the Bonannos, broke him down and killed him along with a runner of his named Rudy Perfido. Peter Licavoli couldn't retaliate, it would have been too much to bite off. He had to eat it.

Years later, I was at the Sahara Hotel in Tucson and Batts came in. He said he had to talk to me, so we went out to his car. He told me he had a freshly whacked guy in the trunk and would I help put him away. I'd already helped him with desert burials.

"Who is it?" I said.

It was a one-eyed Jewish guy from LA named Jules, who they called Julie. Batts said he had a hole ready to go by Rocking K Ranch.

So I told Batts, "Look, Charlie, I'm not going for it this time. I don't know why or what this is about, but I'm not up to driving across town thirty miles with a stiff in the trunk that I've got no involvement with. A piece of work is one thing and a favour another. Besides, it's Saturday night and I don't want to change and I've got a woman stopping in to have a drink. This joint is hot and the cops are probably checking us out right now. Find somebody else this time, and don't come at me on the spur of the moment anymore with shit like this. This is how guys get busted. No disrespect intended." He went and drove off.

Almost a month later, Batts came into the hotel, acting as if he owned the world. We were having a few drinks. It was a slow night, no band playing. I asked him what was up. It was seldom we saw him downtown. He was sort of in the bag, but he said he was meeting a guy down here later. After a few drinks, I said, "Hey, look, no hard feelings about that night a few weeks back."

"No sweat. It's over." He smiled. "Hey, back in the day, I had to put two away by myself. It took all night. In fact, they're all in the same area by Rocking K Ranch. I might open a burial service there in my old age."

"Anybody I know?" I asked.

He smiled. "No. You don't know them. This was before your time out here. But they were friends of mine and I did them as proper as could be, all things considered. Yeah, one was a real gentleman. He just got caught up in the life." For about five seconds, I saw some sadness come over Batts as if he was actually sorry for his chosen profession. His guy never showed up at the hotel, so he had a couple more drinks and left.

Later, my buddy, Sal, arrived and I ran this all down to him. He said when him and Batts were partners in Tucson Vending Company, Batts got drunk one night and was all melancholy about killing Joe Hootner, who he said was a good guy. He talked shit about Rudy Perfido, but he liked Joe.

So that's what I know about your old man. He seemed to have had a rep as a good man. And he probably was. He just got involved with a bunch of crooks on a different level than him. Bad decision. It's all about decisions.

It was a real fucking *Shawshank Redemption* moment when a tobacco-chewing guard wearing reflective shades wheeled a squeaky cart across the desert, piled high with books sent to us by readers of Jon's Jail Journal, with a hundred prisoners mobbing around the desert, watching the cart hungrily. Shaun waved a few of us over to help carry the books to his cell. Checking them out, we were as excited as Ivan Denisovich when he came up on some extra tails and gills in his fish-eyeball soup.

When most of the fellas had left the cell, I sniffed *The Electric Kool-Aid Acid Test* by Tom Wolfe. "I just love the smell of new books."

"Me, too," Shaun said. "What do you think about all these books – Updike, Murakami, Rushdie, Bret Easton Ellis, and your favourite, Tom Wolfe?"

"Let me tell you something," I said. "I've been doing time since I was a kid, in and out, in and out. Thanks to these books, this is the best I've ever had it. There was a time in my life when the fucking

TV meant everything to me. It used to mind-fuck me every night. Now I've got these books, I don't even turn the motherfucker on. From this cell, I'm travelling the world. Whether it's Tom Wolfe taking me to a five-bedroom townhouse on New York's Fifth Avenue with green marble floors, or Robert Fisk taking me to Tora Bora in the mountains of Afghanistan with Bin Laden and the Mujahideen – I'm there, bro. These books are getting me out of the fucking cell."

The next day, I said to Shaun, "Now, out of the books from yesterday, I'm really excited about this one: *The Great Thoughts* by George Seldes."

"What's so good about it?" Shaun asked.

I flipped to the introduction. "It's right here. Blaise Pascal: 'Man's greatness lies in the power of thought.' And Marcus Aurelius Antoninus: 'Our life is what our thoughts make it.' And here's Emerson: 'Great men are they who see that spiritual is stronger than any material force, that thoughts rule the world.'"

"It's powerful stuff," Shaun said. "I need to work more on my spiritual side."

"These quotes are making me realise that I'm wasting my thoughts hating on people. For me to lay up and hate is like having a goitre on my neck." I pointed below an ear. "Sometimes I just lay on my bunk, thinking about motherfuckers I hate and fantasising about ways of killing them. It's a goitre that keeps growing and growing, and I've got to cut it off. I'd like to get it surgically removed, but there ain't no surgeon in the world with a scalpel sharp enough to cut this fucker off."

"So how are you going to fix it?" Shaun asked, smiling.

I put the book down and threw up my arms. "Aurelius is gonna be my surgeon! Pascal is gonna be my surgeon! Emerson is gonna be my surgeon! Life is nothing but thought, is it? I could go to a restaurant and order a rack of lamb with mint jelly, rice pilaf, French bread, a bottle of Cabernet Sauvignon and, for dessert, Kahlua parfait made with vanilla ice cream, and maybe I'd finish with a Baileys Irish Cream and coffee, and hell yeah, I'd enjoy it at the time, but I'd also enjoy thinking about it afterwards as well. Just like I can lie on my bunk and instead of hating on motherfuckers and thinking of ways to whack them, I can enjoy picturing when I was on the run in Waikiki and Maui, and how beautiful it was. It's all about thoughts. This is an epiphany for me. Look, my goitre's shrinking." I tapped my neck. "When I feel hate invading my space, I'm gonna combat it by reading this book or whatever else I can get my hands on. The more I read, the more my thoughts turn to philosophy. I was watching some show on PBS about the Norwegian explorer, Roald Amundsen. To get to the South Pole without dying he lived with the Eskimos for a few years, and learnt how to live in harmony with that environment. That got me thinking: prison is my environment. I ain't going nowhere for the rest of my life, except on a trip to the hospital every now and then. Instead of fighting my environment, I need to be living in harmony with it. I can't be raising my blood pressure 'cause I didn't get called to Property when I was supposed to. I've gotta go with the flow. Why should I be blowing gaskets over the small shit when there's people getting blown up in Iraq, mudslides are killing thousands in the Philippines, and there's earthquakes in Turkey? Shame on me."

As much as I enjoy reading philosophy, I'm gonna warn you about the vanity of philosophers: *I'm smarter than you. I'm so smart, listen to me.* Philosophers are people who don't wanna go out and work in the hot sun. They lay around under the shade of trees, write books and give lectures, so the unwashed will say, "Man, he's smart. He's so intelligent. Let's have him over for dinner."

I really think in my heart and mind, I could have been a book critic. I've only got a ninth-grade education, but I can recognise good writing. I've never enjoyed an author as much as Tom Wolfe. When I read *A Man in Full*, I didn't want to finish the motherfucker. I wanted to read a page a day to savour it. I happen to think that his *Bonfire of the Vanities* is almost right up there with *A Man in Full*. I laughed at the black preacher and the pompousness of the Masters of the Universe.

When I first read the two jabronies, Clancy and Grisham, I ended up asking myself, *Is a Big Mac better than a fucking Wendy's burger?* I'm not knocking success or Wendy's or McDonald's, but it's food for the unwashed. That's why I've never read *Harry Potter*. Clancy is always trying to take me to South America, where the drug cartels are torturing and murdering motherfuckers or to a submarine at the bottom of the ocean to fight the Russians. He can't do it, no more than Grisham can take me to a courtroom. Listen, I've been in courtrooms. What Grisham writes fiction about I've lived.

I've read plenty by John Updike. Most recently, *Toward the End of Time*, and I'm getting ready to reread *Rabbit, Run*, written in 1960. When I read his descriptions of grave robbers in the tombs of Egypt, I thought, *My God, that's good writing.* His sheer descriptive ability on a scale of 1 to 10 is 9½. But I'll be honest with you. I think Updike's got some marbles loose upstairs when it comes to writing about sex. I think he's a borderline child molester. He gets way too graphic on the young kids and stuff.

Updike is right up there with Wolfe, but Wolfe sets the table a little bit better for my feast, and he dims the restaurant lights. I can spend a day or a week in the prison library, and I can't find anything better than Wolfe for escapism. Spending the rest of my life in a nine-by-six cell – don't get me wrong, I deserve to be here, I ain't crying – I want to read something that takes me out of here. Thanks to Wolfe, I've been on the basketball team at DuPont University, where I've also been to a frat party – me, Two Tonys, whacker of men.

The guy who brought me *The Da Vinci Code* said it was silly. I didn't even bust it open. It was like someone giving me a bologna sandwich when I had a locker full of filets.

My reading started before TV with comic books and funny papers. I'm an under-educated person, but I went on to read some of the finest authors in the world, including the fucking drunk, Hemingway, as well as Steinbeck, who is one of the best. No shoot 'em up bang bang here comes the chopper let's make a run for it with our AK-47s.

Haruki Murakami is real good. He took me to the Gobi Desert, where the Mongols and a Russian were torturing Japs. I could feel the wind. It gave me a chill. The fear was there. I was thinking, *How the fuck is the protagonist gonna get out of this?* even though he was a Jap and the Japs had whacked my cousin in Okinawa. I give Murakami props. The only thing is, he's not too logical when it comes to plotting a story, which Wolfe excels at. But Wolfe would never take me to the bottom of a well in downtown Tokyo. Updike might. He took me on an excursion in *Toward the End of Time*.

Other authors hate Wolfe 'cause of his genius. Take Norman Mailer, who won the Pulitzer for *The Executioner's Song* about Gary Gilmore getting the death penalty. But the book was only a documentary on paper – transcripts of Gary Gilmore's brain.

I like Hunter S. Thompson. I went through the sixties when it was cooking, and I never dropped a hit of acid until I was forty-six and in the joint. Hunter was a freak, a psychedelic acidhead.

I've gotta give Ken Kesey kudos for *Cuckoo's Nest*, and Heller for *Catch-22*. They had early success, but their later books bombed. Writing is a hit and miss thing. Look at Mario Puzo. *The Godfather* was good, but anything he wrote after that was pure shit.

Lincoln by Gore Vidal is one of the best historical novels, along with his *Burr*. But his *1876* never grabbed me. Burr – Vice President of the United States – whacked Alexander Hamilton – Secretary of the Treasury and one of the Founding Fathers – in a duel in New Jersey by the Hudson River. In those days, if you had a beef with someone, you could whack a motherfucker in a duel and nothing would happen to you. I wish they'd continued that law. Maybe then, I'd have a shot at being the Vice President instead of being in this motherfucker for the rest of my life, wondering what we're eating for chow and whether the chow trays are clean.

Reading the Algerian Frenchman, Camus, was depressing. Look, you can scare me, thrill me, make me laugh, but don't fucking depress me.

The Bank of America's president probably reads the same

books as me, and I could rap with him about them and connect – just like if Putin came to town, we could sit down and play a game of chess even though I can't speak Russian. Discussing the military manoeuvres of the British Empire with the Prime Minister is probably out of my league, but we could kick around the books we've read. He ain't always lived at 10 Downing Street, studying geopolitics. Somewhere along the way, he's read some books.

Books bring me joy. I confess I do like a cheeseburger every now and then, but if we are going out for dinner, I'm not gonna drive through a McDonald's or stop at a Subway for meatball sandwiches. I'm gonna take you to the Fleur de Lys, where I'll order oysters on the half shell with horseradish sauce and a cold Heineken. Your taste and my taste might be refined, but not quite the same, so maybe you'll order roast duck with mango sauce or tournedos Rossini or chateaubriand. Having been introduced to the fine dining of literature, I stay away from junk food as much as possible.

In August 2006, the blog readers sent more questions.

"One reader asked about coming to prison," Shaun said, pen in hand, ready to scribble my response.

"I remember," I replied, "at The Walls when the big grey bus drove up with the fish in it. Twenty-five guys from Alhambra Unit would get off, get their chains undone, and walk to Cell Block 1 for orientation. Everybody – the white gang members, the Mexicans and blacks – would be looking at the herd of fish, checking out who's who, who's weak, who's fearful, who's strong. A fish with fear radiating from his eyes, with his shoulders humped and his head down, they'd know they could prey on. A swaggering motherfucker, with his head held high and all tatted down would be a potential comrade. The gang leaders are always looking for new members. If I'm George Dubya Bush, I want more Christian conservative Republican members, but I'm not gonna just let anyone in. It's just the same in here."

Frankie, a Mexican American friend of mine, who'd served over twenty years, piped in with, "The gang members look at fish as furniture for all corners of the room. Each fish fits in somewhere, whether he's a chair or a table. A fish may get punked out and be a piece of ass. If he's coming in with jewellery or a Sony Trinitron TV then he's a source of money."

"Imagine," I said, "the gang members watching the fish come in as wolves on the side of a grassy hill on the plains of South Dakota watching a herd of elk. The wolves are lying there looking for any signs of weakness in potential prey. Maybe a limp in an elk, an old-timer trotting behind the herd, or a young elk that's strayed too far from its mother. Once the wolves pick out their prey, the alpha wolf will somehow communicate to the pack that this is the one we're going after. Gang members are looking for the same. Maybe a guy with an aura of fear who won't make eye contact is a child molester they're gonna shank. Or a scared-looking kid who's too polite. They'll approach the fish friendly at first. A probate from the same race will roll up to the newcomer and say shit like, 'Wassup! Where you from? Let's go eat.' Over days and weeks, the fish will divulge certain information to his new friend. Whether he's in for murder, rape, burglary. Whether he's doing two years, five or life. Whether he likes or hates the other races. If he's a white guy with a Mexican wife, they'll know he's not for them. But maybe he has other uses. Does he get a weekly visit from someone who'll smuggle dope into prison? How much money does he have on his books? And they're always looking for sexual prey, punks, someone to turn out. At The Walls they were looking for bleeders, people who could bleed twice a week for $6.50 from Cutter Lab."

"What if you refused to give blood?" Shaun asked.

"They'd bust your fucking head in."

"So what kind of body language would you recommend a fish portrays when he arrives at prison?"

"Make eye contact," I said. "Talk to motherfuckers. Keep your head up. Try not to show fear or apprehension – although everyone feels it. Don't be too polite, but don't be too disrespectful. If somebody fucks with you, get busy."

"What about stealing things in prison?"

"In the joint you should abstain from taking people's property 'cause, firstly, you can get hurt, and secondly, it's not the right thing to do. Readers may be saying, 'But Two Tonys has robbed, stolen, conned, and now he's saying taking someone's Snickers and two bars of soap is wrong,' so let me tell you something: there ain't nothin' worse than a jailhouse thief. Also, extortion of property by gang members ain't right. It's hard enough in here with the boot of the man, society, on our necks, to then have to experience man's inhumanity to fellow man from your brothers in chains: shit like protection rackets, quid pro quos, I'm gonna give you two boxes of cigarettes a week to handle my problems. Here the strong prey on the weak and the smart take from the strong."

"Is it safer to be feared or liked?"

"Here, being feared can hurt you or can help you. If you're too feared, motherfuckers might wanna take you out. I whacked a motherfucker out of fear. He scared me, so I had to get there first. There's a happy medium. Love in prison is a word thrown around a lot, but if you get right down to it there ain't too many motherfuckers who love you in these fucking shithouses. You're on your own. Respect is a more common emotion, and a form of fear. I respect The Rock out of fear. I'm not gonna pull his moustache and poke him in the eye if I see him in a bar. That's respect."

"What about politics in here?"

"Prison politics have changed since my first time down in 1980. There was a code. If you were a good person of your race they wouldn't beat you down and take your shit. They'd show you the ropes, the dos and don'ts. If some Mexican or black dudes ran up on your store bag and said, 'What you got in there? I'm hungry. Give me some,' and you had no allies, you were in big trouble, so you needed six or seven white guys to roll over to prevent a situation. The peckerwoods weren't supposed to exploit you later on, but they did. I saw a fish, a guy who'd been in prison for two days, on the rec field. An Aryan Brother rolled up to him and said, 'Trade me your jeans.' In front of everyone, he relinquished a pair of brand-new Levis. His best and only response should have been, 'Hey, you know what, these are my fucking jeans.' I went to the Aryan Brother and said, 'You've really fucked that kid's head and rep up. You've ruined him. He'll be known as the guy who gave up his jeans on the rec field for the rest of the time he's in the pen.' He replied, 'Well, he could have fought me.' Politics changed when the prison STG'd [classified as a Security Threat Group] the gang leaders and sent them to supermax. The cons used to run prison. Department Of Corrections runs it now. The days of the old, wise-cracking con talking out of the side of his neck are gone."

"Is it possible to lead a virtuous life in prison?"

"Not always. For example, when something bad's going down, you feel it. It's in the air. You know it's about to happen. I saw a guy one time they were getting ready to kill. I knew him and something told me to warn him, but I didn't do it. They killed him. The virtuous thing to do would have got my ass killed. You can't be too virtuous in here. If I see a guy coming out of a cell with some jabroni's TV that I don't give a fuck about, I'm not gonna get involved. If it's a crime partner's TV, yeah, fuck, let's get it back. In society, you see your neighbour's house getting robbed and you call the cops. In here that's a no-no."

"Is prison a revolving door for most prisoners?"

"You've got a lot of institutionalised prisoners. State-raised from the cradle to foster homes to juvenile hall to county jails to prison. These guys hit the gates, get out and can't cope with it. They're freer in here than with the bunch of worker ants I see on TV at 5:30 AM on the freeways, bumper to bumper, bunched up line after line, all heading downtown. Here we don't decide what we eat, wear, or what doctor we see. If this is all you've known your entire life, how are you expected to get out there and get a job, buy clothes, get to work, pay bills? It's a drain on a motherfucker who's not ready for it. You've got to be a well-oiled machine. The tiniest infraction – a speeding ticket – and the whole machine is kaput. Suddenly, you're down $175, so you've got to boost some canned ham from the meat department at Safeway so you can eat. When I wave goodbye to motherfuckers like Grim at the gate, I know they're coming back. Slavery is a state of mind and prisoners are mentally conditioned to be in prison."

"One reader asked why you use the word fuck so much?"

"My thesis on the word fuck is: it's like saying DWI or any other acronym. When the Puritans first came to this country, after leaving sunny ol' England, they had their rules and regulations they established when they got off the fucking *Mayflower*. Legend has it that one happened to cover fornicating in public. The legal term was For Unlawful Carnal Knowledge. Abbreviated in legal terminology to F-U-C-K, to save them time. Back then, when they busted a guy from the marketplace behind a bale of beeswax, boffing away, they arrested him and took him to pilgrim court, and explained to the judge it's for F-U-C-K. So I'm not swearing. Swearing is like saying something like, 'You punk-ass son of a bitch.'"

"A guy called Bill wrote to ask if you'd whack someone for him?"

"I'm in here for life. I'm in a real comfortable spot in my life right now. I don't see any reason to have to whack a motherfucker again. I stay out of the line of fire. I don't get in other people's business. There's a quote I read every day: 'Don't interfere with something that ain't bothering you none.' That's my Ten Commandments right there. That's my Exodus, Matthew, Mark, Luke and John rolled into one."

Spending hours every day with Shaun, working on my life story and answering blog-reader questions, we became so close, I told him that I was starting to feel like he was the son that I never had.

"That means a lot to me." Shaun was on the stool in my cell, clutching his pad and pen as usual. "I really appreciate our friendship."

"How's your mom and pops doing?" I asked, resting on my bunk with a cup of coffee.

"They're good," he said.

"I only saw your parents by chance when I was outside Medical. I was thirty feet away from them in an eight-by-ten cage separated by two fences with razor wire. As corny as this may sound, I could see they were nice people. They smiled and waved, and I said, 'Welcome to America.' They were both good people who loved their boy. And it's because of them you are who you are."

"I think you're right."

"I know I'm right. And a lot of people ain't as fortunate as having family like that. Have you guys always been a tight family unit?"

"Growing up we were, but after my sister and I graduated from university, we left home and travelled overseas. I ended up this side of the planet, and my sister ended up on the other side, in Japan. The distance drifted us apart somewhat, but my arrest pulled us back together."

"Then a good thing came out of your arrest. I can tell you were well-raised. That you were nurtured by people who cared about you. To stay alive in here, I have to read people upon meeting them. Some I have to be around a little while to figure out. Some I have to be in positions of adversity with. Others I look for controllability and wind-up-ness, so I can send them on missions like those eighteen- and nineteen-year-olds George Dubya Bush's sending to Iraq. My point is this: I'm a good judge of character. You're not perfect, Shaun, but I can tell by talking to you, trusting you, and discussing things with you I normally wouldn't with others, I don't detect any malice, greed or deceptiveness from you. You seem to be genuinely interested in my life. And you're out of your environment in here. You know that?"

"Being in prison?"

"Yeah. But at the same time you've managed to maintain yourself and nobody really fucks with you. That's because of the way you carry yourself, not like a swaggering tough guy like Ken who wants to cave skulls in 'cause you didn't buy him a jar of coffee. You seem to have a knack for staying out of people's business."

"Thanks a lot for saying that. It means a lot to me coming from someone with as much respect as you." I showed Shaun a recent picture of my daughter, Niki, with her husband and two kids. "You must be real proud to see Niki doing so well," Shaun said.

I smiled. "If you get out before me, which you will unless I can get a hundred and ten years knocked off for good fucking behaviour or I kick down a million bucks to the tight-ass Arizona Clemency Board, and you touch base with Niki, I'd like you to promise me one thing."

"Sure, I will."

"Remind her how much I love her."

In December 2007, when Shaun's release was confirmed, I was consumed by a sad feeling that made me weary. The problem with growing close to anyone in this motherfucker is that you get ripped apart when the guy hits the gate. When it was time to say goodbye, I joined Shaun near the rec-field fence.

"I can't believe I'm never gonna see you again," Shaun said, wearing a baseball cap, gazing through the chain-link.

"Me, too, little bro. But I'm sure glad we crossed paths on the road of life. Out of all the motherfuckers I've ever met, you've changed my way of thinking the most."

"I really appreciate that. But ultimately you've changed your way of thinking," Shaun said. "I've learnt a lot from you."

"You need to take some fucking credit!" I said, smiling. "And stop being so fucking humble."

"Alright. I'm glad I've helped you," Shaun said.

"That's more fucking like it!"

"I'm not good at saying goodbyes, so I'm gonna head back," I said, my voice getting emotional. I could hear it in Shaun's voice, too.

"I love you, Two Tonys. I'm never gonna forget you. I'm gonna keep writing to you."

"I love you, too, my little bro." I stared at Shaun, capturing his image to take back to my cell. I raised my hand and patted my heart, showing love and respect. "L&R, little bro. L&R." Tears formed behind my glasses.

"I'll always remember your PMA and what Ivan Denisovich went through. L&R, Two Tonys."

I turned and walked away. When guys get released, they promise to write to you, put a few dollars on your inmate account and send you some books to read, but you never hear from most of the motherfuckers again until six months later when they get busted with a dope sack and end up back in this shithole. I figured it would be different with my Brit friend. As the days went by, I missed his English ass and I still do. He kept in touch, sent me books, and hooked me up with some pen pals. He was a bloke who did his number in his own style, but he did it good. I – and some others – always had his back even when he didn't know it.

CHAPTER 18

'Cause of the increased frequency of cellmates murdering their cellmates, the fucking geniuses at the Arizona Department of Corrections came up with a new rule: housing cellmates with like crimes. They tried to put a mass murderer in with me who I didn't get along with. For refusing a new cellmate, I did ninety days in the hole in Tucson. After that, they shipped me to a unit I'd never been to before at Buckeye prison, where I knew a lot of the fellas from the old days and other yards. One guy, McGee, I'd known for twenty-eight years. I hadn't seen him for twenty-three. He was a half-ass shot-caller back in his younger days, and was close to that dude, Skull, the Aryan Brother I had to snuff out.

I was put in Building 2, but after three weeks, they moved me to Building 1, where McGee lived, and five friends of Skull I felt I should be careful around. McGee and I had seen each other through the rec-field fence, going and coming to chow. In Building 1, McGee's cell was right above mine, so we could talk through the vents, but there were two other cells in our vent, so it was light talk. "How you been? You seen so and so?" *Yaddy yaddy ya* bullshit. We agreed to talk at recreation, while taking laps around the track.

We met, hugged and started lapping. Just the two of us. Me: sixty-six. Him: sixty-two and grey-haired, but in great shape. Prison does that to some guys. So I started it off. "Look, I know Skull was your guy and you had love for him, and so did I at one time. But he got out. He got full of that fucking meth and he got real disrespectful and real ignorant. You know how he was. He was dangerous. I couldn't wait for him to whack me or to do something to my daughter. I did what I did. It's a shame, but it's over. It was a me or him thing. You would have acted as I acted."

McGee agreed with everything I said. I ain't no fool. I've been to a few tea parties. Sometimes when a motherfucker is agreeing with everything you throw his way, it's time to tighten your vigilance. I scoped out the yard. It wasn't like the old days. Buckeye is a modern twenty-first century prison. Gun towers. Guards walking around. I was on a let-me-do-my-time-and-go-home yard. Or a let-me-do-what-I-can-of-my-life-sentence-and-die-in-peace yard. McGee assured me he understood. While he loved Skull, he knew Skull was a wacko, and if he were in my shoes he would have probably done the same.

So I grilled him a little bit about others on the yard. One in particular had a nasty rep. He was big back in the day. Mean, crazy and tough. I knew him twenty-six years ago and stayed away from him. They called him Mekong Mike. He was a vet who'd seen a lot of shit over there and did a lot of crazy stuff. He was for real. I knew that much. But he was also close to Skull and he was in my building. We'd passed each other maybe ten times. But no eye contact. No swagger. No good vibes. I felt the vibe Mekong Mike put on me, so I asked McGee about him.

"Mekong Mike's a Jesus freak now. He's hung up all his spurs. He walks with God. The Skull shit is over. No need to get paranoid. Relax. Enjoy the yard. It's mellow. It's our fucking retirement home."

"Right on. That sounds good to me."

So we went on. McGee took me over and introduced me to a few young guys. All buffed up. Tatted down. If you've seen *America History X*, you know the type.

Now look, I don't want to sound vain or nothing, but I've got a rep that precedes me. Some of these kids had heard of me and I was picking up good vibes. A lot of respect. McGee and I were old, but we both had respect. We were not rape-os or chomos or rats. We were a couple of OGs – Old Gangsters. We earned our spurs back on Florence prison yard, where white guys always had to go two to three deep to the showers, always on full tilt in case the Mexicans or blacks jumped off. It was like that back then.

Most of these kids were shitting yellow, while guys such as me, McGee, Skull and Mekong Mike were representing. The other races had theirs, we had ours. Respect ours, we'll respect yours. Otherwise, fuck it.

Back in those days, if a new arrival showed heart he wasn't alone. We'd stand with him. If he had the heart of a piss-ant, then he did his time as a weakling. The guards let it go on 'cause it made their job safer and easier. We all did our best to keep the lid on. It would blow at times, but afterwards, it would settle down.

It's the man's system now. The state has thirty prisons to break up gangs and tough guys. The holes are deep and dark and insane. You get scared just going to them. Prison is an adapt-or-suffer world, so the smart ones adapt. Go to rec. Read. Watch TV. Enjoy this time drama-free. You don't have to check your balls at the warden's office. Just try to use your head. But keep in mind there are still motherfuckers whose brains are locked into that old shit. And if you hit the button, you can get killed. But you stay away from those guys. Don't borrow. Don't lend. Just a "Hi!" or "Right on!" and keep your distance. I've been in both time frames. Now is better. Less stress. The old epoch was fun at times. But lots of stress.

McGee introduced me to this kid, Warrior, with the face of a choirboy, the build of a young Mike Tyson and polite as hell. I picked up good vibes from him. He was real respectful in his manner. We talked for a little while about Tucson.

Then a lame called Skids came over. "Hey, Two Tonys. You remember me back in 1984 South Unit?" *Yaddy yaddy da.* He wanted to lap a couple with me.

"Sure. Why not," I said. McGee hung back, kicking it with Warrior and some others. I started taking laps with Skids. We went by four young, in-shape Mexican Americans, known as eses. They had tats. Mexican war eagles. Aztec chieftains. Real political stuff. Noticing them, I didn't stare or make eye contact. They had an air about them that radiated, "We're all that and a bag of M&M's," as if their shit had no odour.

One of them called my name, so I turned to him, and he said, "When did you get here?"

"Hey! How you been?" I said, acting like I recalled him, but I didn't.

"Cool, man. Good to see you again."

Skids and I resumed our walk. "Who are those guys?" I asked Skids.

"The one you talked to is Tono. They think they're bad-asses. They just hang out together and look down their noses at most of the Mexicans."

"I picked up on that yeah-we're-bad vibe." Passing the eses doing push-ups and stuff, I gave Tono a nod and an alright. He returned the nod.

Later on, walking along with Skids, I heard a voice and the shuffle of feet coming up behind me fast. "Move! Move!"

Skids and I spun and jumped out of the way. The eses raced by. "What's up with that shit?" I said, aggravated.

"Oh, that's nothing. They're just jogging a lap."

"Oh, yeah. They just roll up behind us and yell, 'Move! Move!' like we're a couple of lames. That's no respect. I gotta let them know not to run up on me like that." I took off after them. They were finishing their lap on the other side of the track.

Following me, Skids said, "Oh, they didn't mean nothing. They're good guys." The weak motherfucker was shitting, but I didn't give a shit. I wasn't counting on him or anyone else. I was in the zone and hot. Brand new in this building, I wasn't gonna get yelled at like some old punk! It was never gonna happen again.

Here's my motto on respect: standing up for yourself is a way of life. Fuck the ass-kickings. I've woken up in hospitals with tubes in my nose. It hurts, but it heals. Losing that respect is forever, it never heals. Word travels fast in prison, just like on the battlefield. Everyone in here knows who the fearless guys are – guys who, centuries ago, would have painted their faces blue, picked up axes and spears, and fought alongside William Wallace on the misty Scottish highlands. Just like we all know the ball-less guys in here who, if they were on the plains of Normandy, facing a British army with longbows led by the Black Prince, would tell the guys at the front that they needed to go to the back lines to eat a soup.

In Buddhism, it's said that you can't make me mad; the only person who can make me mad is me. But everyone has something that if they're called it, they're gonna react to or consider themselves pretty damn weak. If someone crosses that line by calling you something, or taking your Walkman, for example, that's when you have to step up and say, "This is who I am." Sometimes it's a hell of a price to pay. You're gonna lose your good time and privileges, such as visits and access to the inmate store, but how else are you gonna live with yourself? If you don't stand up, it opens all kinds of doors to other motherfuckers.

Now, I wasn't rushing in like a fool. They were mean want-to-be-tough dudes. So I was gonna have my say and let the chips fall. Fuck the hole, the gun tower. I go, they go. I knew they could rat-pack me, but I wouldn't be yelled at. I wasn't trying to recruit others either. I was solo. Skids took off for McGee. Approaching the eses, I heard McGee yelling for me to wait. *Fuck waiting!*

I went up to them, and I said to Tono, "Hey, ese, understand what I'm saying here: when I'm walking laps and you guys are coming up behind me, you don't have to start yelling, 'Move! Move!' like I'm a lame. All you gotta do is give me a, 'Coming through,' or a, 'Behind you.' It's a track. I'll move over for you. Show respect, and you'll get respect. Tono, you know that."

"Oh, we know you'll move," one said in a shitty tone.

McGee arrived with Warrior, and an old pal of mine, Cowboy. Skids didn't come. He was back with the water cooler, watching. "Hey, ese, I don't know you and you don't know me," I said, "but I'll tell you right now, I ain't the one to be moving on demands. It will be what it will be." Then I just walked on, by myself. McGee stayed behind and engaged them in conversation. As I made a lap and was getting ready to pass them again, McGee was ahead on the track by the gate.

A guy came up behind me: Warrior. Now he's Mexican

American, so I wasn't sure what was up. As we passed the four eses, he started talking about Tucson. "Hey, fuck those guys," Warrior said. "They ain't all that. I already got down with the one yelling, 'Move! Move!' He tries to be hard. I've seen him do that with others."

"Well, I'm not coming out here to be yelled at. I don't yell. I won't put up with it."

So that was my first night at rec and some shit almost flew. It would have been a shame. We'd all go to the hole. I'd probably be hurt. But the big shame would have been to come out to rec and walk and have those four assholes yell at me every rec period. In prison, there are rules. They're unwritten, but they're there and have been for years. Adapting to a twenty-first-century prison is important, but so is respect and pride.

I checked around about Warrior. He had beefs with a lot of bullies who thought they could muscle him. He fooled them. Choirboy face and all. But he wasn't crazy. He just wanted his respect like we all do. We became close. What's funny is the four eses never yelled at me again. I even talked to Tono a few times. I never liked them. They all got busted with dope and had to go to the hole. They seemed to have trouble adapting.

Warrior and a couple of other good guys hung out together. I was the old man, but we all enjoyed each other's company. As each was released, I missed him, but there were always new friends coming along. Only the actors changed. The roles remained the same.

CHAPTER 19

You've heard me say over and fucking over that I didn't kill any-body that didn't have it coming. Let's expand on that. If I get a job at the circus and a motherfucker tells me all I've got to do is put my head in a lion's mouth three times a day for $200 a time, and then one day the lion chomps on my head and takes out an eye, an ear, half my fucking jaw and nose, and I get out of the hospital after they've stitched my face back together, I can't blame the lion. How the fuck am I gonna blame the lion? I'm getting paid for it. I'm reaping the benefits of putting my head in the lion's mouth. It's the same in de bizness. There are certain recourses open to a person who has been faulted in the criminal world. He can't take his case to those stiffs at the Supreme Court. In certain criminal organisations such as the Cosa Nostra or biker gangs there are hierarchies and you can plead your case, but nine times out of ten you've gotta do what you've gotta do and be able to live with the consequences.

There are people in here serving life without parole irrespective of the circumstances of the murder. Some should never get out. Yeah, some motherfuckers need a good killing. People that hurt kids, old folks, nice ladies on their way to the mall, guys on their jobs or resting in their homes. Kill kill kill the chomos, the rapos, the abusers of the weak. Shank them in their fucking windpipes. Kill the ones who have got it coming. Send them to a better place. Fuck their childhood, their old grey granny in the front row of the court. Kill them. Let God sort them out. That's His job.

But there are also some who present no danger to society. Like a guy who leaves a New Year's Eve party after having too many glasses of Mumm or Piper-Heidsieck, who runs over some other poor guy, and the next thing he's in the county jail. He made a mistake, but there's no malice, no forethought. There are some in here for killing people who were trying to kill them. If I crack your head in with my clock, and try and strangle you with my stinger cable, and you jump up with a pen and stab me in the ear and I die of a cerebral haemorrhage, you wouldn't deserve life in prison. That's self-defence. If a robber breaks into your house and your kids are asleep upstairs and you blow him away, you might end up on death row in states with retreat-to-safety laws. There's a computer nerd in here serving twenty-five to life 'cause his buddy was shot dead by the owner of a store they were stealing from. As an accomplice, he was charged with the murder.

It's the people with money who make the laws, and that don't make them right. This country was founded and built by law-breakers. George Washington broke the law. Politicians these days just rewrite the laws to suit themselves, especially those two liars who are lower on the shithead scale than shower scum: Bush and Blair. Thomas Jefferson said that it's the duty of patriots to whack frauds like Bush and Blair in order to restore the tree of liberty. I don't see no one stepping up to the plate, and that's 'cause we're taught that following the leader is the right thing to do. Choose the laws you like and fuck the rest, like Bush and Blair have done, plundering the world in the name of global counterinsurgency. And people still buy into that shit!

If I were ever released, maybe I could get hooked up with a job as a greeter at Harrods or Walmart, and perhaps work my way into the gun department, so I could show some motherfuckers the wonders of a two-inch snub-nose Colt. Hey, I can dream can't I? I probably would be a danger to society, but maybe I wouldn't be if I had a bungalow, with some staples to eat, some soup to warm up for lunch, and a good plasma TV. But what would I be missing if I had all of that? The adrenaline. Does adrenaline count for anything? Yes. With all due respect to people of the world: crime can be fun even when it's not profitable. If I ever got out, I like to think I'd do the right thing and stay out of trouble. That I would not seek to harm no one. I fantasize about fishing trips and ball games and playing with my grandson at the park. That's a nice normal fantasy, a healthy fantasy, which is easier on my hate goitre, but the reality is that it ain't gonna happen. Neither is me getting out and putting my hack defence attorney's grey matter on the inside windshield of his car, which is also a fantasy of mine as the motherfucker sold me out. What is trashier than a fucking attorney?

But I've got to be honest with you. I shouldn't be allowed out of this motherfucker. Prison was built for me. I accept that and live with it. I'm doing it every day, and trying to have fun playing a little chess, watching TV shows like *Big Brother*, and making myself a nice roast-beef supper with a bag of iced-down Coca-Cola, and having good conversations with my friends. I'd hate you to have the misconception that I'm sad at never getting out. Doing my thing out there put me in here. It's done. I can do this time for as long as I'm alive. I can't do all of it, but I'll do what I can. I'm doing it. No one else. Me. And I like doing it feeling good.

Let me tell you about a day several months back. At 5:30 AM, I went to rec. It was still dark. I walked fifteen laps or two miles at a good fast clip. The sun hadn't come up yet, but as I was walking my laps, here it came. It might have come up over the landfill area the garbage is dumped in, but it was still beautiful. I stopped to watch it rise. I can understand a rice farmer on the Nile Delta 5,000 years ago, tending his fields in the night and all at once here comes this bad-ass fucking sun. No wonder they worshipped it. It's a natural high. By myself, watching it rise, I got all inspired. There were about ten guys out there that early, but I exercised alone. Inspired by the sun, I did push-ups, squats, back arms, and I even sprinted forty yards a couple of times.

After rec, I went for chow. Scrambled eggs. Cold cereal. Fried potatoes. Two oranges. One milk. There was good rap at the table discussing Michelangelo, the Sistine Chapel and the pervert Pope Julius II. After a hot shower, I watched the Wachovia Golf Tournament and busted open a ramen beef soup.

Recently, I reread Sol's *Ivan Denisovich*. It keeps me inured to the conditions. Silly, I know, but it works. If old Ivan did it in those Siberian conditions with all those inbred Slavs, I can do it here in sunny Arizona with French toast and pancakes. No fish-eyeball soup for me.

There are guys lying up in cancer or burns wards, doing much worse. If I allow myself to get all sad with woe-is-me bullshit, then I'm a weak-ass motherfucker. I don't think I'm institutionalised. It's just that I'm a realist. I'm here. I'm not going anywhere, so I've got to accept it and make the best of the bad situation I put myself in. Like a cancer patient does or a car-wreck victim, except my situation is self-inflicted due to bad choices and not considering options and penalties.

After I was found guilty of one of the murders, I was called back to court for sentencing. A witness got up on the stand, acting like a loving victim. She went on about never wanting me to have a happy day again or to smell roses and all that bullshit and how much I should suffer. If she had a video camera on me today, she'd be pissed. I ain't got no roses to smell, but fuck it, I'll smell some aftershave and make-believe it's roses.

CHAPTER 20

Here's what I wrote to my Brit friend, Shaun:

Jan 2008

Hey Pal, I received your most welcome letters. I was so happy to read that you are back in sunny ol' England surrounded by those that have got love in their hearts and minds for one of the best blokes I've run across in my prison years (from the heart). Now I don't have to tell you (but I will), stay the fuck away from all the silly shit that life will throw in your path. In simple talk, "Do the right thing." Enough said.

It's 6:30 AM Sat morning here. I'm a shower porter. I'm going to break for now. Duty calls and these showers have to be cleaned, so these geeks can wash their cruddy asses and balls. Woe is me. Crime doesn't pay, but I sure enjoyed some of it along the way. Fuck it. It is what it is. I'm not complaining. These fucks treat me better than I would them.

It's 2 PM. Here in Buckeye it's not so bad, especially now that they moved the Tucson guys into dorms. There's 50 guys per dorm, 3 shitters, 3 showers. Yea. You get up in the morning, grab your toothbrush, go to put a nice brush on the pearlies and there's big ol' Slingblade sitting there taking a noisy shit, and there's a line of people waiting to dump. No thanks. I'll pass. This place is OK as far as yards go. The guards are not as picky as Tucson. They let a man do his time. Oh, they do their job – a man has to expect that. But it's nothing like the bullshit in Sheriff Joe Arpaio's jail.

Grim caught a murder case. Something about some dead Native American swinging in the wind. Who knows and who gives a shit. My biggest concern is what time chow is and what's on the tube, or if I've got a good book to read. Hey! I'm reading *The Constant Gardener* by Le Carré. It's slow but I'm staying with it. I read *The Looming Tower* about Osama bin Laden. It was good. Check it out if you can take time from your pubbing, you bloody bloke.

I've enrolled in horticulture school. Yeah, I've decided to devote my life to planting plants instead of blokes who cross me. In fact I'm seriously thinking of opening a horticulture store when I get out in the next century. But if I don't make my release date then, oh well, it's still a good class to get out of my single cell and keep my mind busy. That along with my shower porter job and rec five times a week, I keep active.

Your nemesis Ken's here. We don't speak. He's a fraud and a pooty-butt. But he's not in my building. That's good.

Hey, I was glad to read that you're safe and had a good homecoming with Mom and Pops. I'll bet baby sis is happy to have her wild and raving bro back. Send a picture or two of you and the folks if you can. Stay strong, my Limey friend. Let me hear back from you. I'm excited about your future. Give the folks my L&R and tell them to let up on your leash a bit at a time.

Get back with me mate,

Two Tonys

PS Oh yeah, you saw Norman Mailer passed, well fuck 'im. He talked shit about our boy Tom Wolfe, plus he never put a penny on Two Tonys books. Maybe he'll be my celly in hell. I'll give him the blues and assign him shitter cleaning duty 24/7. The fraud. And that goes for his author pal, Jimmy Breslin.

Hey, the godfather's son, Bill Bonanno, died. He was as full of shit as a Xmas turkey. He tried to write. Forget about it! He sucked. His only claim to fame was his daddy. I was present when some big shots talked shit about Bill. Plus he had me put in his work. He was ball-less. He's better off dead. At least the worms will appreciate his fat ass. Hey, I hope I don't sound bitter, but to be honest I'm just glad I outlived the bastards. Fuck 'em.

Hey bro, I don't want to get on a roll. I hope I haven't already.

Believe me, life is good. I'm as happy and content as can be expected. Humor helps a lot. I like to laugh, and I do every day. I'm 67 and healthy. This ain't a Russian gulag. So let the good times roll. Let's do this thing!

Hone your skills. You got good skills.

Mar 2008

Greetings & Salutations,

Forgive me for taking so long to answer your letter dated 2-10-08. What can I say? "I've been busy" or more like "I've been lazy." It's like this, did Michelangelo just pick up a brush on demand and start turning out masterpieces? Hell no!

I'm trying to slow down on my cursing and foul language. I can't explain why. I guess the only thing I can say is that it's the right thing to do. I mean I don't have the best vocabulary on the planet, but I know a few words. It's not like I'm a George Dubya Bush – a real giant of English verse. But I like to think that if fate should ever move its huge hand and you ever throw a cocktail party that I was invited to, I would not be an embarrassment to you with all your English friends. Do you know any dukes or earls? How about a baron or two? But I'd really prefer a countess or maybe a baroness. How's this sound: "I say there, my lady, may I get you another spot of tea or a glass of sherry?" I mean I wouldn't want to appear thuggish to your friends, if that situation should ever arise, which it won't. But I can dream, can't I?

Hey, bro, time to get serious. I've got some sad news for you. Your friend She-Ra cut off his nuts Friday afternoon. Yeah, I said cut off his nuts like in testicles. Poor guy. I can't help but feel bad for him. They choppered him out and he's in hospital as I write this. I'd seen him the day before and he seemed in good spirits. But you never know what currents run through a person's mind. Anyway, whatever, he dealt with it as the poets say "in his own fashion." But wow, I always thought I was a tough old bloke, but imagine cutting your own nuts off. Uh, no thanks. I'll pass on that one. Now I can see myself cutting off another guy's nuts, sort of as a payback for a personal affront. You know what I mean. But my own! Uh, I'll wait for the next bus, you go ahead, enjoy yourself. I don't mean to be cold, but I feel bad for him. I hope She-Ra's all right and he finds what he's looking for, which I gather is a vagina.

Ken finally left. He got picked up by California. They had some kind of beef on him. Probably smelling bike seats in front of the YMCA or some shit like that. Now he can go to those California yards and tell all those guys how he was a big man in AZ, "Running those yards." Yeah, right. I'll never forget the time I put him on his fat ass in front of the whole yard. I just got lucky, but sometimes even a blind hog will find a truffle. Hey, bro, I'm gonna miss him. Yeah, right, like a dose of syphilis. I'll always remember him walking around wiping his runny nose with the back of his hand then wanting to shake hands later or reach into your chip bag for a chip, catching attitude when told to fuck off. We never spoke for the last year. We just glared at each other. Those Calif guys will show him how the cow ate the cabbage once they figure out he's a fraud. OK, time out hating. You know me. I've really got a lot of love in my heart, just not for frauds.

Hey bro, how's the folks? Give them my love. Has your being back wore off yet? Do you have a job? A car? A girlfriend? These are things I want to know. "Why?" you ask. Because I have an inquiring mind. I'm sort of living vicariously through you. In fact as I pay my penance for past sins and a wayward life and I am scrubbing down the showers, I often stop and as I'm getting all the pubic hair out of the drains, I'll ask myself, I wonder what Shaun is up to now, and I'll picture you out in your English garden enjoying your tea and scones or a nice kidney pie as the hounds run by chasing the fox down.

OK, bro, keep in touch, and be pulling for Obama in the race. He's crooked as hell but they all are. He's one of those southside Chicago blacks, they ain't nothing nice. God bless 'em. Let those young blacks get an issue. It's Obama's turn to stick it to the great unwashed. His turn to piss on their heads and tell them it's raining. I'm sorry. Do I sound bitter? I'm really not. You know me. I'm just venting. I saw one of those so-called men of God the other night on TV. He was selling handkerchiefs anointed by God, and I thought of all the poor folks getting fleeced. Then I thought fuck 'em. If he don't get them then the plumber will or the insurance man or the doctor or the lawyer. Bottom line is this: there will always be an England and there will always be suckers.

Write me, ye bloody bloke, ye prince of the misty isles, you ex con from AZ.

Your pal,

Two Tonys

PS) Read *The Kite Runner*, really good, an 8½ to 9 out of 10. Khaled Hosseini wrote it. I'm reading *Oil!* by Upton Sinclair next, also a book called *Martha Peake* by Patrick McGrath, a Londoner. It's different. I'm enjoying it. You might like it.

You remain strong out there. No silly shit in your path.

Hey! Kudos to Bonnie Prince Harry. I like that kid. In fact he's my favorite royal. And he's got a good eye for the lassies. Yes, he does. Maybe he should be king. I guess I'm just a Britophile at heart. It's me Irish blood, I guess, me lad. Cheerio!

March 2008

Greetings & Salutations,

I received some good books from one of your Brit friends in London. He sent me some Poe, some *Into Thin Air*, and *Little Big Man*. All 3 seem interesting, but my point is that was nice of the bloke.

Everything around this place is just as fucked up as normal. You asked about my highs and lows of the week here. My high of the week is Thurs night, I phone my kid in Phoenix. I talk to my grandboys ages 10 and 2½, sometimes my son-in-law. And I enjoy that call. They visit and that's a lot of enjoyment. I love them all a lot. OK, that's enough. I'm getting melancholy. I can't afford to get melancholy in this shithole. A man has to stay strong.

Would Ivan Denisovich get melancholy? I don't think Two Tonys can afford it.

You asked for my favorite movie. There's a few. One is *Unforgiven* by Clint Eastwood. It was great. He was really fucked up. He did a lot of bad shit over the years. But in the end, when he pulled the plug and said fuck it, he really stepped up to the plate. *Cool Hand Luke* is a good watch. He was my idol. He just dealt with shit when it came his way. Also a movie called *Ryan's Daughter*. Rent it. It's good. This Irish guy is a rat and they blame his daughter and he lets her take the fall. It's a good flick. Check out the scene where the English officer is watching the sunset on the beach, missing the Irish girl. Like I said, it's good. I wouldn't steer you wrong. I'm the one who introduced you to Tom Wolfe when you were still reading Stephen King as you waited for your Big Mac and diet soda with fries. Besides, it's an English movie. Yeah, I said English. You guys do put on a much better flick than that Hollywood shit. Just look at *Masterpiece Theatre*. My favorite was *I, Claudius* (16 weeks long). I was on the streets and had just got in a predicament where I was hurt and had to heal up for a few months, so I discovered *Masterpiece Theatre*. It's the best. You mentioned Tom Wolfe. Fuck yeah, he's still my boy. If you run across a better author, please tell me.

If I could rewind any part of my life it would be a Saturday night in 1974, Anchorage, Alaska. It's Saturday. My rock 'n' roll club is packed. I've had a few drinks. I'm feeling good and I go in the back of the bar to my liquor room to get a bottle or two, and my bartender is snorting some coke. So he offers me some and I try it. Bang! I grow about 2 feet. I get a lot handsomer, wittier and wiser. I love it. Then a short time later it begins to fuck up my whole life. That's what I would rewind. Drugs, what a fuck-up they are. Look, I'm 67 years old now, and my daughter who I love more than anything in the world has two of the cutest boys I've seen. Now you know I'd like to pick them up and spend the weekend, but no, I'm doing this time. It's my fault, but it's still fucked up no matter how I try to sugar coat it with my PMA.

I've been in crime since I was a kid. It was a neighborhood thing, a peer thing. But this other shit. This so-called whacking thing. When the fuck did it show up? Sure we cracked a few heads and even broke a couple of arms, but this taking life thing started DD (During Drugs). Was it all business? No. Some was a get-even for a so-called affront to me. Yeah, I was a tough guy for 10 seconds and now I'm a shower porter and an asshole for 141 years. It not only changed my life, but many other things. Victims got Mom, Dad, kids, sisters, but they got in de bizness or fucked with the wrong people. It boils down to bad decision making on all sides. Drugs, yeah bro, I'd re-do that shit. I'd keep my mind wired on success. I don't want to sound like I'm snivelling because the world hates a sniveller. I'll do this time, or what I can do of it. But if I could rewind, as you call it, I'd rewind the fucking drugs. Don't fuck around, Shaun! But you know that, don't you?

Hey mate, do good and know I'm pulling for ya. But let it be known from the East End to the West End – you're my horse even if you never win a race.

Hey! I miss ya,
Two Tonys

Oct 2008

Hey friend,

I guess I owe you an explanation as to why I've been slow in getting back to you. The big one is that I'm going through a little bend in the river right now. Without going Dr Sanjay Gupta on you, here's what's up. I've been sick. It's a funny kind of sick. A few weeks ago I'm called to Medical for a blood test. 5 vials. Then a week or two later they did it again, but it was a retest. Then a few days later the Dr calls me up there and tells me I'm scheduled for a serious test at St Mary's, and the reason is my tests are off the chart with negative results for the big C. So I'm waiting to go.

Now it ain't no big fucking deal. But I just want a yea or nay so I can settle down. As soon as I can get some answers, you'll hear from me, and one way or another I'll settle in and get down to writing you more. I know you understand where my head is at, plus I'm not feeling real good.

Hey! Sorry I haven't written you more. But I'll make it up to you big time. We'll go where no man or woman has dared to go before. If God, Buddha, Muhammad, Fate or Mother Nature fucks with me, then it's on big time. In the words of that great sage George Dubya Bush, "Bring it on."

Thanks for the mail!

Stay strong,

Your pal,

Two Tonys

Jan 2009

Hey Shaun & The Blog Readers,

With all sincerity, I want to thank all of the bloggers who took the time to not only think of Two Tonys, but to sit down and throw an encouraging blog comment at him. It helped. That's no bullshit. I never expected that. Wow! Do I have that coming?

OK. Took some time off but I had to do some pondering. Here are a few things that I've been pondering. I'm on some serious meds. They're highly toxic. Real cell killers. Bad. But I'm told they'll kill a good cell if it interferes or tries to get in the way of a bad cell's mission. So I get sick, do some puke and bingo, I'm a new man.

I feel real good about the blog and all of the encouragement. I like you folks. I don't want no sympathy. Like I told a friend who comes by every day to give me that poor-old-Two-Tonys crap, "What can I do? What do you need?" I mean every day! Finally I told him, "Fuck all the bullshit! Talk shit to me! Try to pick a fight, but don't talk shit about my liver. I love my liver, and holes or no holes, don't fuck with it!" Now he's come undone. I've got some serious gold in my teeth. Now he's asking for my gold upon my demise. Fuck it! It's to the victor go the spoils. First there before the hearse driver gets what he can pry out. But I better be dead. Joke.

I'm sending you my Dr's report. They tell me this type of cancer is more common in Europe, Asia and Africa. I can't tell, but check it out and give me your thoughts.

Principal Diagnosis: Hepatocellular carcinoma

A CT scan revealed a moderate degree of hepatomegaly. A diffusely infiltrating mass was seen replacing the entire left lobe of the liver in both the medial and lateral segments. Patchy areas of hypervascular nodular enlargement were also seen through the right lobe of the liver, measuring from 3mm up to 12mm. An enhancing tumor thrombus extending into the left portal vein and into the right main portal vein were also noted. The radiological diagnosis was that of a diffuse infiltrative and multicentric hepatocellular carcinoma with portal invasion.

The patient entered the hospital for beginning treatment with sorafenib (Nexavar). At the time of discharge he is on 400 mg p.o. twice a day. Metoprolol will be added to his regimen of captopril and verapamil. It is important that he not miss any doses of sorafenib, as we would lose some ground in treatment.

Can anyone get me some info on this chemo drug they got me on called Nexavar? It's toxic as hell. This is not to cure me. It's just to try to stretch it out and get me a few more months. Dr said he gives me 90 days without it. Maybe 9 months to a year with it. So let's go for it! But I've got a feeling when it comes, it's going to come hard and fast.

When I said this thing I got ain't no thing. I lied. My machismo popped up. That was my tough guy talking. It is a thing. Those folks that wrote about me and it, I wish I could take them all out for a cold beer, ham sandwich and a game of pool. But the best I can do is say thanks. The nurses tell me the time will come when I'll have to make a choice between quality of life and quantity of life, referring to this chemo poison and my choice to continue. Well, a lot of folks just upped my quality of life. Thanks! When I read your comments, they almost brought a tear to my old red eyes, but I fought it off and it was hard. I tell myself tough guys don't cry, even when they're by themselves. But we all know that's bullshit. We all cry. But you must never cry about the hand you are dealt in the game of life, because like Ol' Blue Eyes sang, "That's life."

The last I checked we were all dying, so enough of the sad shit. It's back to Jon's Jail Journal. Back to adventures, and exploits. Let's go for shits and giggles and satire. You want me to keep writing, so let's go for it! Stay tuned.

Feb 2009

My daughter who's 100 miles north came with my son-in-law and my youngest grandson. The kid's 3 and wild and says I'm a monster and wants to throw rocks at me. He's a cutie, says what he wants and basically does what he wants. My daughter's coming back with her 12 year old. He doesn't know why I'm in this shithole, but he suspects. So I'm feeling I'm going to have to take him for a few laps and try my best to explain without fucking up his brain. He'll get several stories. I'm thinking it's best if I weigh in, leaving out all of the details. What do you think? I can't just go out there and say, "Oh yeah, kid, your ol' granddaddy snuffed a few motherfuckers along the way, but they all asked for it." I've got to figure this out or ponder it real good. Or should I just shut the fuck up?

Hey, what if when I get over to the other side and all those assholes I put down are waiting for me? Fuck 'em! I've got to have a few old pals over there. If not, fuck 'em. I'll just have to deal with them. What can they do, kill me?

Mar 2009

Greetings My Pal From The Misty Isles, The Land of Pendragon, Churchill, Sir Drake, The Great Monte Savior of the Free World, and Amy the Great. I'm talking Winehouse here. Not the Liverpool Winehouses, but the London Winehouses. Am I correct? I like Amy, and if I could get to London, I'd like to hang out with her. I'd straighten her out. Not in a mean way. But help her in a nice way.

It's 6:30 AM over here. I've been up since 3 AM doing the things we do. Clean my area. Straighten up. Do part of my store list.

I've got to go to pill call around 8 AM, and have them give me my chemo and pain pills. They look under my tongue. Degrading? Yes, but it's all part of my journey. Humbleness and degradation has a big part.

Now that doesn't mean I just pull the plug. You know, I go to pill call twice a day, and there are around 40–50 guys that all get turned out at the same time, and stand in a long line while each guy gets his pills and goes through the same ritual. "Tongue up! Show the sides of your cheeks!" Now I've got a buddy here who goes with me to get his issue also. He's cool. He's one of those Italian Stallions out of Phoenix. We try our best to enjoy our trip. We laugh at some of these phoney motherfuckers, who, on the walk up there start grunting, groaning, baby-stepping along. And if they catch someone checking them out, it's even worse. They really turn it on. Oh poor me. Poor me. I'm sick. I'm sick. Pity me. Now that kind of shit gives me strength to climb my mountain. And I enjoy that. Look, if we're climbing a mountain and we're all hooked on a line, we don't want 3 or 4 weak-asses who cry, snivel and gripe all the way.

Look, I've received a lot of our blog buddies' comments telling me to fight the fight. I feel that everyone is sincere and considerate. So this is what I'm up to. My goal is not really to find a cure for this bullshit. I guess I just want to show my old ass off and try my best to go out, not complaining or snivelling, but as the man I think I am. We discussed pain and suffering before. Yeah! I copped to being scared of it. But after researching it, pondering on it real hard, I come to the finding that it's there, but we have to fight to endure it. Where is it? It's in the mind. Pain is just lying there waiting to stick its head up and root in self-pity, weakness, unknowing.

The worst of cancer is the actual physical pain itself. It is the motherfucker who separates the strong from the weak. Was Hemingway weak when he crawled down in that basement in Ketchum, Idaho, and ate the end of that 12-gauge? I think he just pondered what lay ahead and the rough tough guy he was, he said, "Fuck it!"

I get a lot of mail from family and friends saying that a time will come when quantity of life will take a back seat to quality. I'm pondering the truth to that. I sure as fuck ain't got no quality in this shithole. It don't exist in this camp (the worst I've seen). So fuck it.

We could stay up all night and debate is there a heaven or hell. We just got to wait and see. It would be great if I could have a road-to-Damascus epiphany like Saul of Tarsus did. But I haven't. I guess at times, I try to hedge my bets. But that's normal. Don't you think?

Good luck with your adventure in the Big Smoke. I am really happy for you, and I do believe in you. You're unique and have a clear-headedness to go with that when you use it. Everybody you speak to in the schools won't understand you, so fuck 'em. But you've got a real chance to help some youngsters have a life, so get out there and do it. You're going to be great. I believe that.

Hey bro, watch that nightlife. It will come up and bite you right on your red ass. But you know that, don't you? I believe you when you tell me you've got a plan and you intend to work it. But to quote: The best-laid plans of mice and men often go awry. Put yourself on a short leash. I know you will. Big cities eat people up, but you get in there and do what you've gotta do. Chris in Phoenix had a good comment on your manic side kicking in and trying to fuck up your plan. Be on guard.

I'd like to thank you sincerely on your choice of books. I'm just getting into *Shantaram* and *The Shack*.

Hey, permit me one more shout out to all our friends who emailed nice thoughts and prayers to me. It's really pepped me up. So thanks friends! Like I tell my pals out on the yard who wanted to mollycoddle me (but I put a stop to that shit), I'll deal with this bastard as best as I can. No baby-stepping, hunched-over lifestyle for me. This is my fight. I appreciate the written words from our pals, and I feel like we're all in our own way pals. I will keep you all posted on my condition, and it will be my adventure. I don't plan on doing a Hemingway. Your comments help me, and I appreciate them.

Two Tonys

Mar 2009

How deep I can write now that I'm facing death is up in the air. It's like that killer broad, Barbara "Bloody Babs" Graham, first woman to be gassed in California's death row. The hacks strapping her into the chair told her, "Don't worry. You won't feel a thing." She replied, "How the fuck would you know?" Yeah, I can't help but agree.

A blog reader, Cat Eyes, wrote to me:

I don't know what to say except isn't death a mandatory part of life? I've never been confronted by my own death, only life so far and can't imagine what you are feeling, perhaps you might see it as an exit … you are after all getting out of prison, just not the way you would have hoped. As we say in French when someone is going on a trip … Bon voyage. Make it a good one. I enjoyed discovering your character in Shaun's written words. These I suspect will be the most difficult yet fulfilling last months of your life because you are high on emotion. Be well. Love Cat Eyes

I responded:

Cat Eyes, I agree death is a part of life, and perhaps if I were sitting in a nice house watching grandchildren play, or in a mansion waiting for my young trophy wife to come down the stairs, so we can get in the Lamborghini to go to dinner, sure I'd worry about death, and who she will be loving after my death. But this old life I'm in is nothing like that.

To be real honest with you, the dying is not scary, it's the suffering and pain of dying that worries me. I guess I'm a coward along those lines. Those whose lives I had to take went fast, adrenaline was flowing, survival value was full-tilt boogie. They died in seconds. Now how long is a second? If you're walking along the beach at sunset with Heidi Klum a second is over fast. But if your balls are on a hot grill, a second is a lifetime. We'll find out as this thing in me progresses.

Gareth wrote:

Hey Two Tonys, I do wish you all the best in dealing with this bend in the river. You are clearly a man of strong character and ideals – whilst some would argue that, I believe you believed in everything you were doing in your past – we all choose our own world to live in and yours, whilst not aligned to mine, was your choice.

I responded:

Thanks for the good wishes and the undeserved character ideals I seem to possess. I modestly agree with you on my character. I'll put it up with anybody's on a level playing field, all things considered. I made a lot of wrong decisions, some resulting in death for others. But as I always said, even before *Chicago*, they had it coming. We were all players in the game. And I'd be lying if I said I didn't enjoy it. Excitement galore. My ideals were not up to standing a lot of times as I look back on my life, but I do say people enjoyed my company. Many were apprehensive. Some just wanted to hang around for a few days, months or years. But it was my life. I was a junkie for fun and excitement. I guess I still am. But I don't see too much of that stuff in my future.

Leigh wrote:

I wish you the best Two Tonys! Cancer is a tough battle but then I would say you're no stranger to tough. I hope you'll show them all and pull through.

I responded:

Yeah, I think I'm as tough as the next guy, but this cancer is going to be tougher and will win. What choice do I have other than to develop a fuck-it-c'mon attitude? I hope I can hold on to it when the shit hits the fan. I like to think modern medicine will give me a hand. But it's true, I'm scared, Leigh.

May 2009

Shaun, My main guy, Jim Hogg, a 280 lb hunk of rock some refer to as Rolling Thunder. Well, he's always looked out for me in here. When I came back from the hospital, he met me at the gate and told me I've been moved to his pod. He is right across from me and he is godsent. He does so much for me, I feel both guilty and old. He's my big-headed boy, and I got big-time love for him. But he goes home soon and I'll miss him a lot.

You know, as screwed up as my life has been, I'm fortunate with friends who actually want to look out for me. There's a group of good solid nasty white boys I've known for quite a while who came to me and wanted me to move to their pod. Jim Hogg was with me, and told them I'm staying with him till he leaves. They put up an argument, but to no avail.

Hey! What can I say? Good guys all of them. Maybe society doesn't care for them and probably with their own good reasons. But these are my people, and everyone knows it. I earned their respect and love not by being here, but by my conduct.

And while I don't want to make this the T.T. loves T.T. blog,

I've done some reflecting and pondering of my life's journey. And as fucked up as it is now, there's poor souls out there in the same boat as me who have worked, paid bills, raised families, went to church … but are lonely and don't have nowhere near the love and moral support I'm getting. As I reflect on this life, I realise, yes, I've taken guys out and they didn't get 6-7-8 months to reflect on their fucked-up deeds. It was 1-2-3 – see ya – *bam!* – it's over.

OK, moving on. If you remember my BW and Roy story, I've done that several times. Interfered in hits when possible or when I thought they were out of line. From prison yards to gangster business. I saved a few lives. Pulling a 3 year old from a ranch well and assisting in his resuscitation. That's like saving a life. A life of a child, that's a good life. I don't want a medal or any of that shit. What's funny about the kid and the well is that his mom made me a whole chocolate pie, my favorite, the next day. But within 3 months, the kid's old man is putting out word he's going to blow my head off if I step on ranch property.

When I get up and read these blog comments from Ghost, Jose in San Diego, Jayne, Barry from up there in Tonopah, Will, your mom and dad, Geoff, Big W, Cindy, Sue O, August, Hammy, all of these folks have inspired me with good advice, strong-hearted advice, fuck-the-odds advice, and I don't know what to say.

I don't consider myself a religious man. I'd like to have that blind faith that's in songs, written in books, shouted about on street corners. But I can't honestly say, "Oh yeah!" I've lived this life of robbing, stealing, killing, and now as the moment nears, I can't jump up and say, "OK. Forgive me. Sorry about all the sadness I caused families. I'm now a good Christian." I'm having trouble in my mind with that. Sure I can say it.

You know, since word hit the yard I'm on my last legs or soon will be, I've had at least 5 inmates come up to me. 2 gave me books on Jesus and 1 on Jehovah. One had his people send me a student bible to study. Their thoughts are nice.

Now these ain't pooty-butt guys. They're guys you would get scared about if you run into them in an alley. They're not chomos or rapos. They're guys, I guess you would say, who're all looking for change and answers. I'm not rude. I take their books out of politeness. But to be honest, I haven't cracked one of them open.

I told the oncologist last week as we met over the TV-set hook up, "Hey, Doc, let's keep it on the up and up here. I'm not afraid of death. In fact I'm trying to look at it as a possible new journey." I told the Dr what I fear is the pain. He told me they can and will handle the pain. We'll see. Don't let this thing I got make your heart sad. I sort of deserve a little ass-kicking.

C'mon, let's get back to having fun at the blog. What do you want to kick around? War? Politics? The Mafia? Prison?

Shaun, I'm really happy with your progress. Now get to work.

L&R,

Two Tonys

ps) Jim Hogg wants to write to you. I'm worried about him and his release. But what the fuck? Look at the adventure. This place becomes a nest and some of these guys are like baby birds. My advice: Fly, motherfucker, fly.

Oct 2009

Hey Shaun,

What can I say? Let me start with I'm sorry I haven't written to you sooner. Now let's move on with an update on my condition. Obviously I'm still kicking and fighting this cancer. I had a real bad time a while back with that chemo and shit. It's a bad motherfucker. But I didn't lay down on it. I'm still battling. Like your Liverpool lads sang, "I get by with a little help from my friends." And you're one of them.

I received all your mail and always intended to answer, but I'm whacked-out on morphine, so let me try to make up for it. I'm glad to see you are moving up in the literary world. I knew you would as long as you kept your head and heart on the prize. This is good. I'm proud of you.

Hey mate, our friend, Frankie and me kick it a lot. You're with us and it's all good positive rap. No bad shit do I allow to come to me. I've got PMA, and this is 10 months I've been in the fight, which was supposed to be over 6 months in. I know I can't cure this, but I can do my best to hang out. I don't want to make this a snivel letter. Me and Frankie will keep in touch. No more long spells of silence. I'm sure up about my dog Frankie being here. I catch him trying to baby me like I'm an old broke-dick cancer patient. Well, he's right on one of them. 1 out of 2 ain't bad. I check him. I tell him I'll kick his ass if he keeps it up. He's to treat me as always. No pity. No empathy, or any of that bullshit. Yeah, mate, I've got good memories of you. You came along and enriched my fucked-up life. I'm grateful for that. I'll write you more because I seem to be doing a lot better.

Hey bro, I've got this funny feeling I'm holding this cancer at bay by keeping my spirit up and not giving up. There's something to that. I visit my Dr for the big C in December. I'll keep you posted.

So allow me to give a big shout out to you, your fam, and all of our blog readers who thought to give an old fuck such as me a nice thought and a prayer.

I quit the chemo, bro. It was too much of a robber on quality days. I'd rather have quality than quantity. The Grim Reaper ain't shit. Good friends and good thoughts and memories along with a few prayers, and who knows, shit does happen.

I haven't been reading too much. But I get this magazine, *Vanity Fair*. My kid sends it to me. I told her, "Hey! That's a broad's mag." She laughs and tells me a lot of men read it. So I don't give a fuck. If my kid wants me to read it, I read it. Now I'm enjoying it. Good articles.

Her and my grand babies are doing good. She's got a good solid decent old man, and I'll die happy and relieved because they're all good and safe.

Hey, I'll cut this short. You give my Love & Respect to Mom, Pops and baby sis, and keep a big slice for yourself, me lad from over the pond. I'll write more next time.

You stay strong and healthy.

Two Tonys

Mar 2010

Hey English Cuz,

What can I say? "I'm sorry" has to be getting old to you, so I won't even go there. I've been getting your mail, books, plus good moral-support letters.

First, allow me to write you with congratulations on your good turn of events in your literary career. This is great. No one can say that you don't deserve this. I personally observed your hours and days working in your cage of a cell while many around you were busy whacking their puds or spreading drama with a mix of hate and envy. You were busy hunched over at your little metal slab of a desk in a heat-infested cell working your bald head off, with your eyes on the prize and the spoils that come with it. Cocktail parties. Limos. European baronesses, countesses. Dare we even dream of the ultimate? Tea with Her Majesty! Yes, we do dare to. This is how railroads, tunnels, Great Walls of China are built: with one man's dream. Yes, my friend, dream on. Don't let it die. I'll bet on you every time your name's on the card. "You go, Limey boy, you go." Please keep me posted, and I'll start to keep up on my writing. I was just down, bro. But I've got some real good news at this end for me to share with you and our blog readers.

As you might be aware, I was told in December 08, I had terminal cancer and given an estimate of 3–6 months to live. This was done by a civilian oncologist who was 90 fucking years old, and under an advisory position contract with the Department of Corrections. I was issued chemo, which I knew from my 9th grade education was a killer worse than cancer. Anyway, I quit the chemo, and I truly believe that's why I'm still alive. This Dr didn't want me to quit, and told me if I did I had 90 days to live. Fuck it! I told him 90 days without that shit is better than a year on it. I quit, and I'm still standing. I went from 200 lbs to 140 lbs, but I'm feeling great.

Now in over a year as his patient, I saw the guy once in person. That was at a hospital back in 2008. The rest of my so-called exams were from a matchbox office on prison grounds staring into a 16"

TV screen with a nurse next to me to poke where the good Dr told her to. Now don't get me wrong, I'm grateful for any help I get, and the truth is after my wicked past, any help is probably too much, but I'll still take it. So now I'm on this morphine twice a day, and I stay doped up. It's a good pain fighter and seems to do the job (for now).

About 2 months ago, my Dr, the old man, along with St Mary's Hospital, had their contracts not renewed, and I got moved down here to Lewis Complex. You know the place we met, when I came out of the hole to a rock-star greeting, and you were mesmerized by my welcoming committee.

Getting back to the story I started. So now I have no oncologist, even though I didn't really have one back then. The old Dr was just pissing on my head, laddie, telling me it was drops from a soft summer rain. So I'm up here in Lewis, and early one morning they come and chain me up, put me in the back of a new Ford with two guards, and tell me I'm gonna see a doctor. They drive me in style, radio playing, comfortable back seat, good scenery. I'm doing it. We pull up to a new building in Casa Grande about 100 miles from here. It's a medical lab, 21st century, and it is modern. The three of us are shown an exam room, and after ten minutes a nice Asian Dr comes and introduces himself to me, shakes my hand and examines me as best he could. Then he proceeds to explain to me that we're all different. The old Dr should never have told me that shit at any rate. He ordered all new blood work. Cat scans. Etc. He explained that they were now under contract with DOC, and he's my oncologist. This is great. He explained that after my new tests are complete, him and the surgeons will discuss the results, and they may do a treatment called T.A.C.E. It stands for Transcatheter Arterial Chemoembolization. They run a tube up through my thigh to my liver, pump chemo, then take the tube out. Bingo, lots of bad cancer cells die and perhaps I live a little longer. Time will tell. I'll be sure to keep you posted. I'm so excited.

I imagine a lot of people wonder why I'd want to go on living in here. Why the fuck not? I've quoted Shakespeare many times to the effect of, "A wall does not prison make. It's all in the fucking mind."

Love to you and your family and all good blokes and birds across the seas.

Two Tonys

Apr 2010

Hey! It's me. Guess what? I fell off the john two nights ago. My pals got help for me. Bottom line is I've been moved up to a medical complex, a big building. It seems they have a wing of cells here for blokes such as I. I'm speaking medical talk. They're doing things to me but not too much. I don't know, bro. This could be the end of the road for me. Time will tell. They're talking a lot of making-me-more-comfortable shit, but that's OK with me. I've got my own room, TV, remote, change of diet, change of meds, more nurses on demand. I'm messed up now as I write. I would and should have wrote you more, but I was lazy. You're in my thoughts and prayers.

Good news on your school speeches and come up in the writing world. Know this, you're a damn good man, and you've enriched my life and soul. Knowing you, I can feel your love and friendship even as I sit here waiting for my number to come up.

Hey, bro. I'm short on stamps till store day, so until then I'll cut this off. I've got a few blogs left as soon as I get a little more energy. My daughter will get in touch if my number comes up, so you can have a pint on my sorry old ass.

L&R,

Two Tonys

May 2010

I'm still in the medical complex, but this is all up in the air. What makes me suspicious is they're treating me too nice. (We'll see.)

They might send me back to a yard or keep me here. I can't get to the decision maker.

Hey, I'm real proud of you. Not only as a true friend, but also for your achievements. I know you'll keep it up and the sky's the limit. Maybe you'll even make it to *Larry King Live*. Pond to pond of course. All I ask is as you struggle on, stop and give me a good thought. Now get your bald ass in there and get on with it.

L&R from over the Atlantic!

Two Tonys

CHAPTER 21

I lean towards the theory that it's in the nature of humans to kill each other. History is replete with civilisations fucking over people lighter, darker, taller, fatter or skinnier than them. From Hitler gassing the Jews and slaughtering over ten million Russians – and look what that got the Nazis: chomping down on cyanide caps – to the Aztecs sawing open chests, plucking out beating hearts, and beheading women while they danced to the mother goddess before flaying them, wearing their skins and selling their remains to the meat market.

Yes, more people are killed when there are warlike leaders like Hitler, but there have been societies of warlike people, too. Take the Mongols and Huns riding across Poland, where some peasant motherfucker is getting water from a well. The next thing he knows, he's thrown across a saddle horse, taken to a hut, sold to someone, and ends up in a town with a name like Tosokh, where he's somebody's wife for the next seven years and all he's fed is warm mare's milk. If you don't call that warlike, then what the fuck do you call it?

In the modern world, people kill each other over the colours they're wearing – Bloods versus Crips – and the all-time favourite, religion – Sunnis versus Shias, Catholics versus Protestants … More Germans died in the Thirty Years' War over religion than in both World Wars. It's just like being caught up in the war between the Gambino and Bonanno crime families. It's fucked up, but it's not new. We're always gonna be killing each other. Religion is just as good an excuse as a pound of cocaine. It's all killing. If you read scripture, who killed more than God, Yahweh or Jehovah? Nobody. If you choose to buy into that program, then you believe he killed a lot of fools.

Most people claim to believe in God, heaven and hell, but they don't want to die right away to go to heaven. They'll fight to live under severe conditions 'cause they're half-assed atheists. They don't want to be, but they are. They're unsure about the other side. Their minds have been polluted over centuries by child-molesting popes, whore-mongering kings ... They want to believe death brings mansions of gold, the reuniting of loved ones and orgies with virgins. But are they sure? The exception is those extremists who do a hell of a job on their suicide nutcases. They've really got them stuck on stupid. At least the Christian preachers just want your life savings. The clerics in some of those madrasas want your guts on a wall. Wow!

The sicko who tried to help sickos, Freud, said people who follow religion are nuts, which may be the case for suicide bombers, but his theory doesn't apply to most people. People follow leaders. People are afraid not to be religious, and it seems the right thing to do when everybody else is claiming to believe. It filters right on down to employment advancement, even marriage and acceptance in friends. People go along to get along. They play the role, especially the presidential candidates. Do you really think that one of them would stand up on TV and give his or her true thoughts on God, Jesus Christ or religion in general? Hell no. She or he would never last. Plato said no one has ever died an atheist. I say that was bullshit back then and ever since. Marx, Stalin, Van Gogh, Carl Sagan, plus all the rest.

I read about Martin Luther the German friar, Ulrich Zwingli and of course the great founder of the Church of England and serial killer of wives, Henry VIII. The great unwashed bought into their bullshit, just like they lapped it up from those Medici and Borgia popes. Jesus wasn't joking when he said people are sheep. It's scary. These days, the media feed the unwashed whatever they want them to believe. People's minds are so full up with shit like Britney getting her head shaved that they don't even know when they go through airport security that their kids are getting checked out by some child-groper working for four dollars an hour with an X-ray machine that tells him what you had for supper, how digested it fucking is, how many green beans are in your colon, how many wires are in your bra, how many pubic hairs you've got and whether you've got crabs.

Look how many people were killed by the Spanish Inquisition, who used a metal-cap device to slowly crush your skull, which popped your eyeballs out and shattered your teeth before you died, and look at how many women were tortured and killed for witchcraft. The Bishop of Würzburg alone had 9,000 women burned. Black-robed priests used red-hot pincers to tear off breasts. Some were hung upside down and sawn in half. All in the name of religion.

Jesus didn't torture women. He seemed to be a smart man with a lot of mojo, some good, some questionable. Was he a prophet? The son of God? Did he rise from death? Or was that all PR for the industry built on the back of him? He didn't write anything down, did he? We only read what hustlers wrote. He had all these mooches hanging on him: the so-called Twelve Apostles plus more. Scammers like Peter and Paul went all over the Mediterranean cashing in on JC's crucifixion. Do we believe them? At one time in our lives, we all doubt their sincerity, honesty and motives. Anyone who says they don't is lying. That goes from the pope to the cab driver. The hustlers kept JC alive, so they didn't have to plough the fields or lift. Same goes for the pope. Who has the answers? Billy Graham? Jimmy Swaggart? Hustlers, all of them.

Even though I don't know a lot about her, I do think Mother Teresa was on the right track. But throughout history, those Catholics have been a brainwashing bunch. Look at the House of Medici. A ruthless bunch with their hands out in the name of Jesus Christ. That's how they got the mooches' change and they wanted you to kiss their ring. Think about it. The last good thing a pope did was to help bring down the Soviet Union with his undercover work, his behind-the-scenes trips to Poland meeting the founder of Solidarity, Lech Wałęsa. Now the pope's an old fraudulent motherfucker. What kind of sick fuck covers up for child molesters, moving them around parishes or countries, where they can molest more children when they should be coming to prison to get shanked in the stomach and their dicks cut off? All I know for sure about heaven is that child-molesting priests don't go there.

The four Christian gospels – the word of God, yeah right – all seem to run with the same theme. Do what we say. Believe as we believe. Don't question or doubt what we say, and if you do so we'll give you eternal life in a heaven of gold and mansions. Not a bad deal. Oh, one more thing, we're not gonna work, plough fields, fish, hunt, cut trees, so you folks all chip in and feed us, clothe us, provide our housing and put us on a pedestal above you common mooches 'cause we know things about heaven and how to get there. Trust us, but here's the catch: if you don't do any of these things we ask, then you're going to burn in a fire pit forever. That's basically the message. These guys, just like everybody, had to justify their existence. A dinosaur hunter has to find a bone every now and then or how else will he receive funding for his next project. If not, he might have to lift or plough as the great unwashed do. It's all hustle.

Somewhere along the way religion became a money scam. A farmer ploughing the field got sick of looking at a mule's ass, so he put a robe on and walked around all day, and people came to him for advice and brought him his daily bread. He thought, *Fuck, this is an easy ride!* and he snatched and molested a kid every now and then. Religion became chomos on pedestals telling people to give them their money 'cause God has reserved them a place in the sky.

Imagine God in the sky looking down, and you're looking up, asking him to forgive you 'cause you sinned. A few billion people all asking for forgiveness to some eye in the sky. Instead of religion, it should be called control. What controls you? The Catholic Church. Protestant. Moslem. Jewish. Buddhist. It's all about control. Look, I know when I do wrong. I think about it and I have a little talk with myself. I've felt worse about the attitude I've had towards friends and loved ones than shmucks I've whacked or mooches I've robbed. I'm Arizona Department of Corrections controlled, but physically only, not in mind. I sure as fuck ain't asking them for forgiveness or Jesus Christ, Muhammad, Billy Graham, the Nazi pope, the Dalai Lama or the judge. Well, maybe the judge. That's who a motherfucker should pay homage to and pray to is the judge, but only before sentencing 'cause the judge is a fool that can really forgive you of your sins. All the rest are a joke.

Look how far humankind has progressed. Walking on the moon. Computers. Planes and trains. Medicine. Cloning. Transplants. Now think about some Greek or Roman or Egyptian thousands of years ago, standing in his temple, burning incense or slaughtering his bull while he asks for his prayers or sins to be granted or forgiven by some horned God or some dude living up on Mount Olympus. Now here we are thousands of years later and we've still got mooches getting down and praying for rain for a good crop or to win the lottery or not to get AIDS. It's control. If you're Church of England, King Henry VIII would be real proud of his control over you 500 years later. The great fornicator was a good one to start a religion. He was like all the rest who want control.

Perhaps it's best that I don't believe that there is life after death, otherwise I'd be burning in a fire pit for all eternity 'cause of my crimes. The religions of all ancient civilisations offered a carrot and stick. The Babylonians. The Greeks. The Egyptians. Hittites. Just to name a few. The deal closer was always eternal life in the other world. Throughout nearly all of these religions, there was always a son of God who happened to come back to life after death. No, I don't believe in miracles. Do you? If you do, let me ask you a question. Have you ever seen a miracle? Exactly. I rest my fucking case. That shit – Jesus walking on the water, Noah putting two of everything on the fucking ark, God impregnating Mary by Immaculate Conception – was crammed down my throat as a kid at Sunday school.

The eternal-life message appealed to kings and rulers, who told the mooches whatever bullshit they wanted to hear to keep them under control. If you and I were leading 100,000 or more through the Sinai Desert with people warring all around us, we'd come up with a few rules and beliefs like don't shit too close to camp, don't fuck the goats, don't steal your neighbours' barley and let's all worship the same deity. And while we're at it, let's cajole that first generation into teaching their offspring to believe. Once we get our people through the desert, and we're safely in our castle, we don't want the people living outside of our walls to be heathen barbarians plotting to rape our ol' ladies and steal our booty. We want nice motherfuckers who go to church and pray and not to think about jacking all the money we fleeced from them. They can all get brainwashed by child-molesting priests.

China's got Buddha. India's got cows. Moslems have Muhammad. Japs have Shinto. We've got Jesus Christ. There are so many forms of religion and selections or choices, people choose one that fits their fancy. Catholic. Methodist. Church of England. Mormon. I could go on and on. The masses are weak for religion 'cause they're afraid of death. Believing in the hereafter justifies their mooch existence. I'm talking about the kind of dumb motherfuckers whose only care in the world is when *The Simpsons* comes on. And God bless them, even though they elected George Dubya Bush and consistently put cocksuckers like him in power, who throw that Christian shit at us, while sending young guys to kill and die and get their noses and schlongs blown off in Iraq, slaughtering women and kids in the name of democracy and Christianity when it's really in the name of fucking money and oil. I don't see the brotherly love taught by Jesus Christ in Bush's eyes. I see incestuously fucked-up genes. If we got on a bus in downtown LA, ninety per cent of the people on board would know the latest Angelina Jolie drama, but have no fucking clue about how much Halliburton and the Carlyle Group are making from genocide in the Middle East.

The mooches I've referred to so far should not be confused

with the stupid motherfuckers on this planet who you could put in a pool of pig-shit, give them some rice and they'd still find something to laugh and joke about. Actually, I like to think I'm one of them: having the time of my life stuck in a bucket of crap right up to my neck.

The positive bottom line of religion is that Buddha, Confucius, Jesus Christ and Muhammad all basically taught that if you treat the person next to you like you wanna be treated, you can be all right in this fucking world. If I'd done that over my life, I wouldn't be where I am today. Now that might sound strange coming from a thief, robber, hustler, kidnapper, multiple-homicide motherfucker like myself, but I've got a soft side. I've never beat a kid. Even though I don't believe in life after death, a part of me likes to believe in my heart that there's something more to life. But how the fuck can anyone alive answer that? Billy Graham can't answer that. Tammy Faye Bakker – the old mascara-eyed crook who was always crying on *Larry King Live* and got busted for a religious scam ripping off old people's money – sure as hell can't answer that.

Here's how I look at life after death: if I go to New York City and tear down the Empire State Building, the concrete, wood, marble and shit will continue on as atoms. One of my favourite quotes is by Melissus of Samos: whatever was, always was and always will be.

I don't think that death is the goal of life, especially if it's to reach the other side. We all struggle to stay alive. Simply put, I think death is a destination more than the goal. But also, at times, death is welcome, which is something I contemplate as I endure the pain of cancer.

CHAPTER 22

What the fuck's up with these dudes that go and climb Mount Everest? Let's take a look at that. Number one, they've got big fucking dollars. It takes more than chump change. They've gotta get their gear, airfare and travel expenses. They've gotta hire a guide, Sherpas, oxygen tanks and tents. They've gotta take time off their hustle. The cost has to be well over one-hundred grand. But that probably ain't shit to most of those fools.

Here's what I don't get, but I'm starting to focus in on. Me and you – let's say – are a couple of silver spoons, and one of us says, "Hey, I've got an idea. Let's go to the most inhospitable environment on the planet. A place where it's below freezing. Where nothing can grow. Where the wind's blowing gale force. Where the slope is almost straight up. Where we can't breathe without oxygen tanks on our backs. Where just the act of putting one foot in front of the other is pain. Where we'll sleep in a little tent and heat our Meals, Ready-to-Eat on butane burners. Where we'll suffer for days – but when we come back and belly up to the bar we can say we did it. No, it's not Monte Carlo or Cancún or the South of France for us. We're gonna suffer and have fun doing it."

Now I ask: where the fuck is the fun in that? Does that sound like fun to you? That wouldn't be fun to me. Doesn't that then mean that the fun is in their minds?

It's like the great Bard said, "There is no happiness, no sadness." They do not exist. It's in their minds. Their minds tell them they're on an adventure. A challenge. A struggle. That's their reward. And while they're psyched up like that they're free of those fucking prisons called conditioned minds.

Now I ask you: can a person who's just been diagnosed with cancer develop the same frame of mind? Or a person who's just been given a life sentence or two? Or sent to the hole to suffer with no books, TV, radio, visits, coffee? I think they can and some do. They know pain is coming, but they feel a sense of reward by enduring the pain.

Now this train of thought opens up a whole bunch of shit – from suicide bombers to organ donors. Criminals. Heroes. It's a line of thought that sort of mystifies me.

Look at O.J. Simpson. He's so rich in material, yet so poor in brain thought. He'll be out on parole in six years or even earlier if he kicks down some baksheesh to the right appeals-court judge. How do you think he feels now on his little journey, which is a slam dunk for guys like me?

I like to think I'm strong in mind. That I could take a dose of Abu Ghraib or the Guantánamo Bay prison – just to see what's up. But I don't know about that waterboarding shit or hanging by the thumbs. To endure that you have to be committed real strong to what you're into.

But imagine what a trip to endure that adventure, that challenge, that suffering to climb Everest. That would be strong and rewarding – for some people.

Back in 1989, I did a piece of work, a drug robbery. I took my profit and went to Detroit for a few months, you know, to allow things to settle down, to allow the guy's hurt feelings to subside from the I'll-get-even shit.

In Detroit, I went to a wedding reception of an old pal. A big hall. A sit-down dinner. Wine. Champagne. A band playing. Bridesmaids. Ushers. Lots of showy dresses and tuxedos. I saw a lot of guys I grew up with, neighbourhood guys, some close, some not so close, but still pals. I spotted a guy I remembered, Ronnie. He looked good. We were both about the same age: forty-eight. We bullshitted for a little while. He was in real estate doing well. He was legit, normal, classy, a really good-looking guy as he was when we were kids. He always had good manners and style. I said to myself, *What a lucky guy. He does what he does. I do what I do. That's that.*

After saying goodbye to Ronnie, he never came up in my mind until 1993. I was in my cell in scumbag Sheriff Joe Arpaio's jail, and the guy next to me brought a *Time* magazine. I was flipping through it, and guess whose mug was looking out at me on one of those pages with his name in a caption below it? Not one photo but two: before and after shots. The before was a shot that appeared to be taken around the time I crossed paths with Ronnie at the wedding reception. It was a head shot with him wearing a blue tuxedo. He looked good, handsome, the kind of guy you'd want your sis to go out with. The other shot showed him bald, skinny, face sunken in. It didn't even look like him.

Now, why was he in the mag? The article was about Dr Jack Kevorkian a.k.a. Dr Death, who'd just helped kill Ronnie by assisting his suicide. They'd interviewed the doctor and some of Ronnie's friends. They all said he'd wanted it that way. That he was in too much pain to endure life. Up in Arpaio's jail, I thought, *Here's a guy who less than four years ago I envied for his life. Now look what's transpired.*

My point is: life is one of those things you can enjoy while you have it regardless of whether you're struggling to put one foot in front of the other in a snowstorm on Mount Everest or lying on a bed with tubes in your nose in a hospital with cancer or lying on a cell floor reading a *Time* mag or even hanging from a waterboard in Gitmo – you can be one bad motherfucker and that's your reward. Doing it.

We've all got our own Mount Everests to climb. I guess some are just higher than others depending on our states of mind.

O.J.'s mountain is just a little old hill to me. But not to him. To him it's almost unclimbable. And therein lies the meat of the whole thing. It's all in the mind of the beholder.

Advice from an old lifer who was a tough guy for twenty seconds and an asshole for 141 years. Life ain't no thing, but a chicken wing. It's ephemeral. So never give up. Attitude is everything. Let's do it. When life throws some shit on your shoes, get a stick, clean it off, deal with it. Yes, life has hard spots, but if you accept life with a fuck it, you can deal with things better than if you expect it to be a big ol' stroll across Waikiki Beach.

Disappointments: expect them 'cause they will come. Difficult tasks like climbing Everest are good to attempt even if you don't achieve them 'cause they build character. Living through life's bullshit can be rewarding. Divorce. Death of a loved one. Fired from a job. A buddy fucking your ol' lady. A baby's first words or steps. A killing. A loving. A bankroll. An ass-whupping. They're all life. A monk living frugally is deprived of living and tasting the things I believe build character. To lock yourself up in a cell until you die, having never tasted life's ups and downs, well, what the fuck's that all about? *Oh, I am a monk. I can do this.* Hell no!

Let's make the most of life 'cause sooner or later we're all gonna die. You can't learn that in a book. You have to learn that – mistakes and all – by living. And never forget in the turmoil of life's struggles, it's good to stop and smell the roses – or in some cases, the jailhouse aftershave.

Life is a book we live. My book was good. You're holding it in your hands. I tasted it all. Good and bad.

Death is a part of life. They go together like pork chops and apple sauce. True believers in the Pearly Gates can't wait to die.

Don't mourn for me 'cause I've lived a life.

EPILOGUE BY
SHAUN ATTWOOD

In September 2010, Two Tonys' daughter emailed:

Just wanted to let you know that my dad passed away last night. I received a call from the chaplain this morning. I visited him last Sunday in Tucson, he was really sick. He had gotten pneumonia a couple of weeks ago, and really never recovered from it. When I saw him, he couldn't speak and didn't make much sense. I am convinced he is much better off now. That medical unit in Tucson is miserable, and he always feared spending his last days suffering there. Thank God he was only there for less than a week. Thanks so much for being a great friend to him. I know they are hard to come by in there.

You can read more about Two Tonys in Prison Time which is available worldwide on Amazon

GET A FREE BOOK:

JOIN SHAUN'S NEWSLETTER AT

SHAUNATTWOOD.COM

SHAUN'S BOOKS

English Shaun Trilogy
Party Time
Hard Time
Prison Time

War on Drugs Series
Pablo Escobar: Beyond Narcos
American Made: Who Killed Barry Seal?
Pablo Escobar or George HW Bush
The Cali Cartel: Beyond Narcos
We Are Being Lied To: The War on Drugs (Expected 2019)
The War Against Weed (Expected 2019)

Un-Making a Murderer:
The Framing of Steven Avery and Brendan Dassey

Life Lessons

Pablo Escobar's Story (Expected 2018)
T-Bone (Expected 2022)

SOCIAL-MEDIA LINKS

Email: attwood.shaun@hotmail.co.uk
Blog: Jon's Jail Journal
Website: shaunattwood.com
Twitter: @shaunattwood
YouTube: Shaun Attwood
LinkedIn: Shaun Attwood
Goodreads: Shaun Attwood
Facebook: Shaun Attwood, Jon's Jail Journal, T-Bone
Appreciation Society

Shaun welcomes feedback on any of his books.

Thank you for the Amazon and Goodreads reviews!

SHAUN'S JAIL JOURNEY STARTS IN HARD TIME NEW EDITION

Chapter 1

Sleep deprived and scanning for danger, I enter a dark cell on the second floor of the maximum-security Madison Street jail in Phoenix, Arizona, where guards and gang members are murdering prisoners. Behind me, the metal door slams heavily. Light slants into the cell through oblong gaps in the door, illuminating a prisoner cocooned in a white sheet, snoring lightly on the top bunk about two thirds of the way up the back wall. Relieved there is no immediate threat, I place my mattress on the grimy floor. Desperate to rest, I notice movement on the cement-block walls. *Am I hallucinating?* I blink several times. The walls appear to ripple. Stepping closer, I see the walls are alive with insects. I flinch. So many are swarming, I wonder if they're a colony of ants on the move. To get a better look, I put my eyes right up to them. They are mostly the size of almonds and have antennae. American cockroaches. I've seen them in the holding cells downstairs in smaller numbers, but nothing like this. A chill spread over my body. I back away.

Something alive falls from the ceiling and bounces off the base of my neck. I jump. With my night vision improving, I spot cockroaches weaving in and out of the base of the fluorescent strip light. Every so often one drops onto the concrete and resumes crawling. Examining the bottom bunk, I realise why my cellmate is sleeping at a higher elevation: cockroaches are pouring from gaps in the decrepit wall at the level of my bunk. The area is thick with them. Placing my mattress on the bottom bunk scatters them. I walk towards the toilet, crunching a few under my shower sandals. I urinate and grab the toilet roll. A cockroach darts from the centre of the roll onto my hand, tickling my fingers. My arm jerks as if it has a mind of its own, losing the cockroach and the toilet roll. Using a towel, I wipe the bulk of them off the bottom bunk, stopping only to shake the odd one off my hand. I unroll my mattress. They begin to regroup and inhabit my mattress. My adrenaline is pumping so much, I lose my fatigue.

Nauseated, I sit on a tiny metal stool bolted to the wall. *How will I sleep? How's my cellmate sleeping through the infestation and my arrival?* Copying his technique, I cocoon myself in a sheet and lie down, crushing more cockroaches. The only way they can access me now is through the breathing hole I've left in the sheet by the lower half of my face. Inhaling their strange musty odour, I close my eyes. I can't sleep. I feel them crawling on the sheet around my feet. *Am I imagining things?* Frightened of them infiltrating my breathing hole, I keep opening my eyes. Cramps cause me to rotate onto my other side. Facing the wall, I'm repulsed by so many of them just inches away. I return to my original side.

The sheet traps the heat of the Sonoran Desert to my body, soaking me in sweat. Sweat tickles my body, tricking my mind into thinking the cockroaches are infiltrating and crawling on me. The trapped heat aggravates my bleeding skin infections and bedsores. I want to scratch myself, but I know better. The outer layers of my skin have turned soggy from sweating constantly in this concrete oven. Squirming on the bunk fails to stop the relentless itchiness of my skin. Eventually, I scratch myself. Clumps of moist skin detach under my nails. Every now and then I become so uncomfortable, I must open my cocoon to waft the heat out, which allows the cockroaches in. It takes hours to drift to sleep. I only manage a few hours. I awake stuck to the soaked sheet, disgusted by the cockroach carcasses compressed against the mattress.

The cockroaches plague my new home until dawn appears at the dots in the metal grid over a begrimed strip of four-inch-thick bullet-proof glass at the top of the back wall – the cell's only source of outdoor light. They disappear into the cracks in the walls, like vampire mist retreating from sunlight. But not all of them. There were so many on the night shift that even their vastly reduced number is too many to dispose of. And they act like they know it. They roam around my feet with attitude, as if to make it clear that I'm trespassing on their turf.

My next set of challenges will arise not from the insect world, but from my neighbours. I'm the new arrival, subject to scrutiny about my charges just like when I'd run into the Aryan Brotherhood prison gang on my first day at the medium-security Towers jail a year ago. I wish my cellmate would wake up, brief me on the mood of the locals and introduce me to the head of the white gang. No such luck. Chow is announced over a speaker system in a crackly robotic voice, but he doesn't stir.

I emerge into the day room for breakfast. Prisoners in black-and-white bee-striped uniforms gather under the metal-grid stairs and tip dead cockroaches into a trash bin from plastic peanut-butter containers they'd set as traps during the night. All eyes are on me in the chow line. Watching who sits where, I hold my head up, put on a solid stare and pretend to be as at home in this environment as the cockroaches. It's all an act. I'm lonely and afraid. I loathe having to explain myself to the head of the white race, who I assume is the toughest murderer. I've been in jail long enough to know that taking my breakfast to my cell will imply that I have something to hide.

The gang punishes criminals with certain charges. The most serious are sex offenders, who are KOS: Kill On Sight. Other charges are punishable by SOS – Smash On Sight – such as drive-by shootings because women and kids sometimes get killed. It's called convict justice. Gang members are constantly looking for people to beat up because that's how they earn their reputations and tattoos. The most serious acts of violence earn the highest-ranking tattoos. To be a full gang member requires murder. I've observed the body language and techniques inmates trying to integrate employ. An inmate with a spring in his step and an air of confidence is likely to be accepted. A person who avoids eye contact and fails to introduce himself to the gang is likely to be preyed on. Some of the failed attempts I saw ended up with heads getting cracked against toilets, a sound I've grown familiar with. I've seen prisoners being extracted on stretchers who looked dead – one had yellow fluid leaking from his head. The constant violence gives me nightmares, but the reality is that I put myself in here, so I force myself to accept it as a part of my punishment.

It's time to apply my knowledge. With a self-assured stride, I take my breakfast bag to the table of white inmates covered in neo-Nazi tattoos, allowing them to question me.

"Mind if I sit with you guys?" I ask, glad exhaustion has deepened my voice.

"These seats are taken. But you can stand at the corner of the table."

The man who answered is probably the head of the gang. I size him up. Cropped brown hair. A dangerous glint in Nordic-blue eyes. Tiny pupils that suggest he's on heroin. Weightlifter-type veins bulging from a sturdy neck. Political ink on arms crisscrossed with scars. About the same age as me, thirty-three.

"Thanks. I'm Shaun from England." I volunteer my origin to show I'm different from them but not in a way that might get me smashed.

"I'm Bullet, the head of the whites." He offers me his fist to bump. "Where you roll in from, wood?"

Addressing me as wood is a good sign. It's what white gang members on a friendly basis call each other.

"Towers jail. They increased my bond and re-classified me to maximum security."

"What's your bond at?"

"I've got two $750,000 bonds," I say in a monotone. This is no place to brag about bonds.

"How many people you kill, brother?" His eyes drill into mine, checking whether my body language supports my story. My body language so far is spot on.

"None. I threw rave parties. They got us talking about drugs on wiretaps." Discussing drugs on the phone does not warrant a $1.5 million bond. I know and beat him to his next question. "Here's my charges." I show him my charge sheet, which includes conspiracy and leading a crime syndicate – both from running an Ecstasy ring.

Bullet snatches the paper and scrutinises it. Attempting to pre-empt his verdict, the other whites study his face. On edge, I wait for him to respond. Whatever he says next will determine whether I'll be accepted or victimised.

"Are you some kind of jailhouse attorney?" Bullet asks. "I want someone to read through my case paperwork." During our few minutes of conversation, Bullet has seen through my act and concluded that I'm educated – a possible resource to him.

I appreciate that he'll accept me if I take the time to read his case. "I'm no jailhouse attorney, but I'll look through it and help you however I can."

"Good. I'll stop by your cell later on, wood."

After breakfast, I seal as many of the cracks in the walls as I can with toothpaste. The cell smells minty, but the cockroaches still find their way in. Their day shift appears to be collecting information on the brown paper bags under my bunk, containing a few items of food that I purchased from the commissary; bags that I tied off with rubber bands in the hope of keeping the cockroaches out. Relentlessly, the cockroaches explore the bags for entry points, pausing over and probing the most worn and vulnerable regions. *Will the nightly swarm eat right through the paper?* I read all morning, wondering whether my cellmate has died in his cocoon, his occasional breathing sounds reassuring me.

Bullet stops by late afternoon and drops his case paperwork off. He's been charged with Class 3 felonies and less, not serious crimes, but is facing a double-digit sentence because of his prior convictions and Security Threat Group status in the prison system. The proposed sentencing range seems disproportionate. I'll advise him to reject the plea bargain – on the assumption he already knows to do so, but is just seeking the comfort of a second opinion, like many un-sentenced inmates. When he returns for his paperwork, our conversation disturbs my cellmate – the cocoon shuffles – so we go upstairs to his cell. I tell Bullet what I think. He is excitable, a different man from earlier, his pupils almost non-existent.

"This case ain't shit. But my prosecutor knows I done other shit, all kinds of heavy shit, but can't prove it. I'd do anything to get that sorry bitch off my fucking ass. She's asking for something bad to happen to her. Man, if I ever get bonded out, I'm gonna chop that bitch into pieces. Kill her slowly though. Like to work her over with a blowtorch."

Such talk can get us both charged with conspiring to murder a prosecutor, so I try to steer him elsewhere. "It's crazy how they can catch you doing one thing, yet try to sentence you for all of the things they think you've ever done."

"Done plenty. Shot some dude in the stomach once. Rolled him up in a blanket and threw him in a dumpster."

Discussing past murders is as unsettling as future ones. "So, what's all your tattoos mean, Bullet? Like that eagle on your chest?"

"Why you wanna know?" Bullet's eyes probe mine.

My eyes hold their ground. "Just curious."

"It's a war bird. The AB patch."

"AB patch?"

"What the Aryan Brotherhood gives you when you've put enough work in."

"How long does it take to earn a patch?"

"Depends how quickly you put your work in. You have to earn your lightning bolts first."

"Why you got red and black lightning bolts?"

"You get SS bolts for beating someone down or for being an

enforcer for the family. Red lightning bolts for killing someone. I was sent down as a youngster. They gave me steel and told me who to handle and I handled it. You don't ask questions. You just get blood on your steel. Dudes who get these tats without putting work in are told to cover them up or leave the yard."

"What if they refuse?"

"They're held down and we carve the ink off them."

Imagining them carving a chunk of flesh to remove a tattoo, I cringe. He's really enjoying telling me this now. His volatile nature is clear and frightening. *He's accepted me too much. He's trying to impress me before making demands.*

At night, I'm unable to sleep. Cocooned in heat, surrounded by cockroaches, I hear the swamp-cooler vent – a metal grid at the top of a wall – hissing out tepid air. Giving up on sleep, I put my earphones on and tune into National Public Radio. Listening to a Vivaldi violin concerto, I close my eyes and press my tailbone down to straighten my back as if I'm doing a yogic relaxation. The playful allegro thrills me, lifting my spirits, but the wistful adagio provokes sad emotions and tears. I open my eyes and gaze into the gloom. Due to lack of sleep, I start hallucinating and hearing voices over the music whispering threats. I'm at breaking point. Although I have accepted that I committed crimes and deserve to be punished, no one should have to live like this. I'm furious at myself for making the series of reckless decisions that put me in here and for losing absolutely everything. As violins crescendo in my ears, I remember what my life used to be like.

SHAUN'S INCARCERATION CONCLUDES IN PRISON TIME

Chapter 1

"I've got a padlock in a sock. I can smash your brains in while you're asleep. I can kill you whenever I want." My new cellmate sizes me up with no trace of human feeling in his eyes. Muscular and pot-bellied, he's caked in prison ink, including six snakes on his skull, slithering side by side. The top of his right ear is missing in a semi-circle.

The waves of fear are overwhelming. After being in transportation all day, I can feel my bladder hurting. "I'm not looking to cause any trouble. I'm the quietest cellmate you'll ever have. All I do is read and write."

Scowling, he shakes his head. "Why've they put a fish in with me?" He swaggers close enough for me to smell his cigarette breath. "Us convicts don't get along with fresh fish."

"Should I ask to move then?" I say, hoping he'll agree if he hates new prisoners so much.

"No! They'll think I threatened you!"

In the eight by twelve feet slab of space, I swerve around him and place my property box on the top bunk.

He pushes me aside and grabs the box. "You just put that on my artwork! I ought to fucking smash you, fish!"

"Sorry, I didn't see it."

"You need to be more aware of your fucking surroundings! What you in for anyway, fish?"

I explain my charges, Ecstasy dealing and how I spent twenty-six months fighting my case.

"How come the cops were so hard-core after you?" he asks, squinting.

"It was a big case, a multi-million dollar investigation. They raided over a hundred people and didn't find any drugs. They were pretty pissed off. I'd stopped dealing by the time they caught up with me, but I'd done plenty over the years, so I accept my punishment."

"Throwing raves," he says, staring at the ceiling as if remembering something. "Were you partying with underage girls?" he asks, his voice slow, coaxing.

Being called a sex offender is the worst insult in prison. Into my third year of incarceration, I'm conditioned to react. "What you trying to say?" I yell angrily, brow clenched.

"Were you fucking underage girls?" Flexing his body, he shakes both fists as if about to punch me.

"Hey, I'm no child molester, and I'd prefer you didn't say shit like that!"

"My buddy next door is doing twenty-five to life for murdering a child molester. How do I know Ecstasy dealing ain't your cover story?" He inhales loudly, nostrils flaring.

"You want to see my fucking paperwork?"

A stocky prisoner walks in. Short hair. Dark eyes. Powerful neck. On one arm: a tattoo of a man in handcuffs above the word OMERTA – the Mafia code of silence towards law enforcement. "What the fuck's going on in here, Bud?" asks Junior Bull – the son of "Sammy the Bull" Gravano, the Mafia mass murderer who was my biggest competitor in the Ecstasy market.

Relieved to see a familiar face, I say, "How're you doing?"

Shaking my hand, he says in a New York Italian accent, "I'm doing alright. I read that shit in the newspaper about you starting a blog in Sheriff Joe Arpaio's jail."

"The blog's been bringing media heat on the conditions."

"You know him?" Bud asks.

"Yeah, from Towers jail. He's a good dude. He's in for dealing Ecstasy like me."

"It's a good job you said that 'cause I was about to smash his ass," Bud says.

"It's a good job Wild Man ain't here 'cause you'd a got your ass thrown off the balcony," Junior Bull says.

I laugh. The presence of my best friend, Wild Man, was partly the reason I never took a beating at the county jail, but with Wild Man in a different prison, I feel vulnerable. When Bud casts a death stare on me, my smile fades.

"What the fuck you guys on about?" Bud asks.

"Let's go talk downstairs." Junior Bull leads Bud out.

I rush to a stainless steel sink/toilet bolted to a cement-block wall by the front of the cell, unbutton my orange jumpsuit and crane my neck to watch the upper-tier walkway in case Bud returns. I bask in relief as my bladder deflates. After flushing, I take stock of my new home, grateful for the slight improvement in the conditions versus what I'd grown accustomed to in Sheriff Joe Arpaio's jail. No cockroaches. No blood stains. A working swamp cooler. Something I've never seen in a cell before: shelves. The steel table bolted to the wall is slightly larger, too. *But how will I concentrate on writing with Bud around?* There's a mixture of smells in the room. Cleaning chemicals. Aftershave. Tobacco. A vinegar-like odour. The slit of a window at the back overlooks gravel in a no-man's-land before the next building with gleaming curls of razor wire around its roof.

From the doorway upstairs, I'm facing two storeys of cells overlooking a day room with shower cubicles at the end of both tiers. At two white plastic circular tables, prisoners are playing dominoes, cards, chess and Scrabble, some concentrating, others yelling obscenities, contributing to a brain-scraping din that I hope to block out by purchasing a Walkman. In a raised box-shaped Plexiglas control tower, two guards are monitoring the prisoners.

Bud returns. My pulse jumps. Not wanting to feel like I'm stuck in a kennel with a rabid dog, I grab a notepad and pen and head for the day room.

Focussed on my body language, not wanting to signal any weakness, I'm striding along the upper tier, head and chest elevated, when two hands appear from a doorway and grab me. I drop the pad. The pen clinks against grid-metal and tumbles to the day room as I'm pulled into a cell reeking of backside sweat and masturbation, a cheese-tinted funk.

"I'm Booga. Let's fuck," says a squat man in urine-stained boxers, with WHITE TRASH tattooed on his torso below a mobile home, and an arm sleeved with the Virgin Mary.

Shocked, I brace to flee or fight to preserve my anal virginity. I can't believe my eyes when he drops his boxers and waggles his penis.

Dancing to music playing through a speaker he has rigged up, Booga smiles in a sexy way. "Come on," he says in a husky voice. "Drop your pants. Let's fuck." He pulls pornography faces. I question his sanity. He moves closer. "If I let you fart in my mouth, can I fart in yours?"

"You can fuck off," I say, springing towards the doorway.

He grabs me. We scuffle. Every time I make progress towards the doorway, he clings to my clothes, dragging me back in. When I feel his penis rub against my leg, my adrenalin kicks in so forcefully I experience a burst of strength and wriggle free. I bolt out as fast as my shower sandals will allow, and snatch my pad. Looking over my shoulder, I see him stood calmly in the doorway, smiling. He points at me. "You have to walk past my door every day. We're gonna get together. I'll lick your ass and you can fart in my mouth." Booga blows a kiss and disappears.

I rush downstairs. With my back to a wall, I pause to steady my thoughts and breathing. In survival mode, I think, *What's going to come at me next?* In the hope of reducing my tension, I borrow a pen to do what helps me stay sane: writing. With the details fresh in my mind, I document my journey to the prison for my blog readers, keeping an eye out in case anyone else wants to test the new prisoner. The more I write, the more I fill with a sense of purpose. Jon's Jail Journal is a connection to the outside world that I cherish.

Someone yells, "One time!" The din lowers. A door rumbles open. A guard does a security walk, his every move scrutinised by dozens of scornful eyes staring from cells. When he exits, the din resumes, and the prisoners return to injecting drugs to escape from reality, including the length of their sentences. This continues all day with "Two times!" signifying two approaching guards, and "Three times!" three and so on. Every now and then an announcement by a guard over the speakers briefly lowers the din.

Before lockdown, I join the line for a shower, holding bars of soap in a towel that I aim to swing at the head of the next person to try me. With boisterous inmates a few feet away, yelling at the men in the showers to "Stop jerking off," and "Hurry the fuck up," I get in a cubicle that reeks of bleach and mildew. With every nerve strained, I undress and rinse fast.

At night, despite the desert heat, I cocoon myself in a blanket from head to toe and turn towards the wall, making my face more difficult to strike. I leave a hole for air, but the warm cement block inches from my mouth returns each exhalation to my face as if it's breathing on me, creating a feeling of suffocation. For hours, my heart drums so hard against the thin mattress I feel as if I'm moving even though I'm still. I try to sleep, but my eyes keep springing open and my head turning towards the cell as I try to penetrate the darkness, searching for Bud swinging a padlock in a sock at my head.

OTHER BOOKS BY SHAUN ATTWOOD

Pablo Escobar: Beyond Narcos

War on Drugs Series Book 1

The mind-blowing true story of Pablo Escobar and the Medellín Cartel beyond their portrayal on Netflix.

Colombian drug lord Pablo Escobar was a devoted family man and a psychopathic killer; a terrible enemy, yet a wonderful friend. While donating millions to the poor, he bombed and tortured his enemies – some had their eyeballs removed with hot spoons. Through ruthless cunning and America's insatiable appetite for cocaine, he became a multi-billionaire, who lived in a $100-million house with its own zoo.

Pablo Escobar: Beyond Narcos demolishes the standard good versus evil telling of his story. The authorities were not hunting Pablo down to stop his cocaine business. They were taking over it.

American Made: Who Killed Barry Seal? Pablo Escobar or George HW Bush

War on Drugs Series Book 2

Set in a world where crime and government coexist, *American Made* is the jaw-dropping true story of CIA pilot Barry Seal that the Hollywood movie starring Tom Cruise is afraid to tell.

Barry Seal flew cocaine and weapons worth billions of dollars into and out of America in the 1980s. After he became a government informant, Pablo Escobar's Medellin Cartel offered a million for him alive and half a million dead. But his real trouble began after he threatened to expose the dirty dealings of George HW Bush.

American Made rips the roof off Bush and Clinton's complicity in cocaine trafficking in Mena, Arkansas.

"A conspiracy of the grandest magnitude." Congressman Bill Alexander on the Mena affair.

We Are Being Lied To: The War on Drugs

War on Drugs Series Book 3

A collection of harrowing, action-packed and interlinked true stories that demonstrate the devastating consequences of drug prohibition.

The Cali Cartel: Beyond Narcos

War on Drugs Series Book 4

An electrifying account of the Cali Cartel beyond its portrayal on Netflix.

From the ashes of Pablo Escobar's empire rose an even bigger and more malevolent cartel. A new breed of sophisticated mobsters became the kings of cocaine. Their leader was Gilberto Rodríguez

Orejuela – known as the Chess Player due to his foresight and calculated cunning.

Gilberto and his terrifying brother, Miguel, ran a multi-billion-dollar drug empire like a corporation. They employed a politically astute brand of thuggery and spent $10 million to put a president in power. Although the godfathers from Cali preferred bribery over violence, their many loyal torturers and hit men were never idle.

Hard Time New Edition

"Makes the Shawshank Redemption look like a holiday camp" – NOTW

After a SWAT team smashed down stock-market millionaire Shaun Attwood's door, he found himself inside of Arizona's deadliest jail and locked into a brutal struggle for survival.

Shaun's hope of living the American Dream turned into a nightmare of violence and chaos, when he had a run-in with Sammy the Bull Gravano, an Italian Mafia mass murderer.

In jail, Shaun was forced to endure cockroaches crawling in his ears at night, dead rats in the food and the sound of skulls getting cracked against toilets. He meticulously documented the conditions and smuggled out his message.

Join Shaun on a harrowing voyage into the darkest recesses of human existence.

Hard Time provides a revealing glimpse into the tragedy, brutality, dark comedy and eccentricity of prison life.

Featured worldwide on Nat Geo Channel's Locked-Up/Banged-Up Abroad Raving Arizona.

Prison Time

Sentenced to 9½ years in Arizona's state prison for distributing Ecstasy, Shaun finds himself living among gang members, sexual predators and drug-crazed psychopaths. After being attacked by a Californian biker in for stabbing a girlfriend, Shaun writes about the prisoners who befriend, protect and inspire him. They include T-Bone, a massive African American ex-Marine who risks his life saving vulnerable inmates from rape, and Two Tonys, an old-school Mafia murderer who left the corpses of his rivals from Arizona to Alaska. They teach Shaun how to turn incarceration to his advantage, and to learn from his mistakes.

Shaun is no stranger to love and lust in the heterosexual world, but the tables are turned on him inside. Sexual advances come at him from all directions, some cleverly disguised, others more sinister – making Shaun question his sexual identity.

Resigned to living alongside violent, mentally-ill and drug-addicted inmates, Shaun immerses himself in psychology and philosophy to try to make sense of his past behaviour, and begins applying what he learns as he adapts to prison life. Encouraged by Two Tonys to explore fiction as well, Shaun reads over 1000 books which, with support from a brilliant psychotherapist, Dr Owen, speed along his personal development. As his ability to deflect daily threats improves, Shaun begins to look forward to his release with optimism and a new love waiting for him. Yet the words of Aristotle from one of Shaun's books will prove prophetic: "We cannot learn without pain."

Un-Making a Murderer:
The Framing of Steven Avery and Brendan Dassey

Innocent people do go to jail. Sometimes mistakes are made. But even more terrifying is when the authorities conspire to frame them. That's what happened to Steven Avery and Brendan Dassey, who were convicted of murder and are serving life sentences.

Un-Making a Murderer is an explosive book which uncovers the illegal, devious and covert tactics used by Wisconsin officials, including:

– **Concealing Other Suspects**
– **Paying Expert Witnesses to Lie**
– **Planting Evidence**
– **Jury Tampering**

The art of framing innocent people has been in practice for centuries and will continue until the perpetrators are held accountable. Turning conventional assumptions and beliefs in the justice system upside down, *Un-Making a Murderer* takes you on that journey.

The profits from this book are going to Steven and Brendan and to donate free books to schools and prisons. In the last three years, Shaun Attwood has donated 20,000 books.

ABOUT SHAUN ATTWOOD

Shaun Attwood is a former stock-market millionaire and Ecstasy supplier turned public speaker, author and activist, who is banned from America for life. His story was featured worldwide on National Geographic Channel as an episode of Locked Up/ Banged Up Abroad called Raving Arizona.

Shaun's writing – smuggled out of the jail with the highest death rate in America run by Sheriff Joe Arpaio – attracted international media attention to the human rights violations: murders by guards and gang members, dead rats in the food, cockroach infestations…

While incarcerated, Shaun was forced to reappraise his life. He read over 1,000 books in just under six years. By studying original texts in psychology and philosophy, he sought to better understand himself and his past behaviour. He credits books as being the lifeblood of his rehabilitation.

Shaun tells his story to schools to dissuade young people from drugs and crime. He campaigns against injustice via his books and blog, Jon's Jail Journal. He has appeared on the BBC, Sky News and TV worldwide to talk about issues affecting prisoners' rights.

As a best-selling true-crime author, Shaun is presently writing a series of action-packed books exposing the War on Drugs, which feature Pablo Escobar and the Cali Cartel.